The Long Hunt

The Long Hunt

Death of the Buffalo
East of the Mississippi

Ted Franklin Belue

STACKPOLE
BOOKS
Guilford, Connecticut
Blue Ridge Summit, Pennsylvania

STACKPOLE BOOKS

An imprint of Globe Pequot, the trade division of
The Rowman & Littlefield Publishing Group, Inc.
4501 Forbes Blvd., Ste. 200
Lanham, MD 20706
www.rowman.com

Distributed by NATIONAL BOOK NETWORK

British Library Cataloguing in Publication Information available

The Library of Congress has cataloged the hardcover edition of this book as
follows:

Belue, Ted Franklin.
    The long hunt : death of the buffalo east of the Mississippi /
Ted Franklin Belue. — 1st ed.
      p. cm.
    Includes bibliographical references (p.) and index.
    ISBN 0-8117-0968-X
    1. American bison hunting—East (U.S.)—History. 2. East (U.S.)—
History. I. Title.
SK297.B45 1996
799.2'7277358—dc20   96-30671
                                         CIP

ISBN 978-0-8117-7116-0 (paper : alk. paper)

♾™ The paper used in this publication meets the minimum requirements of
American National Standard for Information Sciences—Permanence of Paper
for Printed Library Materials, ANSI/NISO Z39.48-1992.

To my father, Frank Owens Belue, and my mother, Myra Janell

Contents

Acknowledgments

IN THE FIVE YEARS SPENT LABORING ON *THE LONG HUNT* MANY A DEBT was incurred and many thanks are due, the first to Larry Doyle, of Murray, Kentucky, who suggested the topic. The Tennessee Valley Authority, which manages the largest buffalo herd on public land east of the Mississippi—nearly ninety head—at TVA's Land Between the Lakes, a 170,000-acre tract spanning western Tennessee and Kentucky, funded a portion of the work.

H. David Wright of Gray Stone Press, a native Kentuckian, modern-day Long Hunter, and artist of remarkable sensitivity, provided his friendship, insights into eighteenth-century life, and art. Neal O. Hammon, historian and author on the Commonwealth, gave vital commentary on early forays into Kentucky. Charles E. Hanson, Jr., Director of the Museum of the Fur Trade in Chadron, Nebraska, offered kind words in the compilation of the bibliography. Laura Herrington granted access to the Loren Herrington Collection of Indian artifacts. Michael J. Taylor, a virtuoso artisan of eighteenth-century Indian wares, supplied information about Woodland Indians. Stephanie Zebrowski, of Zebrowski Publishing, steered me from grievous errors with her incisive research on buffalo in Pennsylvania. Her wit was an added boon.

At Murray State University, in Murray, Kentucky, much appreciation is due to the staff at the Forrest C. Pogue Special Collections Library and at the Harry Lee Waterfield Library. Dr. Kenneth C. Carstens, of the Department of Sociology, Anthropology and Social Work, provided unpublished data on George Rogers Clark's 1780-81 Fort Jefferson occupation. English professor Dr. Jerry A. Herndon bore countless manuscript rewrites with fortitude. Hal Rice at the Faculty Resource Center helped with illustrations.

Others who provided advice, assistance, and encouragement include Dr. Charles J. Balesi, Evanston, Illinois; Win Blevins, Bozeman, Montana;

Dr. Joan G. Caldwell, Tulane University Art Collection, New Orleans, Louisiana; Gwyneth Campling, James L. Jackson, and Liz Turner, Royal Collection Enterprises Limited, Windsor Castle, Berkshire, England; Dr. Kenneth Cherry, University Press of Kentucky; Dr. Thomas D. Clark, Lexington, Kentucky; Marcus Cope, Land Between the Lakes, Tennessee Valley Authority; Randy Corse, Osage Beach, Missouri; Sharon Cunningham, Union City, Tennessee; Dr. Nelson L. Dawson, The Filson Club; Tony Gerard, Shawnee Community College; Dr. Josephine L. Harper, Joanne Hohler, and Harold Miller of the State Historical Society of Wisconsin; Randy Martin, Martin and Company Advertising, White's Creek, Tennessee; Peter Matthiessen, Sagaponack, New York; Dr. Timothy C. Nichols, Albertville, Alabama; Palle Ringsted, The Royal Library, Copenhagen, Denmark; Daniel J. J. Ross, University of Nebraska Press; William H. Scurlock, Scurlock Publishing; Jean Sherrill, Orlando, Florida; Robert and Margaret Sisk, Skiatook, Oklahoma; Sherry Stribling and George "Butch" Winter, Pioneer Press; Dr. Richard Taylor, Kentucky State University; and Jack Turbeville, Shepherdsville, Kentucky.

The greatest thanks go to my wife, Lavina Turbeville, for her abiding love and patience, and for keeping hearth and home intact during the onslaught of the buffalo.

Introduction

THE HISTORY OF THE BUFFALO IS A TRAGIC ONE, YET THE TELLING OF that tale is curiously unbalanced. Most buffalo books spend the opening chapter citing obscure reports of buffalo east of the Mississippi River, then focus on the huge western herds, their relationship to the Plains Indians, and the buffalo's near extinction.

Few people realize the killing of the buffalo began in the East, not in the West. And it began long before the brief era of the coming of the railroad, the .40-90 Sharps rifle, and "Buffalo" Bill Cody.

The story must be told. Yet to tell it by omitting the beginnings of America presents a fragmented history. Reducing the slaughter to an exercise in horn counting and ignoring the Spanish, French, and English intruders, the New Orleans buffalo tongue markets, the French and Indian War, Richard Henderson's 1775 Sycamore Shoals Treaty, and the invasion of the Long Hunters into the Cumberland Valley distorts the picture. Such events devastated the buffalo.

In 1991 Larry Doyle, then Manager of Land Stewardship at the Tennessee Valley Authority's Land Between the Lakes, and Marcus Cope, biologist and buffalo herdsman for the TVA-LBL, suggested writing a booklet on the eastern buffalo. A sea of unused material was left after the project, and it seemed a shame not to finish this heretofore unwritten chapter in American history. *The Long Hunt: Death of the Buffalo East of the Mississippi* is the result.

This is not a book on the natural history or life cycle of the buffalo—although to establish context, chapter 1 gives a glimpse of buffalo prehistory. Nor is it an analysis of the ecological changes that swept the land with the coming of Anglo settlers. Rather, the intent is to tell the true story of buffalo hunting east of the Mississippi, with emphasis on hunters and their skills, and to place that saga in the larger setting of the exploration and settling of eastern North America.

There are two reasons why the buffalo in the East vanished: Over-hunting wiped out their ranks, and destruction of their habitat destroyed their range. Simon Girty, an adopted Seneca, American-turned-Tory, and buffalo hunter in the 1760s for the Philadelphia-based trading firm of Baynton, Wharton, and Morgan, framed both issues perfectly in 1782 in a terse speech to a pan-Indian war council at Wapakoneta, Ohio. "The Long Knives have overrun your country," Girty declared. "They have destroyed the cane—trodden down the clover—killed the deer and the buffaloes."

Indians, conquistadors, Jesuits, voyageurs, European explorers, and American frontiersmen kept few tallies of buffalo kills; many such folk thought no more of shooting a buffalo for its tongue than a modern-day plinker thinks of shooting a beer can. Market hunters did not keep methodical records of buffalo kills until the nineteenth-century western slaughter for meat and hides. Such data, where supplied, has been included.

Regarding terminology, the American buffalo is not a true buffalo, like the African Cape buffalo or the Asian water buffalo, but is closer kin to the European wisent, *Bison bonasus,* and is more accurately a bison. American colonists adopted the French terms of *bufflo* and *buffelo* to describe the beast. Father Louis Hennepin, a Récollet friar who spent two years in New France and wrote about his travels, introduced the term *buffalo* to European readers in 1683. John Lawson, who trudged through the Carolina Piedmont for fifty-nine days in 1700 to 1701, used *buffalo* in his book, *The New Voyage to Carolina,* published in England in 1709. Lawson's work went through six reprints, including two German editions, before the term *buffalo* appeared in 1743 in Mark Catesby's *A Natural History of Carolina.* As in those early works, this book refers to bison as buffalo.

Biologists generally agree that the historic buffalo east of the Missis-sippi was the Plains buffalo, *Bison bison bison,* noting that the buffalo arrived late, probably crossing the Mississippi by the late 1500s. Com-pared with the truly huge trans-Mississippian herds, droves in the East were small, rarely numbering more than five hundred head. When travelers across the Blue Ridge reported seeing "vast buffalo herds," such herds often numbered fifty to one hundred head or less.

There is a well-known dissenting voice in such matters. In *A Pennsyl-vania Bison Hunt,* published 1915, Henry W. Shoemaker, an ex-ambassador to Bulgaria, Pennsylvania newspaper mogul, and self-published writer who specialized in werewolves and bawdy tales, contended that Pennsyl-vania buffalo—which, he said, numbered twelve thousand—were wood bison, basing his words on those of Jacob Quiggle (1821–1911). Jacob, at age eighty-nine, told Shoemaker that his grandfather Philip Quigley (1745–?) said the Pennsylvania buffalo was "Like the Wood bison . . . of the Rocky Mountains and Canada Northwest." There is no evidence to corroborate such third-hand speculations. Yet spinners of buffalo lore have so canonized Shoemaker's tales that *The Long Hunt* would be incomplete without mention of them.

This book places emphasis on Illinois, Kentucky, Tennessee, and the southern frontier. The reason is simple: Many naturalists, explorers, hunters, and surveyors who crossed the Appalachians wrote vivid descriptions about buffalo in their narratives, memoirs, diaries, and journals. Earlier reliable accounts are rare; in some, buffalo are confused with elk, moose, and deer. Even more bewildering, sometimes buffalolike terms appearing in the earliest journals are used interchangeably to describe all four animals. It is hard to make a historical case on such convoluted testimony.

Native Americans are important to this work, but its narrow scope did not allow for a historiographic digression about eastern Indian culture, which is more befitting a doctoral dissertation. Nor is this a forum to debate contentions by revisionist historians, ethnologists, and their academic kinsmen over the relevance of terms such as *race, frontier, tribe, primitive, prehistory,* and *culture.* Readers curious about such matters are referred to works cited in the references.

One last word: It is easy to moralize about the killing that led to the buffalo's near extinction. But before casting blame, it is humbling to wonder how this generation will be judged by those inheriting its legacy of acid rain, oil and chemical spills, the disappearance of many plants and animals, overpopulation, toxic waste, pollution, poaching, and the spoliation of the world's great forests, grasslands, wetlands, rivers, and oceans.

Should we not be held to an equal—if not greater—degree of ecological stewardship than our forebears, who, in their limited vision, saw the wealth of buffalo beef, tongues, tallow, and hides as inexhaustible? It is hoped that the lessons learned from this tale of the killing of the buffalo east of the Mississippi will help stop further abuse of the earth and its resources.

The buffaloes were more frequent than I have seen cattle in the settlements, browsing on the leaves of the cane, or cropping the herbage on those extensive plains, fearless, because ignorant, of the violence of man. Sometimes we saw hundreds in a drove, and the numbers about the salt springs were amazing.

> Daniel Boone
> Kentucky, 1769

We found it very difficult at first and indeed yet, to stop the great waste in killing meat. Many men were ignorant of the woods, and not skilled in hunting . . . would shoot, cripple and scare the game without being able to get much. . . . Others of wicked and wanton dispositions, would kill three, four, five or a half a dozen buffaloes, and not take a half horse load from them all. ,

> Richard Henderson
> Boonesborough, May 9, 1775

The Wild Cattle
of North America

BERINGIA. MISTS OF DARK HAZE HUNG IN THE SKY OVER THE SOGGY tundra mat of grass, moss, lichen, and dwarf shrubs. Above, a swirling void of cloud, ice, and fog stretched long and far, as if beckoning one to the earthen abyss below that led to an unseen land.

Subterranean tremors tossed and churned ice floes thousands of feet thick, jolting the huge plates girding the earth. Melting glacial sheets spanning continents moved slower than eye could see, carving up the bone and marrow of creation on sea and on land. Beringia marked an era of rising mountains, of pluvial lakes and seas, and of freezes and thaws that forever altered the firmament above and below the endless Oceania. As the deep basins froze at the northwestern apex of North America, the waters receded, giving way to the chiseled borders of a subcontinent. So rose the jut of rock, marsh, and bayou linking Siberia to Alaska across the Bering and Chukchi Seas. More a part of Asia than North America, Beringia appeared and vanished throughout the millennia of the Ice Age until it sank forever to rest beneath three hundred feet of ocean.

Historians and their academic kinsmen describe Beringia as a land bridge—the link of silt and rock bridged expanses of terra firma and opened stretches of tundra for man and beast. But the term is misleading. Beringia was one thousand miles wide and fifty-five miles long, an earthen thoroughfare between vistas of white, green, and brown that during thaws was coaxed to life by gusts from warm climes.

Migrating from Asia to North America during one of the Ice Age's last interglaciations came the herbivores of the tundra—mammoths, mastodons, musk oxen, sloths, and caribou. Deer, sheep, and moose—prey for panthers and jaguars that tracked the ungulates across continents—trailed along with the herds. *Bison priscus,* the Holarctic wild cow, itself having migrated to the Asian steppes, joined this caravan of antler and hoof. Late in the Wisconsin

Age of the Pleistocene Era—between 25,000 and 40,000 years ago—came Llano man.

Man was an adept bison hunter and may even have held the wild cow sacred. Millennia before mammals trekked across Beringia, paleo artists sketched *Bison priscus* on the smoke-patinaed walls of caverns in France and Spain. The steppe bison—or, more accurately, wisent—depicted in this petroglyphic line art are big, hump-backed creatures. Paleo man killed the woolly bovine with spears tipped with slivers of sharply knapped flint or quartz. Atlatls launched spears and darts with greater velocity, giving hunters more power to kill and keep their distance from dangerous prey.

Hunters on the Great Plains—a veldt extending from Canada to the Rio Grande and from the Rocky Mountains east to the Mississippi—found seas of buffalo grass, needle grass and protein-rich grama grass, a diverse array of forbs, bushes, trees, and a myriad of rivers and streams yielding browse, graze, and water. Arroyos, buttes, mountain breaks, passes, gaps, and gulches gave protection. There was food and shelter for both man and beast.

Reconstructing what happened at this critical hub and explaining how and why it happened are matters of interpretation. Because bulls, scientists say, were easier to hunt than cows, their skeletons appear frequently in dig sites. Fossil clues are based largely upon the skulls of male bison, focusing mostly on horn size. But within a species, horn size varies depending on age and genetics, and the horn sheaths encasing the fossilized cores are usually absent. Thus extrapolations about the speciation of prehistoric buffalo are educated guesses.

Scientists theorize that some mammals adapted to the climatic demands of North America but others became extinct. Huge consumers—the mammoths, mastodons, tapirs, and giant sloths—vanished, only their bones remaining as evidence that they once roamed the Great Plains and well past the Mississippi. As *Bison priscus* died out, other wild cows, most notably *Bison latifrons,* emerged.

Twice the size of the modern plains bison, and bearing a set of horns that measured nine feet from tip to tip, *Bison latifrons* was a formidable brute. The extent of its migratory range is a matter of dispute, but skeletal remains from this hulk of muscle and horn have been unearthed on the plains of Kansas and as far east as Ohio. According to the "successive wave" theory of bison evolution, smaller, more compact bovine stock with smaller horns, *Bison alleni,* came in the wake of *Bison latifrons.* Remains of *Bison alleni* have been identified in Kansas and Idaho. Either

Bison alleni or *Bison latifrons* may have been a distant progenitor of a later species, *Bison antiquus.*

Folsom man hunted *Bison antiquus (figginsi)* about 9,000 years ago. Warriors cloaked in deer or wolf skins approached the beasts downwind, crawling on all fours. When they closed in, the hunters rose to hurl their spears into the hearts and lungs of the animals. Archaeological evidence shows that hunters ran herds into box canyons, trapped them in chutes built of stones and trees, or stampeded them off cliffs. Indians spotting a drove near a fall surrounded them at the rear and flank. A warrior disguised in a bison robe would near the herd, making sure the animals saw him. On signal, the hidden warriors closed in, spooking the bison into flight. As the decoy warrior bolted, the beasts followed him to the drop, galloping to their doom. In 1957 archaeologists discovered the remains of 193 *Bison antiquus* at a Colorado chute with bits of Folsom man's spear points embedded in the bones.

Yet despite its mortality at the hand of Folsom man, *Bison antiquus* thrived from the Pacific Ocean to Kentucky and from the upper Missouri River drainage south to Mexico. *Bison antiquus,* unlike *Bison latifrons,* had no horns, though *Bison antiquus* did sport a thick mane. But a contemporary of *Bison antiquus* from the Arctic, *Bison occidentalis,* was horned and bore a mane. *Bison occidentalis,* which died out perhaps 6,000 years ago, is an important link in the history of the North American wild cow. Some taxonomists believe that *Bison occidentalis* is the ancestor of the modern plains bison, *Bison bison bison;* the Canadian wood bison, *Bison athabascae;* and the European wisent, *Bison bonasus.*

All three of these ruminant subspecies still exist. Of the three, the wisent, which is smaller, leggier, and more streamlined than the Great Plains bison, is most in danger of extinction. Threatening wisent herds—already precariously low—are unstable wildlife policies, civil unrest, poaching, pollution, and habitat destruction. Currently about one thousand wisent roam what is left of the animal's dwindling range, which is now restricted to the haphazardly managed state forests of Russia and Poland. The wisent of the Bialowieza Forest of Poland are perhaps the best-known and least endangered Old World bison.

Canadian wood bison, which are larger, darker, and hairier than the Great Plains bison and carry a higher, more defined hump, roam Wood Buffalo Park on the Alberta border, straddling the Northwest Territories, and on Elk Island, near Edmonton. Because of mismanaged wildlife relocation policies in the 1920s that resulted in accidental cross-breeding between *Bison bison bison* and *Bison athabascae,* however, by the 1950s many wood bison in Wood Buffalo Park shared the genes and morphological characteristics from both subspecies; in areas of such tainted gene pools, genetically pure *Bison athabascae* are rare. Even worse, diseases once unknown among bison, such as anthrax, brucellosis, and tuberculosis, ravage bison populations on several Canadian game preserves. Despite this situation, the official status of *Bison athabascae* was upgraded in 1989 from endangered to threatened.

But the North American bison—the buffalo—is the focus of this work. Tough, long-lived, prolific, able to take extreme cold or heat, swifter than a mustang at full gallop, and having few predators, the Great Plains buffalo seemed as many as the stars in the sky by the time of the coming of the white invaders.[1]

June is bellowing time. Grunts rumbling like low-lying thunderheads are heard for miles, resonating loudly in badger holes. Older buffalo bulls are restless, agitated, and wary, fending off younger rivals with impressive display: wagging black horns, posturing defiantly, abrupt sidelong lunges, head butts, gorings. In early summer—June, actually—mature bulls feel the call to rut. Tension to mate builds slowly, but by July and August, the cows are fully in their two-day heat. Mountings are frequent, unions swift. The bull dismounts but lingers around the cow, eyeing his rivals. If the bull's seed does not bring the cow's womb to life, in three weeks the cow will again come into estrus. Courtship will begin anew. By September rut has ended. Gestation is just over nine months.

Winds blow chilly. By early autumn, a new wool pelage of auburn and brown sprouts from humps to forelocks, from nose to tail, as buffalo robes turn prime. Beards twelve inches long dangle from bulls. Graze sprouts after the rains of late summer and the buffalo feed, adding fat to insulate their taut bodies before winter.

Snow and ice hardly faze the beasts. The old and infirm succumb to plummeting temperatures, and a few weakened buffalo are picked off by grizzlies or cougars or, more likely, by one of the wolf packs that loll around the herds. But the first frosts cause the wild cows to buck and caper, seemingly frolicking in celebration that the heat is gone and, with it, the flies, gnats, and mosquitoes whose bites itch the buffalo's bald flanks of summer.

"King of the blizzard" is what one herdsman dubbed the buffalo.[2] The animals stoically endure lashing sleet and puffballs of snow that pile in drifts higher than a first-year aspen. Herds seek cover in woodlands that circle the pockets of their range. Deep snow is a nuisance but seldom fatal. The beasts' hairy muzzles allow them to plow with impunity through the layers of hoary crust to munch half-frozen flora below it.

Gulps of snow stave off thirst when creeks ice over. Dominant cows seek sunny spots to bask and will stay in them even to the point of starving or being nipped by timber wolves that themselves feel winter's pangs.

By February, robes look grizzled. Snowmelt begins by March, but food is sparse and buffalo begin to become gaunt. Calves—one to a cow, rarely twins—are dropped in April and May. By then the tattered coats shed in frayed, knotted hanks. The animals' naked flanks twitch and shudder as hordes of ravenous insects seek their first blood. And at last comes rain, torrents of it—rain, sun, warmth; rivers swell, the land awakens and shimmers anew, and the buffalo gorge themselves in preparation for the next cycle of rut.

Indians were the true "conquerors of the wilderness." By the time of the historic period, the first Americans—who peopled the land from the rim of the Arctic Circle to the tip of Tierra del Fuego—were far from a homogeneous lot. Native-built metropolises featuring sprawling estates, temple pyramids, centralized governments, and armies of foot soldiers thrived in Mexico. Indian cities rose high on sugarloaf mounds erected on the Illinois prairie bordering the banks of the Mississippi and north and south of its drainage. Historian Francis Jennings contends that the population of North American Indians may have numbered ten million to twelve million north of the Rio Grande.[3]

Seventeenth-century life was a golden age for many Plains Indians. By the 1600s, the Navajos, Athapascan horticulturists who made their log and adobe homes in that region, began to count Spanish horses—either stolen or traded—as part of their wealth. By the time of the Pueblo Revolt of 1680 or a decade thereafter, there was a lively equine trade on the Great Plains.

Horses exerted a profound impact on native culture. Equipped with horses and dogs outfitted with travois poles, families and tribes became mobile. The Dakota used horses so much that their mode of subsistence became nomadic. Horses allowed more settled Siouans—like the Omaha, Iowa, Ponca, Osage, Oto, Mandan, and Missouri—to hunt buffalo, although such tribes did not become as nomadic as the Dakota. Soon Caddoan speakers—the Wichita, Pawnee, and Arikara—and the western Algonquins—Cheyenne, Blackfeet, and Arapaho—began to use mustangs to pursue buffalo herds. By the 1800s, Comanche hunters, who acquired horses from the Utes by 1700, dominated the Southern Plains of Texas and New Mexico.[4] Until about 1880, for perhaps three dozen Plains groups the buffalo was a commissary on hooves.

Indians found wild beef rich and sustaining. A wet bull skin—thick, tough, and hard to tan—laced on a hardwood hoop dried into a rawhide shield. They fleshed cow hides, rubbed in glops of brains, then whipped the dank skins across a rawhide thong to break down the tough fibers to knead them into robes. Such coverings, soft and supple, wore like iron and lasted for years. Robes decorated with dyed porcupine quills and painted with red and yellow ocher mixed with fat became heirlooms.[5]

Leg and back sinews were stronger for sewing than thread from nettle fibers and easier to prepare. Arrows fired from sinew-backed hardwood bows rocketed with startling velocity. Bladders and scrotums became pouches. The stomach lining was an edible stewpot: Native cooks would hang them on a tripod, fill them with water and meat, and toss in red-hot rocks to make the water boil. After the meat was served, the gut bag was eaten.

Coracles made from green (untanned) buffalo hides laced over a wattle of white oak, willow, or hickory strips, were buoyant, stable, and tough. The hair side was to the inside; the part that lay in the water, the skin side, was sun-baked drum hard, and the sinew and rawhide-stitched seams were caulked with tallow and ashes. Sticks piled in the craft's bottom kept furs, food, and weapons dry. After a day on the river, the boats grew soggy and hard to steer. Early in the day, hide boats drew three to four inches of water; by afternoon they drew twice that. Indians poled the craft to shore at dusk to check for leaks and recaulk the seams for the next day's trip. Pulled up on the bank, flipped over and propped up to dry, a buffalo hide boat became a shelter.[6]

Indians shaved summer hides clean of the sparse wool with a sharply honed elk rib bone and tanned the hide or used it as rawhide and sewed it into sundry items. They wove wool into cordage, boiled horns free of their gristle cores to form cups or split them to make spoons and combs, and made rattles from hooves. Sometimes they ground up the hooves to boil in water with rawhide scraps, the penis, eyes, muzzle, and cartilage to make hide glue.

Historic Indians west of the Mississippi, like the Plains tribes of prehistory, drove buffalo into ravines or stampeded them off cliffs. During the 1804–1806 Lewis and Clark Expedition, Meriwether Lewis, William Clark, and their Corps of Discovery floated past a cliff kill site on the Missouri River on May 29, 1805. Lewis wrote:

> Today we passed the remains of a vast many mangled carcasses of buffalo, which had been driven over a precipice of 120 feet by the Indians, and perished. The water appeared to have washed away a part of this immense pile of slaughter, and still there

remained the fragments of at least a hundred carcasses. They created the most horrid stench. In this manner, the Indians of the
Missouri destroy vast herds of buffalo at a stroke.[7]

Natives rejoiced after a big kill. Then they feasted. Often they ate the
meat uncooked. Artist John James Audubon was with a band of Plains
Indians after a buffalo hunt and watched them devour the raw organs
with relish. He sampled some raw tripe and found it "very good, although at first its appearance was rather revolting."[8] Eating raw meat may
have been done for the taste, but it was also expedient. Cooking could be
hazardous; smoke billowing over the next rise could give the hunters
away.

Skinning buffalo was a time for socializing. As the men and women
worked, they ate and told tales of great hunts and of great hunters. Eyes,
livers, belly fat, testicles, and marrow bones were delicacies, as were the
tiny hooves of unborn calves. The natives stewed fetal calves in their gray-
ish blue sacs and cracked open skulls to eat the brains or to dry them for
tanning. The warm milk from lactating cows went to the elderly and the
young. Warriors drank buffalo blood so that they would not lose heart in
battle. Tribal law dictated the division of meat. Camp dogs, then panthers,
buzzards, wolves, and mice—nature's stewards of the dead—ate the rest of
the carcass and left the offal to rot into the soil.

In the winter, buffalo herds crossed rivers when they iced over, making them vulnerable to attack. Or worse, animals packed together sometimes caused the ice to give way, drowning hundreds of wild cattle.
During the spring thaw, Indians downstream benefited by pulling the
floating, bloated carcasses from the water and feasting. For some tribes,
tainted wild beef—lank and blue—was a delicacy.

For millennia the buffalo's domain expanded west of the Mississippi,
their numbers swelling, by popular estimates, to between forty-five million and sixty million. More conservative numbers put their population
at no fewer than thirty million. But based on the Great Plains' domestic
bovine carrying capacity and a synthesis of scientific, historical, ecological, and archaeological analyses, environmental historian Dan Flores
asserts that "during prehorse times the Southern Plains might have supported an average of about 8.2 million bison, the entire Great Plains perhaps 28–30 million."[9]

By the late 1500s, a new ecological niche opened east of the Mississippi,
permitting buffalo to expand their range. The aperture was created by
several dynamic elements: wide-scale native depopulation resulting from

disease introduced by Europeans, relaxed hunting pressure as the over-hunted deer herds declined, and intensive Indian agricultural techniques, especially the systematic burning of land close to the eastern banks of the Mississippi. To exploit these savannas, droves of buffalo coming from beyond the Red, Washita, and Arkansas River valleys swam the Mississippi and, for the first time, entered the American Southeast and the lower Mississippi floodplain.[10]

During the 1600s, buffalo ranged southward to the Gulf coast of Louisiana, Mississippi, Alabama, and western Florida along the panhandle south to Tampa Bay. Eastward their range extended to the Georgia coast near St. Simon's Island.[11] From there it ran north eighty to ninety miles from the Atlantic coast to the edge of the Carolina Piedmont. Buffalo grazed near New Orleans and along the Mississippi to southern Wisconsin, to Lake Superior near Duluth, Minnesota, perhaps to the Fox River in Winnebago County.[12]

Reports of buffalo trails come from Cavetown, Maryland, western New York, and the shores of the Great Lakes in southern Michigan. Buffalo were plentiful in Kentucky and Illinois. Hamburgh, an explorer of the upper Ohio Valley whose full name is now unknown, recorded in his journal of 1763 that he had observed buffalo from the Chicago River southward, as well as in Indiana, Tennessee, and Ohio. Thomas Salmon's *Present State of Virginia,* published in London in 1737, says that settlers at the Huguenot colony of Manikintown, fourteen miles north of Richmond, tried to domesticate buffalo in 1701.[13] "At the bottom of the lake," noted French explorer Armaud Louis de Delondarce de la Hontan in 1687 while exploring the southern shore at the eastern end of Lake Erie, "we find beeves upon the banks of two pleasant rivers that disengorge into it."[14]

In 1714 Marquis Jean-François Rigaud de Vaudreuil allegedly saw buffalo on the southern shore of Lake Erie but not on the northern shore.[15] In 1637 in *New England Canaan,* Thomas Morton described "great herds of well grown beasts that live about the parts of this Erocoise lake." These beasts were "the bigness of a cow, their flesh being very good food, their hides good leather, their fleeces very useful, being a kind of wool as fine almost as the wool of the Beaver, and the Savages do make garments thereof."[16] Most historians believe that "Erocoise Lake" is Lake Ontario, which was called Lake of the Iroquois by the French; it may mark the northeastern limit of the buffalo's range.

From Florida to Minnesota, and from North Carolina and Virginia to Kentucky and Tennessee, hundreds of creeks, rivers, bluffs, hills, lakes, fords, swamps, points, licks, and wallows have been named after buffalo. Such landmarks appeared on maps by 1670, but the earliest known naming of a Buffalo Creek was on October 7, 1728, in the journal of Colonel William Byrd during his sojourn in North Carolina.[17] By 1774, Sivelo Point, or Buffalo Point, in Tampa Bay, appears on Bernard Roman's *Map of Florida*. During the Seminole Wars, Lieutenant Robert C. Buchanan recorded in his journal of 1837–38 that his company "halted for a night at Buffalo Ford" near Lakeland, Florida.[18] Place names do not prove that buffalo roamed a region, but such clues often hark back to diaries of explorers and settlers.

Archaeological evidence of eastern buffalo is rare. Charles C. Jones wrote in 1873 in *Antiquities of the Southern Indians* that "I have seen the skull of a buffalo, with the horns still attached, in good state of preservation, which was plowed up in a field in Brooks County, Georgia."[19] Bones identified as *Bison bison* are listed in a 1941 report from a site dated 1600 A.D. at Irene Mound, in Chatham County, Georgia. H. B. Sherman at the University of Florida identified four bison carpal bones and part of a humerus found in Clay County, Florida, while excavating the site of Fort Pupo, a Spanish outpost built about 1716. In the late 1800s, a Franklin County Floridian unearthed a neck pendant made from a buffalo femur. A man dug up strips of buffalo horn in a mound east of the Black Warrior River, in Hale County, Alabama. In 1903 near Memphis, one Tennessee man discovered part of a buffalo's right humerus and right radius in Menard Mound; another Tennessean named Clarence Moore saw "many bison bones" in a field nearby. Still another amateur archaeologist found the jaw "of a young bison" in a gravel pit in Hamilton County in 1915. Buffalo bones in middens and mounds are rare, but deer and bear bones are common.[20]

Problems arise in plotting the buffalo's eastern range because of the scant archaeological evidence. And the fact that America was geographically amorphous during the earliest stages of white settlement increases the chance for error. In 1749 Swedish botanist Peter Kalm observed that "wild cattle are abundant in the southern parts of Canada . . . which are nearly in the same latitude with Philadelphia; but further to the north they are seldom observed."[21] If his figures are correct, "the southern parts of Canada" Kalm is writing about would be Illinois.

Buffalo herds in the East were never huge, never teeming, never rivaling the truly vast herds that thundered across the Plains until the latter half of the nineteenth century. Nor would buffalo east of the Mississippi figure as prominently in the hide trade as deer skins, furs, or other peltry. Eastern buffalo herds often numbered one hundred head or less. Droves of fewer than twenty were common. On the Illinois plains and around the salt licks in Kentucky and Tennessee, buffalo herds of five hundred to six hundred head were not unusual, but credible accounts of larger eastern herd counts are rare.

Compared with the herds west of the Mississippi, the buffalo to the east were hardly more than stragglers. Ironically, by the late 1500s, man created the niche that permitted the buffalo to enter the East. By the 1820s man destroyed them.

Indians, Barrens, Traces, and Wild Cows

EUROPEAN EXPLORERS SAW THE "NEW WORLD" AS A HOWLING WILDER-ness, an untamed and unsettled virgin land teeming with frightful, unseen things.

Englishmen described the forests as "savage," derived from the Latin root *silva,* meaning "wood." They also used the epithet to refer to forest-dwelling Irishmen prior to the first Anglo forays to North America. But after European contact, "savage" was identified with the fauna and flora in the sylvan glades: panthers, wolves, deer, elk, black bear, opossums, moose, caribou, buffalo, hardwoods, longleaf and loblolly pines, wildflowers, grasses, canes, shrubs, and forbs. And "savages" became the defining term for Indians.[1]

It is no wonder then that white explorers cast the newly discovered continent as a far-off, wild triune: a savage land, teeming with savage beasts, inhabited by savage folk. But it was not so to those descendants of the ancient ones who peopled the land, settled it, farmed it, hunted it, and built homes upon it. Population estimates of Indians living east of the Mississippi vary. John R. Swanton, the chronicler of southeastern tribes, places their number at about 170,000 by 1650. Anthropologist Henry Dobyns raises Swanton's number tenfold.[2]

An array of resources sustained the native people. Fish, crustaceans, shellfish, amphibians, reptiles, insects, dogs, aquatic mammals, hides, beans, squash, fruits and edible trees and plants, medicinal plants and herbs, flint, flour and dent corns of white, red, yellow, and blue kernels, peltry—Indians used them all, depending on their location and the season.[3] Small game—squirrels, rabbits, raccoons, beaver, other furbearers, and birds—was plentiful. Moose, bear, and caribou roamed the far Northeast. In the Southeast, deer, bear, and elk abounded in park-like savannas created by man, as they did in the *pays d'en haut,* the Middle Ground, which included the lands around the Great Lakes (except Lake Ontario, which fell within the domain of the Iroquois), reaching west to the Mississippi.

Indians east of the Mississippi used fire as a means to manage their resources. Igniting "surrounds"—torching dry leaves and grass into rings of fire five or six miles in circumference to drive game to the center to be killed—was a native hunting tactic. And it was often, depending on prevailing conditions and density of flammable cover, a hazardous one.

Fall was the season for fire-hunting deer; by October, browned thatches of grass and crisp fallen leaves readily ignited and bucks in rut were less wary. By the end of autumn, deer tended to become gaunt. From January to March, the Indians hunted bear, chasing the sluggish bruins from their dens with darts of lit cane or killing them in surrounds.

In 1708 Thomas Nairne observed a party of Chickasaw fire hunters. The men lit the land with cane torches in huge, sweeping circles, then stood along the scorched edges of the receding perimeter to wait. Rising flames licked inward, burning leaves and grass, brush, saplings, and cane. Three to four hours later, as the fire began to smolder, hunters with bows raced through the smoke to kill off their prey. A few panic-stricken deer bounded along the flashing margins and hurdled the flames, their white-tail flags flared high. Deer, bear, raccoons, opossums, rabbits, snakes, and turtles all perished in the inferno. "Of all hunting deversions," Nairne wrote, "I took most pleasure in firing rings for in that we never missed 7 or 10 Dear."[4]

Southeastern Indians managed their environment by slash-and-burn agriculture to kill off large trees and by controlled burns. Burning selected tracts served several purposes: It cleared an area from brush and undergrowth for planting, lessened the impact of damage from forest fires by eliminating combustible matter, eased foot travel, made for efficient food gathering (as in the collecting of pecans, hickory nuts, and chestnuts), made hunting easier, and kept homes and towns safe from enemies who might otherwise hide in the brush surrounding them.

Such fires burned fast yet at a low kindling temperature, sweeping past larger, more durable hardwoods but snuffing out hammocks, canebrakes, and underbrush, creating open forests. Firing destroyed juvenile stands of bayberry, sweet gum, red maple, juvenile oak, and hickory. Where longleaf pine seedlings were torched, older pines with fire-resistant bark (their growth more concentrated in the roots), sprouted quickly and displaced deciduous hardwoods with an evergreen mono-culture. "Only in the longleaf pine forests of the southern part of the nation did burning prove detrimental to deer," notes environmental historian Richard White. "Because of fires, longleaf pines dominated a region that otherwise would have been oak-hickory forest with a higher average carrying capacity for deer."[5]

Periodically burning off broad swatches of land killed weeds and less desirable floral species, as well as lice, fleas, chiggers, ticks, and rodents. Burning let sunlight penetrate to the forest floor, encouraging higher yields of forage. Ashes provided nutrients. Bursts of new shoots and tufts of grass created graze and browse that attracted game, especially white-tailed deer.

To keep their families fed, preserve tribal stability, and maintain or increase their bargaining power as skin traders, Indians assiduously guarded their hunting grounds. But in times of overhunting or calamities, bands migrated, trespassing on other tribes' territory. This sparked wars—often abetted by manipulative and genocidal policies of European leaders—between groups like the Chickasaw and Choctaw, Shawnee and Cherokee, Catawba and Cherokee, Natchez and Choctaw, Mesquakie (Fox) and Mascouten.

These Indian-made woodland parks were vast, airy, dotted here and there with timber. The oldest, tallest trees that had resisted the burning towered over seas of cane, grass, clover, pea vine, flowers, and sedges that grew as a variegated carpet of yellows, greens, and browns, splashed with vibrant pastels of wildflowers. Such parks increased the land's carrying capacity and helped create a niche for buffalo.[6]

By the dawn of the historic era, buffalo were a welcome novelty for Indians in the lower Mississippi drainage. In the South, the Cumberland Valley, the Bluegrass region, and the upper Mississippi basin, wild beef supplemented the Indians' fluctuating food supply. Upon entering this new ecological niche, the buffalo thrived. Herds increased. Range expanded.

Europeans called portions of the prairies in the Cumberland and Ohio Valley "barrens," believing that the sparse timber meant the soil was poor. In 1673 cartographer Louis Jolliet had heard of the "country ravaged by fire" and saw the barrens for himself. "At first when we were told of these treeless lands, I imagined . . . the soil was so poor that it produced nothing." But such reports, Jolliet said, were not true: "We have certainly observed the contrary . . . no better soil can be found."[7]

In 1765 English trader George Croghan had his own ideas about the source of such tales. "Some mention those spacious and beautiful meadows as barren savannas. . . . It has been the artifice of the French to keep us ignorant of the country."[8] George Washington was on the Great Kanawha in 1770 when a hunter named Nicholson told him about the barrens at the juncture of the Scioto and Ohio Rivers. "In these plains thousands, and 10,000sds. of buffalo may be seen feeding," Washington wrote.[9] Yet the myth of the "barren land" died slowly; as late as 1786 James Monroe wrote to Thomas Jefferson that the West was "miserably poor . . . and consists of extensive plains which have not had, from appearances, and will not have, a single bush on them for ages."[10]

The barrens came to life in the spring. In 1812 John Ross rode his horse through the barrens near Hopkinsville, Kentucky, finding it "difficult to imagine anything more beautiful." It seemed to be "one vast deep-green meadow, adorned with countless numbers of bright flowers springing up in all directions." Wild strawberries grew so thick that they stained his horse's hooves red.[11]

The largest patch of Tennessee barrens was in the northwest Highland Rim near the Pennyroyal Plain, in the Cumberland bottoms of Stewart, Montgomery, and Robertson Counties. Grasses there were "scrubby and coarse." Hundreds of buffalo grazed them. Blackjack and hickory shaded an undergrowth of gum and hazel. Tennesseans called the region the Big Barrens; Kentuckians knew the veldt as the Kentucky Meadows because the sweep of savanna defined a half-moon from Louisville to the Cumberland.[12] Boggy flatlands—called "pondy woods" or "crawfishy lands"—were unique to the southeastern Highland Rim barrens. The flora of the western Kentucky prairies was like that of the cedar glades in eastern Kentucky's Prairie Barrens, which extended into Middle Tennessee. Touching the western edge of Tennessee, spreading through Mississippi and Alabama, was the Black Belt Prairie.

One settler described the Kentucky Big Barrens as an "open prairie with hardly a stick of timber of sufficient size to make a rail as far as the eye could see." Another marveled at the "waving grasses so tall as to conceal a man on horseback." French botanist André Michaux delighted in his ride through the Big Barrens in 1802. "I was agreeably surprised to meet with a beautiful meadow, the abundant grass of which was from two to three feet high." Parts of the trail Michaux rode cut across the Kentucky counties of Green, Barren, Mercer, Marion, and Allen, entering Tennessee at Sumner County, forty miles northeast of Nashville. He estimated that the Big Barrens comprised "an extent from sixty to seventy miles in length by sixty miles in breadth."

As Michaux rode on, he had trouble finding water. Hot, thirsty, lonely, and at times lost, Michaux's enthusiasm for the Big Barrens had vanished by August 27 when he rode from the tall grass and into the forest, and to his "great satisfaction . . . got into the woods. Nothing can be more tiresome than the doleful uniformity of these immense meadows where there is nobody to be met with." Another rider soon became "satiated with the spreading fields of grass" and experienced "a feeling of desolation."[13]

Sinkholes littered the barrens. Horses bogged down chest-deep in sloughs, kicking up clouds of gnats, flies, and mosquitoes. Water holes and salt licks drew hundreds of animals that came to caper in the mire and dust and eat the brackish dirt. The ground in and about the licks was pocked like a moonscape by long, wide ditches, some ten feet across, that sloped inward and stopped abruptly at one end. These were hedged in on the sides by thin dirt walls five or six feet high; mammals formed the scalloped hollows by devouring the salty clay oozing from the springs.[14]

At large licks called "stamping grounds," the earth was so trodden and grubbed up that no grass grew for acres. Deer and elk browsed bushes bare. Buffalo rubbed sparse, scraggly trees barkless, scratching and knocking the saplings with their horns. And they wallowed. Bulls and old cows went first. Yearlings kept clear. The buffalo would throw themselves on their sides—their humps prevent them from rolling over—then arise, caked in mud, safe from flies and gnats.[15] Marquis Calmes passed through Kentucky in 1775 and described a wallow: "On the trace there was a great appearance of the earth being trod and washed away by reason of the ground being rolled and broken at those places."[16]

Licks, wallows, and stamping grounds were common sights. Canebrakes, savannas, and barrens meshed with forests, giving buffalo cover and pasture. Salt licks provided buffalo with minerals and, in the winter, kept their bowels from binding after eating the fibrous cane. Such was the land roamed by buffalo east of the Mississippi.

Long before Europeans beached their ships on the shores of the Americas, and long before buffalo grazed along the Mississippi's banks, Indians had a thriving system of commerce spanning hundreds of miles. Indeed, observes Dan Flores, it was this preexisting order that whites learned to exploit by altering "the patterns, goods, and the intensity of trade."[17] Before the Christian era, from the north, south, east, and west, Hopewell and Adena cultures flourished along a network of paths and trails. Along this web native traders carried a wealth of exotic goods.

Commodities mined from the Great Lakes included raw copper to pound into arm and wrist bands, reel-shaped gorgets, chest-plate armor, panpipes, and ear spools. Artisans carved catlinite and steatite into pipes and effigies and utilized mica dug from the eastern slopes of the Appalachians, as well as alligator and shark teeth, conch, welk, and iridescent pinkish white freshwater pearls. Workers lugged baskets filled with yaupon holly *(Ilex vomitoria)* leaves for the caffeinated "black drink" from its habitat along the Gulf to trade throughout the Southeast and north of the Ohio. Grizzly bear teeth and obsidian exchanged hands enough to find their way east of the Mississippi. Other trade items included salted and dried meat, body paints and dyes of lampblack, black lead, cassia, red ocher, cinnabar, black locust and bois d'arc (Osage orange) for bowmaking, herbs, flint, quartzite, colored stones, hematite and meteoric iron, gold and silver nuggets, pottery, vegetables, nuts, figurines, peltry, deer hides, salt, exotic feathers, and more.[18]

Historians are not sure how the system was organized or how it operated. During the historic period, some tribes acted as intertribal mediators. The Cree in the North and the Creek in the Southeast, for instance, dealt between factions as merchants and middlemen. This process of barter has yet to be fully understood. But what is known is that trails used for hundreds of years by beast and by man became well-established avenues that facilitated travel and trade.

The Warrior's Path led into Kentucky. The Miami knew it as Athiamiowee, meaning "path of the armed ones," used by Shawnee, Cherokee, Creek, and Catawba to raid one another. In 1784 it appeared on John Filson's "Map of Kentucke." This trace began in the Carolinas and Georgia, and entered east Tennessee past Reedy Creek and the Holston to the Cumberland Gap. From there it ran northward, past the Ouasioto Pass, to Es-kip-pa-ki-thi-ki in Clark County—the last Shawnee town in Kentucky. At Es-kip-pa-ki-thi-ki, the trail forked: One path led to the Scioto, the other to Upper Blue Licks toward the Ohio.

The Great War Path was another avenue. Alabama Creeks hunkered along its bends to attack the Overhill Cherokees who lived in the Blue Ridge. The war road led to Long Island, in east Tennessee, then forked. One prong went past the Holston Valley to what is now Saltville, Virginia; the other cut into Pennsylvania.[19]

By 1600 buffalo paths, or traces, began merging with trails. Traces circled hills and stabbed through tangles of laurel, leading to licks, pastures, rivers, creeks, and canebrakes. Buffalo cut a narrow path in the woods as they walked nose to tail in one long line, threading their way up and down ridges, across creeks, around bushes, rocks, and trees. Their sharp hooves pounded down trails in open land, chipping out dirt and rocks until the paths lay three or four feet below ground level. Banks along the sides rose as high as six feet. In Shelby County, Kentucky, a surviving trace measures forty feet across and four feet deep.[20]

Alanant-o-wamiowee, meaning "the Buffalo Path," cut through north-central Kentucky from Big Bone Lick in Boone County to Maysville in Mason County, 225 miles to the east. South of Big Bone, it ran to Drennon's Springs in Henry County and on to the Scott County town of Stamping Ground—"so named from the fact that the herds of buffalo which resorted here for salt water tramped or stamped down the undergrowth and soil for a great distance around." Limestone Street in Lexington follows part of this old trace.[21] From Scott County, Alanant-o-wamiowee crossed the Licking River in Nicholas County, then ran north to the Ohio to May's Lick. Thirty miles north from Big Bone, the Buffalo Path merged with a network of trails leading to Indian towns along the Ohio.

Indian-marked paths and buffalo traces often overlapped, but telling them apart was easy for hunters. Simon Kenton, a frontiersman who was in Kentucky by 1775, observed that war roads were not worn as deeply as traces, and trees along war roads were blazed and marked with red paint in deeply carved Indian pictographs.[22] Woodsmen like Kenton, Daniel Boone, and Casper Mansker distinguished between paths that just meandered and lead trails—paths that led to licks, rivers, canebrakes, and open land.

Traces from Indiana and Illinois joined at the Ohio near Lawrence, Indiana, emerging again on Kentucky's shore. From there the paths reached the licks west of the Kentucky and went on to the Salt River. One prong went past Athens, crossed the Kentucky near Boonesborough, then branched off to the Cumberland.[23] Settlers gouged traces into wagon trails, and laid railroad tracks on others. Some lead traces evolved into highways and state roads. When asked who Kentucky's roadmakers were, one old-timer replied, "the buffler, the Ingin, and the Ingineer."[24]

No one knows which southeastern Indians first utilized the buffalo. A melange of linguistic groups, confederacies, tribes, and clans lived along the Mississippi's lower drainage. Dr. Charles Hudson, leading authority on southeastern Indians, contends that at least four language families were represented, including "Algonquin (e.g., Powhatan, Shawnee), Iroquoian (e.g., Cherokee, Tuscarora), Siouan (e.g., Tutelo, Biloxi, Catawba), and Muskogean (e.g., Choctaw-Chickasaw, Alabama, Creek)."[25]

Caddoans, Siouans, Muskogeans, and Tunica groups erected villages from the Gulf of Mexico to the Arkansas River. Buffalo gave westerly located Caddoans in the Arkansas country "something of the cultural veneer of the Plains Indians. This tended to increase as they were pushed westward." There were other, less well-represented linguistic families and confederacies in the region, including the Natchez, Chitimacha, Yuchi, Timucuan, and Atakapa.[26]

The Natchez were hunting droves of buffalo—probably numbering under twenty head—at the time of Spanish and French contact. Great Suns—the Head Chiefs—lounged on royal thrones and beds of brain-tanned, hand-painted buffalo robes draped over a mesh of cane mats or upon skin mattresses stuffed with Spanish moss or goose down. During a funeral ritual following the death of Tattooed-Serpent, a brother to a Great Sun, several friends, wives, and loved ones closest to Tattooed-Serpent submitted to death by strangulation. Strong men—two warriors per noose—bound cords of woven buffalo hair about the victims' necks and yanked them taut until death throes were stilled, the bodies lurched forward, and the act was done.[27]

On the new moon of the ninth month of the Natchez calendar, villages began preparing to leave their towns to hunt buffalo. Tribal leaders dispatched scouts to find the herds grazing several leagues away. That done, reports Le Page Du Pratz, a Frenchman who lived among the Natchez from 1720–28, "everyone sets out, young and old, girls and women . . . for this hunt being rough there is work for everyone. Many nations wait until later before going, in order to find the bison in greater number and the cows fatter."[28] Yet even by the time of French colonization, buffalo were getting scarce in Natchez territory because of over-hunting.[29]

Choctaw, Chickasaw, and Upper and Lower Creeks utilized buffalo by about the same time as the Natchez. One French trader observed Choctaw women dressed in one-piece wrap around skirts of buffalo wool blended with fiber: "This fabric is double like the two-sided hand-kerchiefs and thick as canvas, half an ell wide and three quarters long." In winter Chickasaw women wrapped themselves in buffalo calf robes, the wool side turned inward.[30]

Such attire was as emblematic as it was practical. Among the Natchez, customs of symbolic dressing to set apart males and females in south-eastern Indian society began at birth. Women swaddled male infants in panther skins and females in deer hides or buffalo robes. Charles Hudson asserts that among some tribes:

The ideal woman was supposed to be docile and submissive. . . . Men appear to have symbolically associated women with buffalo or deer. Men, in some sense, "hunted" women just as they hunted buffalo or deer. . . . This may also explain why the deer and buffalo are seldom if ever portrayed in Southeastern Ceremonial Complex motifs. The men portrayed the animals whose qualities they feared or admired—not the ones they hunted.[31]

For these hunters living on the banks of the Mississippi, buffalo were a valued commodity. Buffalo flesh was delectable, especially smoked tongues, hump ribs, and tenderloins. Unlike western Indians, eastern Indians rarely, if ever, ate raw meat. Artisans crafted spoons, *micouenes,* of buffalo horn and made a myriad of items from buffalo parts, including saddles, rugs, mats, matchcoats, sashes, bracelets, and garters. Indians stuffed wool into moccasins for insulation and comfort and made hoes from shoulder blades. Fishermen wove cylindrical rawhide fish traps. Warriors laminated cane and rawhide into small, circular shields. Holy men carved buffalo effigies and incised pictographs on pipe bowls and into bone roach spreaders.[32]

Catawba warriors of South Carolina cut off buffalo hooves and bear and panther paws and tied them on their feet to make fake tracks. Cherokee or Delaware hunters—foes of the Catawba—were often enticed by the false spoor and followed it to their doom. In the mid-1760s, Daniel Boone was hunting with some Cherokee in the Blue Ridge when scouts came across a sprinkling of buffalo tracks. Boone was puzzled; though he knew of buffalo, he had probably not hunted them, as the herds by then were more to the west. The Cherokee were wary. "No buffala," one whispered. "Tawbers." Cautious, poised, and with guns on half-cock, they rounded a bend, nearly stepping in a fresh pad of buffalo dung. "Tawber no make so!" someone said, followed by laughter.[33]

North of the Ohio River, by the 1700s Algonquins ate wild beef and made items from the beast. Skins were brain-tanned, but native tanners also used tannin leached from white-oak bark. English explorer John Lawson observed that Indians "wear Shooes, of Bucks and sometimes Bears Skin, which they tan in an Hour or two; with the Bark of Trees boil'd wherein they put the Leather whilst hot, and let it remain a little while, whereby it becomes so qualify'd, as to endure Water and Dirt, without growing hard."[34] A green hide stretched over a sapling frame made a rainproof and sunproof lean-to.[35] Indians carried buffalo skin bags fitted with a strap, called a tumpline, that was wide in the middle, tapered at the ends, and woven of wool or nettle fiber. Leather whangs tied the tumpline ends to the bundle, and the wide part of the strap lay across the forehead so that while the burden was being carried, the bag sat in the crook of the lower back. White market hunters adopted these "happis bundles" to carry loads of meat, though they altered the word to "hop-pus," meaning "to carry."[36]

The Shawnee named the buffalo Mathuetha. Warriors crossing the Ohio at Limestone (now Maysville), Kentucky, in the 1770s ferried over in a buffalo hide boat made of four bull hides; the boat could hold up to twenty men.[37] East of the Mississippi, buffalo boats were less common than on the Missouri, but eastern Indians and white hunters were familiar with their construction. Still, poplar, cypress, and pine dugouts, elm and birch bark canoes, and rafts of logs, skins, cane, and rushes were more common than buffalo boats.

Brain-tanned buffalo robes were winter wear for Indians living in the Middle Ground. Fort Detroit was a focal point of trade. In 1718 a Detroit trader wrote that Potawatomi men wore "red or blue cloth" in the summer and buffalo robes in the winter—the robes secured from tribes who hunted as far west as Iowa.

White traders made the same observation about the Sauk, Fox, and Illinois who lived farther west, where buffalo hunting was confined to Iowa, the Illinois prairies, and the upper Mississippi drainage. There, unlike in the Southeast, herds numbered into the hundreds and were a dependable winter food, making the Sauk and Fox perhaps the most buffalo-dependent Indians in the east. At a Wabash village in 1782, to protest high-priced European and American trade goods, warriors gave up their guns to hunt with bows and arrows. "Three quarters of the Wabash villagers," one trader noted, "were wearing buffalo skins in place of blankets."[38]

Life for Indians living east of the Mississippi was not idyllic. Just as there were times of fat, there were times of lean. In Illinois, the lean times lasted from late winter to early summer, between deer and buffalo hunts and harvest.[39] In the upper Mississippi, winter was an especially "starving time." And worse, skirmishes between tribes and confederacies were common.[40]

Within Caddoan, Creek, Shawnee, Fox, Potawatomi, Winnebago, and other Algonquin and Siouan societies were totemic buffalo clans with buffalo rituals. Buffalo tales do not appear in the oral traditions of southeastern Indians, the League of the Iroquois, or the northeastern Algonquins, though the Alabamas initiated the "buffalo dance."[41] The buffalo was far less central in the lives of eastern Indians than in the lives of the Plains Indians, who farmed less than their Woodland kinsmen; buffalo hunting by Indians in the east was often the exception rather than the rule.

Yet as anthropologist John R. Swanton, whose encyclopedic collection of ethnographic sketches for the Smithsonian Institution remains a landmark in American Indian research, observes, "In spite of the fact that bison disappeared from the Gulf region rather rapidly in colonial times, they were formerly much relied upon as raw material for many purposes, and a knowledge of many of these has come down to us."[42]

By the 1760s, the Delaware, Shawnee, and other Woodland tribes had adapted the horse to hunting. As native hide hunters killed off herds of white-tailed deer, Indians began to depend more heavily on buffalo. As one Delaware told a Virginian in 1768, "The elks are our horses, the buffaloes are our cows, the deer are our sheep, & the whites shan't have them."[43]

Up to about 1700, except in the extreme southeast of Natchez territory, buffalo herds increased, stretching their traces across eastern America. Indians continued their practices of burning and farming, managing the land, their resources, and game herds. But the coming Anglo horde irrevocably altered native life and the indigenous flora and fauna. "Europeans," declares Francis Jennings, "did not conquer wilderness; they conquered Indians. They did not discover America; they invaded it."[44]

Buffalo and Spanish Invaders

ON OCTOBER 12, 1492, A GENOESE SEA CAPTAIN, CHRISTOPHER Columbus, and his crew beached their ships on San Salvador, unfurled their colors, and named their newfound island chain the Indies. What followed after Columbus's discovery was cataclysmic. By 1500 the Indians' world stood poised on the brink of radical change, one that forever altered how they lived, worked, played, and worshiped. The arrival of white aliens in huge dugouts bearing snapping sails put some Arawak-speaking Tainos in mind of gray wings of great birds soaring in from afar. The Indians wondered: Could these pale visitors be from the sky?[1]

The Taino came to the men with gifts, dazzled by these strange folk who had landed on their shores. The intruders were equally dazzled by the encounter—not only by this New World they had "discovered," but by the land's potential. This land and its riches, Spanish invaders of Mesoamerica rightly assumed, would make them wealthy and bring favor at the king's court.

Indians soon learned that these pale folk were not from the sky. The Spanish did not understand the Taino gifts as presents, but as tribute. And the Spanish demanded more. Much more.

Whites invading what became the continental United States found little silver or gold. But the rich land, unique flora and fauna, and diverse native cultures that Europeans saw and wrote about created a New World that became an exotic place of romance, mystery, and always, of untapped wealth. Ironically, the wealth *was* there, but it was not the sort of glittering riches the Europeans had come in search of. Rather, the real wealth in America was its plenteous natural bounty.

Conquistadors were formidable mercenaries feared even by the Spanish government. Living by the sword, they often died by it. After

years of holy war and expansionist jaunts into North Africa, these ruthless adventurers—accompanied by their Roman Catholic fathers, which
helped give this wave of New World imperialism a Crusadelike aura—
came to America in the wakes of the Niña, Pinta, and Santa Maria.
Although armed with pikes, swords, shields, and muskets, the germs the
Europeans carried—influenza, measles, chicken pox, diphtheria, and
smallpox—killed far more Indians than their weapons ever did.

In 1519 Hernán Cortés and his conquistadors invaded Mexico. The
marauders killed and plundered their way through Vera Cruz—Cortés's
terrorist band massacred more than three thousand men in two hours at
Cholula—then headed inland to take Tenochtitlán, the Aztec citadel. It
was there, wrote the Spanish historian De Solis perhaps two centuries
later, that Cortés saw his first buffalo in the menagerie of Montezuma,
the Aztec emperor. De Solis described the *cibola, bisonte,* or *armenta,*
various names for the "the Mexican bull," as "a wonderful composition
of divers animals," having "crooked shoulders, with a bunch on its back
like a camel; its flanks dry . . . its neck covered with hair like a lion: It is
cloven-footed, its head armed like that of a bull."[2] That De Solis is describing a buffalo is beyond dispute. Whether this is an accurate rendering of what Cortés saw two centuries before is a different matter.

Alvar Núñez Cabeza de Vaca—"Cabeza de Vaca" being an ancestral
title taken from Núñez's maternal side meaning "the head of a cow"—
was one of the first Spaniards to see buffalo in North America. In 1528
Núñez's captain, Pánfilo de Narváez, a tough, red-bearded man on a
quest sanctioned by Charles V to outdo Cortés, beached his galleon at
Tampa Bay.

Bouts of mayhem, murder, and retaliatory Apalachee Indian attacks
left a remnant of the Spaniards rowing along the Gulf flats in five soggy,
half-inflated horse-hide boats. Narváez abandoned Núñez—the ship's
treasurer—and three other men on the coast. On Galveston Island,
Núñez lived "among the [Karankawa] Indians, and [went] naked like
them."

Surviving by his wits for eight years, Núñez first was a slave, then became a shaman, and turned to being a trader, dealing in buffalo hides and
other goods. He rejoined his comrades in 1536. Buffalo, he wrote in his
memoirs, which he began in 1537 and published in 1542, "come from
the north, across the country further on to the coast of Florida, and are
found all over the land for four hundred leagues." He said they were "the
size of those [cattle] in Spain." Their wool was long, "like fine wool. . .
and a great quantity of hides are met with inland."[3] Exactly where Núñez

saw the herds or just how far east the buffalo had roamed by the early 1500s is unclear. In 1528 La Florida, meaning "the land of flowers," was a haphazardly mapped, amorphous region from the panhandle extending as far west as Galveston Bay.

Núñez and his companions were the first Europeans to cross that portion of North America on foot, covering about three thousand miles. His writings influenced others to follow in his tracks, altered existing maps, and helped fill in geographic knowledge of the region. His account implies that buffalo were nearing the more eastern regions of North America and may already have entered them.[4]

In 1539 revelations from fray Marcos de Niza touched off a quixotic quest for wealth that reached Spain. His was an exciting tale. While visiting the land of the Zuni and Pueblo in the Southwest, the friar believed he had spied El Dorado—the Seven Cities of Cíbola. Each city, Indians told him, was a citadel with huge caches of ivory, gold and silver, pearls and gems. Affidavits signed by locals confirmed Marcos's speculations, convincing even skeptics of the Seven Cities' existence and of their location. Rumors of de Niza's discovery bode good tidings for conquistadors.

Tales of the Seven Cities spread. In Spain, Alvar Núñez—back from his eight-year sojourn from Florida to Mexico—debated with Hernando de Soto over the feasibility of seeking the Seven Cities. De Soto made plans to go, albeit starting from the Southeast. Ultimately the tales reaped little gold but did reveal to European eyes the vast herds of buffalo in the lands west of the Mississippi.

In 1540 Franciso Vásquez de Coronado and his conquistadors became the first Europeans to campaign in the Southwest. The army was nearly three hundred strong. Two hundred twenty-five men rode horses; one rode a mule; the rest marched, armed with crossbows, two-handed swords, dirks and daggers, and arquebuses—big-bore matchlock muskets ignited by a long, slow-burning cord. Copper gorgets about their necks glowed in the sun. Here and there were coats and breeches of mail, gauntlets, breastplates, and chin pieces. Coronado sat in his saddle in gilded armor. The rank and file dressed in leather jerkins, jackets, and cuirasses to fend off arrows, their morions (high-crested helmets) and rawhide hats adorned with swaying ostrich plumes of black, white, and red.[5]

Coronado's army crossed from Mexico through New Mexico and clear to Kansas, seeing herds of Great Plains buffalo. The men fed on buffalo tongues, short ribs, and hump meat, but they had trouble killing the beasts. The arquebus and, by the 1600s, the *escopeta* (meaning "shotgun") seldom brought down a buffalo with one shot. Reloading the arquebus was a slow, hazardous process. The *escopeta*'s miquelet lock, strong enough to strike sparks from roughly-knapped hunks of New Mexican quartz, was an improvement over the matchlock, but misfires were common.

Coronado never found the Seven Cities of Cíbola, though he and his men wreaked havoc among the Pueblo Indians. His journals show that the Great Plains teemed with buffalo as far east as Kansas. When read in conjunction with the diary of Hernando de Soto, Coronado's journals demonstrate that buffalo were nearing the Mississippi and may already have crossed it.[6]

On May 18, 1539, Hernando de Soto and 600 men, 100 slaves and camp followers, 220 horses, mules, a pack of Irish wolfhounds and bloodhounds, and a swine herd sailed from Havana, Cuba. Within days de Soto's ship landed just south of Tampa Bay, where his expedition—the most famous of all Spanish thrusts into the Southeast—began. Born in 1500, de Soto was a man on a mission. Attaining the rank of Captain at age twenty, he had fought with Pizarro in Peru when the Spaniards massacred the Inca and smashed their empire. Eager to chisel his name into the stone tablets of conquistador immortals, he sought his own Tenochtitlán to best the exploits of Cortés and Pizarro. Not one to flinch at death-dealing in his quest for glory, de Soto's tactics were as lethal as those of his mentors.

Timucuans living near Tampa Bay were the first to feel de Soto's fury when they resisted being made beasts of burden. The conquistadors killed many Timucuans outright, tortured others, or tracked them down to be torn asunder by wolfhounds. The Spaniards impressed Timucuans surviving de Soto's wrath into a death march of slavery. By March 1540 de Soto had pushed past the land of the Apalachees. He had little choice: The Apalachees, remembering Panfilo de Narváez's brand of diplomacy, turned upon this new wave of conquistadors.

Near Florida's northern border, de Soto entered a new ecological niche. There were few deer in the hammocks of pine, cypress, saw grass, and palmetto in Florida's scrub and swamps, but deer were plentiful in the Georgia savannas. Venison kept the Spaniards alive, but de Soto's chronicler makes no mention of buffalo in Georgia. By June 1540 de Soto was bivouacked on an island in the Tennessee River, flowing by the Occaneechi Trace. In the temple of Talimeco (near what is now Augusta), one of de Soto's men saw "breastplates" and "head-pieces of raw-hide." They ate "fresh beef" at a town near the Savannah River, but the Indians did not tell them where they got it. De Soto saw a rack of "cow horns" hung in a village in northern Georgia.[7]

De Soto sent two riders ahead to search the Cumberland Plateau for gold. Beginning the ascent to what is now called Lookout Mountain, they crossed at a river gorge thirteen miles from the confluence of the Tennessee and the Little Tennessee. Called Un'tiguhi' (variously meaning "the whirl," "boiling pot," or "the suck") by the Cherokee, the inlet was a treacherous ford where swift currents and strong undertows boiled through a strait sixty yards across. Men and horses barely made it to shore.

They found no gold, even though they asked a band of Yuchi living near the Indian town of Chisca (near present day Chattanooga) about the yellow metal. Obligingly, the Indians brought gifts of copper, freshwater pearls, and mica. Before the men returned to Georgia, their guides handed them a "cow-hide as delicate as a calf-skin . . . the hair being like the soft wool on the cross of a merino with the common sheep."[8] That this was a buffalo robe is likely, but no mention is made of its origin.

The Spaniards pushed on through the Southeast. Weeks later at what is now Mobile they fought a desperate battle resulting in heavy losses for both sides. Mobile was a turning point. After that, the Indians, retaliating against the invaders who had enslaved and slaughtered their kinsmen and torched their villages, dogged them along the way, attacking in hit-and-run raids. By December 1540 the white men were moving west through north Mississippi, a route taking them near Tishomingo to just south of what is now Memphis.

In May 1541, as they reached the Mississippi, de Soto's army encountered hostile Tunica speakers at the town of Quizquiz, just below what is now Friars Point, Mississippi. There de Soto ordered barges built to cross the river. Leather boots touched Arkansas soil. The men walked northward, driving their horses, dogs, and pigs.

At Casqui, near Arkansas's White River, the whites found a half-devoured buffalo. Tula Indians living south and west of the region, in the western fringes of the Southern Culture Area, heavily exploited the buffalo and were a buffalo-dependent people. Here de Soto's chronicler saw piles of buffalo hides, stores of wild beef, and rawhide shields. As the Tula lived chiefly on buffalo, they farmed less than Indians living farther east of the Mississippi.[9]

Despondent, gaunt, and ill, Hernando de Soto died on May 21, 1542. His men bound his corpse in a blanket weighted with sand, and the Mississippi became his tomb. After fourteen more months of wandering and wading bogs and bayous, on July 18, 1543, about three hundred of the survivors shoved off from the sandy shores of the Gulf coast in home-made boats, sailing toward Mexico. For the Spaniards, minus their leader and reduced to less than half their original number, de Soto's expedition

had been a steady disaster. For the mound-building horticulturist Missis-
sippians—the lineal ancestors to the Creek, Choctaw, and Chickasaw
who, lacking immunity to Old World diseases, were ravaged by epi-
demics—de Soto's rampage through the Southeast left a legacy of
death.[10]

Apparently, neither de Soto nor his men saw buffalo until they
crossed the Mississippi. Other early Spanish adventurers in Florida—including Juan Ponce de León, who visited Calusa Indians in southwestern
Florida in both 1513 and 1521; Tristán de Luna, who in 1559 set out to
establish a settlement on the Gulf of Mexico and explore the interior of
the Tennessee Valley to the Point of Santa Elena, South Carolina; and
Juan Pardo, whose journey from 1566 to 1568 retraced parts of de Soto's
trail in an attempt to create a trade route from South Carolina to Mexico—did not mention seeing buffalo. That such explorers would have
failed to note the novel sight of a wild cow had they seen one is unlikely.

But that does not prove that no buffalo had yet ranged east of the
Mississippi. As scientist Erhard Rostlund observes:

> The narratives of the De Soto expedition imply that the bison, if
> not actually present in the Tennessee River valley in the six-
> teenth century, was found not very far to the north or northwest
> of that river. . . . We have no record of when the first historic
> bison reached Alabama, Georgia, or Florida, but it is possible
> . . . that small unobserved groups or individual forerunners of the
> larger herds to come were on the move in the Southeast as early
> as de Soto's time or shortly thereafter.[11]

Indeed, there may be anomalies concerning buffalo demographics
and range east of the Mississippi. In 1565 Pedro Menéndez de Avilés, re-
garded by some historians as the founder of Spanish Florida, established
the settlement that became St. Augustine. His plans reflected those of the
Spanish crown. French ships from Fort Caroline, a Huguenot colony fifty
miles north of St. Augustine at the mouth of the St. John's River, were
preying on Spanish vessels; the French proved to be an obstacle to trade
in New Spain. In 1566 Menéndez and his army of five hundred men
smashed Fort Caroline and cut down the Protestants.

Menéndez heard rumors of Huguenot settlements cropping up
north of the Carolinas. Tales abounded of a bustling trade between Indians and Frenchmen. In a letter allegedly written circa 1566 to His Most
Catholic Majesty, Philip II, King of Spain, Menéndez reported that

"bison-skins were brought by the Indians down the Potomac and thence carried along shore in canoes to the French about the Gulf of St. Lawrence." In just two years, he wrote, the French had shipped six thousand buffalo hides to France.[12]

Some writers, like Francis Parkman, doubt Menéndez. One anonymous "master-critic" called him "a matchless liar," warning that his name was "not to be conspicuously associated with the truth." Historian H. H. Bancroft rejected the account but thought that Menéndez had told his story as it was told to him, having been deceived by a talebearer. Menéndez waxed eloquent in his letters to Philip II of the fine things that could be done in New Spain: growing sugar cane and vineyards, raising livestock, harvesting freshwater pearls. Whether his claim of "6,000 bison-skins" is spurious, no one can say. And too, in this vague reference from the Gulf of St. Lawrence, "bison-skins" might be a generic term meaning buffalo, elk, or caribou hides. But taken in the overall context of Spanish, French, and English accounts, there is a chance Menéndez was reporting what he knew firsthand.[13]

Perhaps Bishop Gabriel Díaz Vara Calderón recorded the first credible seventeenth-century buffalo sighting in peninsular Florida. While visiting from Cuba, Father Calderón set up missions in Florida (Florida missions were then under his authority) and wrote about Indian life and converting Indians to the Church. The Indians, he noted in 1675, "enter the forest in pursuit of bears, bisons *(cibolas)* and lions [panthers]."[14]

From 1683 to 1686 Marcus Delgado, in an abortive attempt to reach the Mississippi, explored the land of the Creek and Choctaw while searching for a colony of La Salle's men rumored to be living on the Gulf coast. In 1686 he saw buffalo northwest of what is now Marianna, Florida, in Jackson County. Again, near the Little Choctawhatchee River, in the southeastern corner of Alabama (in Houston County), Delgado "observed many buffaloes."[15] Martin de Echagaray reported from Jackson County in 1684 that "the country abounds in cattle ... which produces as good a wool as that gotten from a sheep's back."

In 1693 Don Carlos de Sigüenza y Góngora visited Indians in what is now Santa Rosa County, Florida, and "found buffalo meat . . . buffalo skins . . . spindles and distaffs of yarn of buffalo hair . . . ladles made of buffalo horn . . . and a large frightful buffalo head that was still intact." On East Bay River, Góngora's men happened upon an abandoned camp. Spitted over the smoldering fire were singed hunks of half-cooked buffalo meat; in the center of the ash heap sat a clay pot filled with a rank swill of stewed buffalo entrails.

At another abandoned Indian site, Góngora discovered caches of pulverized buffalo meat and items made from the beast. "What was peculiar here was the fact that the buffalo meat was not only half-cooked as at the other camp, but it had been pounded into very fine, evil smelling powder. . . . Near numerous . . . were ten or a dozen tanned hides of this animal [and] considerable yarn of buffalo hair." On June 25, 1693, in Okaloosa County near the Blackwater River, Laureano de Torres y Ayala saw "numerous buffalo tracks" and a "buffalo trail leading to a ford" across a creek.[16]

Fray Rodrigo de la Barreda, in Liberty County, Florida, between the Apalachicola and Taluga Rivers in 1693, recorded that "a number of buffalo were killed." Near the site he remarked a year later that Apalachee Indians "went on hunting trips for buffalo, of which there is abundance." Andrés de Pez, who was in western Florida the same year, confirmed Barreda's observations. "Many buffaloes, deer, and wild turkeys," he wrote, "are found generally throughout the same region." Father Don Patricio Hinachuba at the Mission San Lorenzo de Ivitachuco, in Jefferson County, mentions "a hunt for buffalo *(civo, cibolo),"* and "Indians coming to sell buffalo skins."

Other Spaniards wrote in their journals about small herds of buffalo they saw in the Southeast. A perusal of the diary of Diego Peña, who in 1716 traveled through parts of Florida, Georgia, and Alabama, shows that Peña frequently encountered buffalo, but their numbers were few.

From the memoirs of Diego Peña: 1716

August 13 [Alachua County, Florida]: The Indians killed two buffalo *(sibolas),* two [domestic] cows and four deer.

August 20 [Alachua County]: Here three buffalo and six deer were killed.

August 24 [near the Suwannee River, in Lafayette County]: There is much game, deer and buffalo, hereabouts. They killed two buffalo, and four deer, and caught many fish.

August 25 [Lafayette County]: At this place there are many buffalo. Two were killed.

August 27 [Taylor County]: Two buffalo and three deer were killed. Many are the buffalo which have withdrawn to this region.

August 28 [Taylor County]: We killed two buffalo and six deer.

August 30 [Madison County]: Three buffalo were killed.

September 7 [Jefferson County]: Three buffalo were killed. The *chicazas* [old abandoned farm fields] abound in buffalo.

September 8 [Leon County]: Five buffalo, two [domestic] cows and eleven deer were killed.

On September 10, "in a boat made from green buffalo hide," Peña crossed the Ochlockonee—a dark, brackish river that flows from Leon County to Gadsden County, Florida—and pushed on, entering Georgia, where he encountered a transitional, more open ecosystem. Fording the Ochlockonee was perilous; heavy rains had swollen the river from its banks, but the Spaniard's buffalo boat served them well. "The hide with its gunwales, ribs and stem holds three persons, or more than a dozen arrobas of baggage." They marched one league and camped. Peña and his men dined on feral cattle that they had rounded up in the abandoned fields of Florida. Buffalo meat, wrote Peña from in Georgia, "is better than that of the cow, the fat is thinner and is tinged with yellow, and has the flavor of mutton." His journal continues:

> September 12 [Gadsden County, near the Georgia line]: A buffalo was killed and two [domestic] cows were killed.
> September 13 [At a Seminole village, in Seminole County, Georgia, near the confluence of the Flint and Chattahoochee Rivers]: I made my abode on some benches . . . carpeted with buffalo skins.
> September 24 [Clay County, Georgia]: Six buffalo were killed.
> September 25 [Barbour County, Alabama]: We camped on a prairie belonging to some Christian [Apalachee] Indians, having a bountiful harvest of corn, beans, pumpkins, as well as the fruits of the forest, such as chestnuts, acorns, medlars, as well as buffalo.[17]

Diego Peña was not the only eighteenth-century Spanish explorer who saw buffalo in Florida. At Fort San Marcos, in Wakulla County, Andrés Gonzáles de Barcia wrote in 1718, "To support themselves, the soldiers had to go out hunting buffalo *(cibolas)*, which are very plentiful."

Possibly the earliest eyewitness glimpse of buffalo in the far Southeast that can be trusted as genuine is from Bishop Gabriel Díaz Vara Calderón in 1675. But writings from a castaway named Hernando d'Escalante Fontaneda predate both Calderón and Pedro Menéndez de Avilés (1566). Sailing on a Colombian ship bound for Spain, in 1551 Fontaneda was shipwrecked at age thirteen on the Florida Keys. He lived in Florida for about fifteen years with various tribes and knew of many more, including the Apalachee, Calusa, Gaucata, Timucua, and Jeaga. By 1566 Fontaneda had made his way back to Spain, where he wrote his memoirs in 1575. During his journeys in Florida, he reported, he stayed for two years with Apalachee Indians, then living near what is now Tallahassee. Fontaneda wrote that the Apalachee ate "deer, foxes, woolly cattle . . . and many other animals."

Historians are not sure what to make of Fontaneda's writings. Both linguist Buckingham Smith (who in 1854 translated Fontaneda's work, *Memoir of Do. d'Escalante Fontaneda*) and ethnologist John R. Swanton doubt his story, believing he made up portions of it. And the provenance of some of the pages from Fontaneda's narrative lead some to think that they may have been written by another hand. Still, much of the writing is an accurate description of the early flora and fauna of frontier Florida, so it seems someone reported seeing "woolly cattle" in Florida in the mid-1500s.[18]

One of the last observations of buffalo sign in Florida was made in 1772. At an unstated location northwest of Tampa Bay, English surveyor Bernard Romans "found the footsteps of six or eight buffaloes, so plain as to be convinced of the tracks being made by those animals." Such a late date in the history of the eastern buffalo is unusual, and it is not certain whether the "footsteps" Romans saw were made by buffalo or feral cattle. Yet that buffalo spoor may have been observed by Romans near Tampa harmonizes with earlier accounts, and this vicinity must represent the extreme southern range of the historic buffalo.

Although the accounts of buffalo in the lower Mississippi drainage in pre-1675 Spanish narratives are likely to be vague or spurious or of questionable authority, Spanish explorers were sighting buffalo throughout the Southeast by the 1670s. Englishmen like James Needham and Dr. Henry Woodward, traveling the inner Southeast in the 1670s, saw buffalo. French fur traders and Jesuits exploring the upper Mississippi basin at the same time were feasting on buffalo meat and recording their observations of herds that numbered in the hundreds. In the Southeast, droves averaged twenty to thirty head.[19]

Spanish territory extended upward from Central America into Mexico, California, much of the American Southwest, Texas, and across to Florida, but Spain's early monopoly on the Americas was not to last. Other nations began hearing of the New World. Soon Indians watched other European ships skirt coastlines for bays, estuaries, and rivers leading into the heart of the continent.

Fleur-de-Lis and
les Boeufs Sauvages

AND SO THE CONQUISTADORS FOUGHT AND PLUNDERED THEIR WAY EAST
of the Mississippi. European quests for land, wealth, glory, and "heathen
souls" sparked a mad rush of New World conquests. No less than the Portuguese, the Italians, the king of Spain, and the Dutch, French king Francis I cast his lot far to the western half of the globe. Two French ships
commanded by Jacques Cartier bearing stark flags emblazoned with the
cross reached the Canadian shores of Cape Bonavista on May 10, 1534.
His orders from Francis I were blunt: Cartier was to search for "a great
deal of gold and other rich things."[1]

Cartier searched. French fishermen living in rude huts on Grand
Banks, Labrador, and Blanc Sablon, Quebec, guided him along the capes,
ports, islands, and islets scattered throughout the Gulf of St. Lawrence. He
inquired among coastal Indians. The Canadian coastline was rocky, cold,
bleak, desolate—"I am inclined to regard this land as the one God gave to
Cain," Cartier scribbled in his journal.[2] Rich things were few. Fish,
geese, ducks, parakeets, and seals abounded, but steering two ships between tilting ice floes in high seas made for treacherous sailing. On land,
mosquitoes and flies devoured Cartier and his men. On September 5,
1534, his two ships slipped back into the harbor of Saint-Malo.

Reports from Cartier's last two American voyages (1535–36 and
1538–43) revealed more dismal news, but with one big difference: Native
towns thrived on the St. Lawrence at the mouths of Saguenay River,
Three Rivers, and southwest almost to what is now Montreal. Indians
lived on meat and maize and dwelt in bark huts. The rich soil reaped
bountiful harvests. Caribou migrated in herds that made the ground
shake beneath their hooves. Bear and moose were abundant. Fisher, mink,
pine marten, otter, fox, and beaver teemed. Cod schooled thicker in the
Atlantic swirl pushing past the Grand Banks than in any other ocean in

the world. Sturgeon ten feet long splashed and rolled in brackish spill-ways like suddenly loosed ricks of cordwood. Whales, dugongs, dolphins, and walruses frolicked along the coast. Vast shellfish shoals emerged from the receding waters at low tide.

There were no spices, no gold or gems in quantities worth mining, but inland, Canada's soil and growing season promised good harvests; the St. Lawrence and its tributaries opened new vistas of adventure and opportunity. French merchants, traders, trappers, and market hunters would find great value in fish and in the fur, skin, hides, oil, tallow, and flesh of New World mammals. And so this huge swath of the New World was well suited for colonization.

New France. Samuel de Champlain's settling of Quebec in 1608 was an Old World milestone, the first European stronghold past the mouth of the St. Lawrence. French territory took in the stretch of the St. Lawrence to the Great Lakes. Farther west were the remote forests of black spruce, tamarack, and cedar of Canada's Alneau Peninsula, border-ing Lake of the Woods. About 190 miles northwest of Lake Superior, Lake of the Woods is in a lush coniferous region, rich in fur and fought over by the Cree, northern Ojibwa, and Minnesota Dakota. A portage southward from Lake Superior led to the Mississippi and its arteries. The Mississippi flowed to the Gulf of Mexico, falling into the sea at the port of New Orleans. Claims along the shores of the Mississippi included New Orleans, Mobile, Kaskaskia, and the upper Illinois country, and west from the branches of the Missouri to the upper Mississippi drainage nearly to the Ohio River, the Great Lakes, to the mouth of the St. Lawrence.

The French learned to deal with Indians. Crown interests and em-pire building came first; here beaver pelts reigned supreme. Using native customs of gift giving and exchanging belts of nettle strung with thou-sands of purple wampum drilled from the spiraled interiors of quahog clams and of white wampum grains made from conch, the French created bonds with Algonquin groups. Skirmishes between factions strengthened the fragile alliances; allied with the Algonquins and Mon-tagnais, Champlain attacked the Mohawks in 1609, driving enmity be-tween the French and the Iroquois Five Nations.

With the French notions of civility came the Jesuits—the vicar's soldiers of the cross—to convert the "sauvages" to the Church, a process which often subjugated natives to the status of pawns for the Crown. These Black Robes, Indians thought, were sachems (holy men) or manitous (spirit beings) or demons whose odd attire, prayers to the one Manitou, chants, ceremonies and sacraments, talking paper (writing), Holy Book,

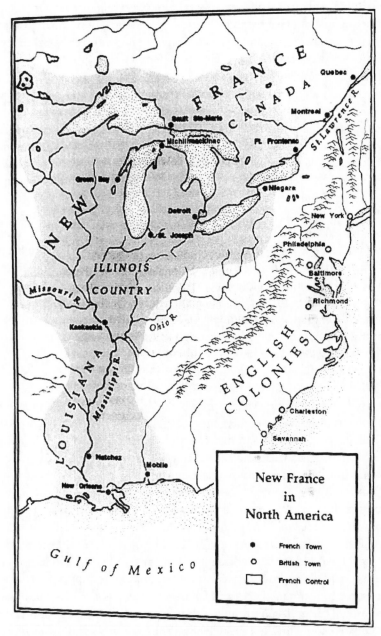

"New France in North America." (Reprinted from Charles J. Balesi, *The Time of the French in the Heart of North America: 1673–1818*. Map by Tom Willcockson.)

and "water sorcery" (baptism) to steal the soul bespoke strong medicine. Friars are firsthand players in the saga of the buffalo east of the Mississippi. Their journals, diaries, and letters teem with precise insights into the role of the buffalo in Indian life; their words are vital to grasping the breadth of wild cow history.

Such was the geographic and cultural landscape of New France. Exploration, colonization, settlement, and conquest demanded subsistence. Wild meat sustained settlers from the St. Lawrence to New Orleans even after domestic herds and crops thrived in towns. (The French imported cattle to Kaskaskia, Illinois, in 1721; farmers harvested wheat in the region by 1714.) Buffalo grazed in the upper and lower Mississippi basin. Herds numbering up to 600 head massed at the confluences of the Mississippi's major tributaries: the Missouri, Wabash, Ohio, Arkansas, Red, and Yazoo. Buffalo were the most easily hunted of all North American big game. For the trifling sum of a big musket ball and a stout black-powder charge, buffalo delivered the most product. French empire builders exploited tongues, meat, skins, robes, wool, and tallow as potential sources of wealth. But attempts to market buffalo failed to make New France self-sufficient. By the end of the French era, one message was clear: The success of New France's economy west of the Appalachians could not depend upon buffalo.

Perhaps the first recorded encounter of Frenchmen with buffalo was in 1565, when Pedro Menéndez de Avilés attacked Fort Caroline in Florida, routing and slaughtering its Huguenot defenders. Nicholas Le Challeux saw an animal in his retreat, "a great beast like a deer, which had a very big head, flaming and staring eyes, pendant ears, and a humped back."[3] Challeux's description may be that of a buffalo.[4]

In the 1600s, voyageurs—professional canoemen—began passing through the Great Lakes and its tributaries to the heart of America. Most voyageurs stood about five feet tall and were sturdily built; fur takers hired short men because of confined canoe space. On water they were workhorses, able to paddle long miles in time to lively *chansons* (songs), resting oars across gunwales on the hour to smoke pipes or brew tea. Over rugged terrain they lugged hundredweight loads of staples, trade goods, and fur packs on tumplines slung across their foreheads, portaging birchbark canoes on their shoulders. Such a life was a hard way to make a living; many voyageurs died from ruptured hernias or drowned, as these woodsmen—deft on water, surefooted on land—were notoriously poor swimmers.

Voyageurs and their unlicensed wood-running counterparts, coureurs de bois, often lived among Algonquins and sired families. Exulting in the joys of a free life, many French woodsmen became acculturated "white sauvages," establishing lasting kinships within tribal societies. "One recognizes them easily by their looks, by their size, and because all of them are tattooed on their bodies with figures of plants and animals," observed Louis Antoine de Bougainville, who in the 1750s came upon a detachment of about 950 voyageurs. Voyageurs were the cornerstones of the fur trade until the early 1900s.[5]

Voyageurs and coureurs de bois exploring the Mississippi and its tributaries were voracious buffalo hunters who gave the wild cows a variety of names: *bison d'Amerique, boeuf sauvage, vache sauvage, buffle, buffe, buffelo,* and *buffalo.*[6] But buffalo were not the only big game whites saw in New France that were new to them; at times, buffalo, elk, moose, and musk ox were called the same names. Some of the "wild cows" described are elk (wapiti to Indians), which Dutch colonists knew as *eland.* Confounding the problem, the Delaware word for buffalo, deer, and elk was *moos.*[7]

Voyageurs stowed salt pork and hardtack, their standard ration, aboard canoes in oak casks. Buffalo beef was a staple. Hunters blew up buffalo bladders to dry them and stuffed them with marrow and fat. Jerk and berries pounded into mush and coated with suet made pemmican to be wrapped in leather bags called *taureaux. Boskoyas*—"bags of grease"— were skin bags of rendered buffalo tallow for lard and for waterproofing leather.[8]

Herds were plentiful in the upper Mississippi. Near Ontario in 1615 Samuel de Champlain saw a band of Ottawa warriors with war shields; he described one as "a round buckler of tanned leather which comes from an animal like the buffalo."[9] In 1662 explorers in Minnesota called the Sioux camped there the *Nation du Boeuf* because the Sioux ate buffalo year-round, hunting them as far as Iowa.[10] Father François Xavier, traveling through Illinois in 1670–71, saw herds of four hundred to five hundred head. Buffalo "furnished adequate provisions for whole villages, which therefore are not obliged to scatter . . . during hunting season, as is the case with savages elsewhere." Xavier esteemed buffalo fat mixed with oats as "the most delicate of native dishes."[11]

In 1672 the Comte de Frontenac commissioned Louis Jolliet and Father Jacques Marquette to find the "great western river" as described by Indians. Jolliet and Marquette and five voyageurs left Green Bay in 1673, descending the Fox and Wisconsin Rivers to the Mississippi. The men canoed to the Arkansas before turning about, convinced that the Mississippi flowed to the Gulf. At Prairie du Chien ("latitude 41°, 28 minutes"), near the Wisconsin, Marquette recorded his first glimpse of the beast Illinois Indians called *pisikou:*

> The head is very large; the forehead is flat. . . . Under the neck they have a sort of a dew lap, which hangs down; and on the back is a rather high hump. The whole of the head, the neck, and a portion of the shoulders are covered with a thick mane . . . the body is covered with a heavy coat of curly hair, almost like that of our sheep, but much stronger and thicker. . . . The savages use the hides for making fine robes, which they paint in various colors.[12]

Sampling a cut of beef, he deemed "the flesh and fat of the *pisikou* excellent, and constitute the best dish at feasts." Jolliet pushed for settlement of Illinois. Farmers could plow the day they arrived and not have to "spend ten years in cutting down and burning the trees." He noted that "game is abundant . . . cows, stags, does and turkeys are found there in much greater number than elsewhere." Settlers could tan buffalo skins into shoe leather and spin buffalo wool into cloth "finer than most of that which we bring from France." Farmers with no oxen could yoke teams of buffalo, Jolliet theorized.[13] But catching buffalo was no sport for the timid. "If a person fires at them," wrote Marquette, "he must immediately after the shot, throw himself down and hide in the grass; for if they perceive him who has fired, they run at him and attack him."[14]

Five years after the travels of Marquette and Jolliet, René-Robert Cavelier, Sieur de La Salle, led fifty-three Frenchmen and Indians from Lake Michigan to the Chicago River, then portaged to the Illinois, pushing down the Mississippi to the Gulf. He named the land along the shore Louisiana for Louis XIV and in 1680 fixed France's claim to the American interior by erecting Fort Crevecoeur on the banks of Lake Peoria.[15] Eager to create trade with France to promote colonies, La Salle hoped to ship buffalo hides and wool down the Mississippi to its mouth, there to be loaded on ships bound for France. "The trade merely in the skins and wool of the wild cattle," he declared, "might establish a great commerce and support powerful colonies."[16]

La Salle's expectations proved naive. Shipping was a problem. River travel was a nightmare of dodging sawyers, shoals, murky riptides, and evading or fending off Indian raids. Storms punctuated by blasting gusts and rips of lighting erupted on the river, leading to loss and death. River trips from Kaskaskia to New Orleans took up to twenty days. Boatmen traditionally launched their vessels on February 1, when high water pushed along at six knots per hour. Winter was the safest time to travel, as Indians living along the banks of the swollen river often moved inland to follow game herds.

Autumn return trips were ordeals that took four months. The best oarsmen rowing from dawn to dusk made no more than twenty miles a day. Cordelling, or towing, boats kept them creeping upstream. A thick hemp rope tied to the bow was yanked along by men on shore slogging in muddy shallows, over buffalo runs, through cane and cattails, all the while slapping mosquitoes, gnats, and flies, picking off leeches and ticks, and sidestepping cottonmouth strikes. Indians attacked. Men deserted. Death from exposure or starvation was common. Deep snow or, worse, ice clogging the channel forced crews to winter along the Mississippi's banks.

In 1678 Louis XIV granted La Salle "the privilege of carrying on exclusively the trade in buffalo skins."[17] He must have despaired during the summer of 1682 as he and his men rowed up the Mississippi and nearly starved, staying alive on a diet of boiled alligator tails. La Salle's men mutinied and murdered him in 1687. Yet his dream of commerce in buffalo robes excited French officials.[18]

Journeying with La Salle was a Récollet friar, Louis Hennepin, whose memoirs include a sketch of a buffalo. He called the beast "a most wonderful animal" and saw traces as wide as a city road and buffalo loping single file in lines leagues long. Buffalo, he wrote, swam rivers and streams "in order to pasture from one land to another." To evade wolves, the buffalo cows swam to sandbars and islets to bear their calves. In northern Illinois, at a kill site between Chicago and the Illinois River, he observed that "the earth is covered with their horns."[19] Published in 1683 in Paris, Hennepin's narrative, *A Description of Louisiana,* gave European readers their first glimpse of America.

Portaging past the marshes of the Kankakee River (near South Bend, Indiana) in December 1679, Hennepin and a remnant of La Salle's crew went hungry from the loss of game because of the Indians' torching the grass to surround buffalo. Miami fire hunters had so devastated the land that Hennepin and thirty-two voyageurs walked for more than 180 miles over scorched earth, surviving on two small deer, swans, and two geese. During this leg of the ordeal, the friar feared the men would desert to "join the Indians whom we discerned by the flames of the prairie to which they had set fire in order to kill the buffalo more easily."[20]

Hennepin and the voyageurs slogged through snow and ice for another 120 miles, "subsisting on the Providence of God."[21] Before them stretched a wasteland scoured with hoofprints and traces. Buffalo bones littered the earth. "These animals are ordinarily found in great numbers there, as it is easy to judge by the bones, the horns and skulls that we saw on all sides." Starving, the men were mutinous when the priest and the voyageurs chanced upon a buffalo mired in a bog. Lashing a cable about the beast, they yanked it from the slough, but "had much ado to get him out of the mud." They killed the bull and gorged themselves.

For several days they found respite at a village where Hennepin observed native fire hunters. "The buffalo seeking to escape the fire, are compelled to pass near these Indians, who sometimes kill as many as a hundred and twenty in a day, all of which they distribute according to the wants of the families."[22] Runners relayed news of a kill to the village's women, who appeared at the site to butcher the animals. "Some of them at times take on their backs three hundred pounds weight ... which does not seem to burden them more than a soldier's sword at his side." A green buffalo hide weighed more than one hundred and twenty pounds. Tanned, the hides were "as supple as chamois dressed with oil." Hennepin patched his cassock with swatches of skin. Smoked jerk, Father Hennepin reported, tasted as if it "had just been killed." A dark broth of boiled wild beef was "the ordinary drink of all the nations of America, who have no intercourse with Europeans."

Father Hennepin and the voyageurs completed their portage on New Year's Day 1680; by January 4, their canoes nosed into Lake Peoria. During their trek, they killed two buffalo. Indians had fared far better. Hennepin wrote that as winter approached, tribes practiced forms of husbandry. Natives took care not to kill all of the buffalo or "alarm them too much," for fear of driving them from their land. "The Indians," declared Hennepin, "have never been able to exterminate these wild cattle, for however much they hunt them these beasts multiply so that they return in greater numbers the following year ... [in] herds of two or even of four hundred."[23]

Father Sebastian Rale traveled the same region almost fifty years later and estimated Indians killed about two thousand buffalo a year, often just for their tongues. Rale is probably exaggerating when he wrote in his *Relation* of October 12, 1723, that "as far as the eye can reach are seen from four to five *thousand* oxen grazing on the prairies."[24]

De Gannes chronicled Indian life in Illinois in 1688, hunting buffalo with Miami, Ottawa, Kickapoo, and Potawatomi. Scouts spotting a herd, De Gannes said, assembled in two lines and hit the ground at a trot to surround them, bursting into a sprint within a mile of the herd, showering the beasts with arrows. In a one-day hunt, they downed 120 buffalo, hacked out 100 tongues, and spent a week jerking meat on racks ten feet long, three feet wide, and four feet high. During a five-week hunt, they killed at least "1,200 buffalos . . . without counting the bears, does, stags, bucks, young turkeys, and lynxes." Indians prized the back meat. "There are two of these in a buffalo. They take it from the shoulder clear to the thigh and from the hump to the middle of the belly, after which they spread it out as thin as they can, making it usually four feet square." They folded the meat slabs like portfolios. Men and women carried eight smoked sides from autumn-killed buffalo; heavier sides from winter-killed buffalo were loaded four at a time. Indians drank water from paunches of dead buffalo after scooping out the excreta, De Gannes reported. "It had a bad taste, but in spite of that, I had the pleasure of slaking my thirst."[25]

Near Mobile in 1700, Henry de Tonti, explorer, promoter of French interests in North America, and ex-partner of La Salle, observed many "bears, buffaloes, and deer."[26] De Tonti does not qualify his observation of many buffalo; by the time of Tonti's arrival, Natchez hunters were slaughtering the beasts. In 1700 Father Jacques Gravier, a Jesuit to the Illinois Indians who helped translate and systematize the Oumamis tongue, affirmed that buffalo were "very scarce" in the Tunica country along the Yazoo River.[27]

Pierre Le Moyne, Sieur d'Iberville, and Andre Penicaut, one of d'Iberville's men, gave more precise estimates of the size of eastern buffalo herds in 1699. That January, d'Iberville sailed to Biloxi. By 1700 he and his men were floating up the Mississippi to the Blue Earth River in Minnesota. D'Iberville's orders, dated July 23, 1698, came direct from the Count of Pontchartrain: He was to ascend the Mississippi; locate a site for a fort; search for pearls, gold, and silver; find mulberry trees for silk; and get samples of buffalo wool and robes.

D'Iberville, the new commandant of Biloxi, recorded specific buffalo sightings in the Southeast.

> March 3, 1699 [Plaquemines Parish, Louisiana]: Our men went hunting and found stags, deer and buffaloes.
> March 6 [New Orleans]: A buffalo was killed . . . and we saw three buffalo on the bank.
> March 15 [at an Indian village in St. James Parish]: They brought us dried buffalo meat . . . and they break up the ground [to plant their gardens with hoes made] with buffalo bones.

March 17 [near Bayou Goula in Iberville Parish]: We saw buffalo
and deer in the canebrakes . . . and [at Indian shrines] bundles of
bison skins.
[Date unknown, at Biloxi]: Buffalo were abundant. . . . we killed
about fifteen.[28]

Andre Penicaut, the ship's carpenter, kept a diary of his adventure.
Begun in 1699 when he arrived on the Gulf coast and concluded in
1723 when he returned to France, Penicaut's journal gives a true glimpse
of the flora and fauna of the Southeast and how natives utilized their
resources. The Natchez, he said, wore "deerskins for summer and buffalo
skins and bear skins for winter."[29]

At Biloxi, he and some hunters "went ashore there and found such a
great quantity of animals that we killed more than fifty wild animals, as
many buffalo as deer." Later, near the same spot, they "killed about fifteen
buffaloes." Near Baton Rouge, he remarked, "Never in my life have I seen
such great numbers of buffalo, harts, and roes as were on that prairie. We
killed five buffaloes which we skinned and cut up." By Lake Pontchartrain they "killed about fifteen buffaloes . . . and the following day we
killed eight buffaloes and as many deer." Near Pascagoula, "the Indians
gave us bison meat . . . they had spoons of bison horn . . . and bison robes."
Hunting along the Mississippi in Minnesota the winter of 1700,
d'Iberville's men and native hunters killed more than four hundred buffalo. "It should be acknowledged that in hunting buffalo," declared Penicaut, "they [the Indians] are more skillful than the French."[30]

For the first two weeks, the diet of wild beef incited fierce bouts of
diarrhea. But by late winter, the men were fattening up, each consuming
daily up to ten pounds of beef and four bowls of broth. Penicaut marveled at warriors who ran alongside wounded buffalo to yank out arrows.
Kaskaskian women sewed dresses from spun buffalo hair that looked like
"the dresses of the women of Brittany or else like the dressing gowns of
our ladies of France, which hang to the floor." Using natural dyes—
bloodroot or wild plum for red, alder bark for yellow—the women dyed
the dresses in resplendent colors. D'Iberville sent samples of the dyed
wool abroad. Again, France proposed developing a buffalo-based textile
industry.

Indians easily captured calves by letting them suckle their fingers as
they led them back to their villages. After the children had played with
them, they killed the calves and ate them. "These little animals," Hennepin concluded, "might be easily domesticated and used to plow the

land."[31] On November 9, 1712, Father Gabriel Marest of Kaskaskia wrote to Father Bartholomew Germon, "We have tried to tame the wild oxen, but we have never succeeded."[32] Some proposed raising buffalo for wool as if they were so many lambs to shear. Monsieur de Remonville added in his letter to Count de Pontchartrain on December 10, 1697, that the buffalo of Louisiana "might be domesticated by rearing up the calves.... We could also draw from thence a great quantity of buffalo hides every year, as the plains are filled with the animals."[33]

In 1701 some Huguenots living near Richmond tried to tame buffalo but found them "too unruly" and killed them off.[34] Sieur d'Iberville issued a decree to breed buffalo to supply wool for settlers at New Orleans: "In four or five years we can establish a commerce . . . of sixty to eighty thousand buffalo skins." Revenue from buffalo and deer skins exported to France, he estimated, would produce "a return of more than two million five hundred thousand *livres* yearly."[35]

In 1704 there was more talk of bringing buffalo hides from Illinois to Gulf ports for shipment to France. Father Hennepin dreamed of shipping kegs of wild beef to the West Indies to sustain French *boucanneers* who supplied ships with cured meat, hides, pigs, and cattle. "This vast continent will be able in a short time to supply all our West India islands with bread, wine and meat," Hennepin declared.[36] *Boucanned* buffalo meat, or jerk, was easily made; the hunks of half-inch meat dried in the sun were called *plats côtes*. "Dried in this manner," Father Julien Binneteau reported, "it keeps for a long time without being tainted."[37]

On October 5, 1721, along the Kankakee River, Father Pierre François-Xavier de Charlevoix observed that "the country becomes beautiful; prairies as far as you can see, where the buffalo travel by herds of two or three hundred." Lake Peoria's banks, Charlevoix said, were "full of game." Along the Wabash and at Fort Pimitoui on the Illinois River were "vast Meadows, well watered, where the wild Buffaloes feed by Thousands."[38] But such herds were often no more than targets for boatloads of marksmen cruising by.

In February 1701, Father Jacques Gravier and a French crew left the Illinois villages of the Tamaroas, Metchigameas, and Kaskaskias to float the Mississippi south to the Gulf. Strong currents pushed them briskly down the river, but the voyageurs pulled up often, traveling slowly. During one five-day span, they made only thirty-five leagues—a distance normally covered in just over two days. The pilot and several others fell sick, forcing the corps to work short-handed, yet Father Gravier blamed the able-bodied crewmen for the slow pace. "Much time," he wrote on

February 11, "was lost in shooting the wild oxen that abound along the river, almost all of which were left to be eaten by the wolves." One buffalo cost them "10 or 12 gunshots" before it fell dead.[39]

Antoine Simon Le Page du Pratz, a French adventurer, landed in Mobile on August 8, 1718, having sailed the Caribbean route taken by French vessels that were New World bound. Du Pratz lived in Mobile, then in New Orleans, and then for eight years among the Natchez Indians before leaving America in 1734. Published editions of his memoirs, *Histoire de la Louisiane,* appeared in France in 1753, 1758, 1763, and 1774. "The buffalo," he told readers, was "the chief food of the natives, and of the French." Tanned robes—"being at the same time very warm and very light"—made for luxurious sleeping. "My bed consisted of a bear's skin and two robes of buffalo ... three canes bent to a semi-circle, one at the head, another in the middle, and a third at the feet, supported a cloth which secured my tester [square canopy over a bed] and curtains." Warm and safe from rain and insects, du Pratz passed many a cozy night. He fared on tongue, hump, and soup of marrow and parched corn. He rendered bulls into tallow—one brute yielded 150 pounds of fat—and saw herds "the least of which exceeded a hundred and thirty or a hundred and fifty in number."[40]

In 1721 the Duke of Orleans, regent of France, named Diron D'Artaguiette the inspector general of Louisiana. That year Fox raids, provoked by duplicity and warmongering on both sides, ignited bloodletting between Algonquin and Siouan alliances, threatening colonists and business interests in New France. French leaders ordered D'Artaguiette to Illinois to "reorganize the government of Louisiana."

On December 22, 1722, the flotilla manned by fourteen oarsmen, accompanied by Father Boulanger and a man named Dulongpré, left New Orleans.[41] D'Artaguiette ordered that stores be kept slim, consisting mostly of Indian corn and salted meat, as he expected to get meat on the way. But even before the trip began, settlers in New Orleans warned that the region was "not sufficiently supplied with buffaloes to support the colony." Natchez hunters, D'Artaguiette reported, had "to go a very long distance to find them."

By February 5 most of the expedition's food was gone. After trading knives and powder and shot to some Indians for "buffalo, bear oil, and other meat," they rowed on. Three days later they saw buffalo tracks. They spotted wild cows on February 13, but did not kill a buffalo until March 12. Grumbling over their bland diet, the Frenchmen lived mostly on salted corn mush and duck.

Once past the mouth of the Arkansas, they slew seven buffalo and a bear between March 15 and 27. On March 31, D'Artaguiette met some traders from the Wabash who had been living among Illinois Indians; the men were en route to New Orleans, their seven pirogues heavily loaded "with salt meat and bear oil." D'Artaguiette arrived at Kaskaskia on April 17. Between April 1 and 13 his crew had killed five buffalo, three deer, three bear, and four turkeys.

D'Artaguiette saw traders haggling with hunters for deer skins, bear and buffalo hides, furs, and beaver pelts to take back to Canada. Illinois women dressed buffalo skins with the hair on, but soon they adopted European tanning methods of removing the hair to dress the "buffalo skins, upon which they paint designs with vermilion and other colors." The intensity of the skin trade stunned D'Artaguiette. Standard fur prices to the company of Marain and Outlas, who sold their hides exclusively to New Orleans fur buyers, were regulated as follows:[42]

Beavers, 34 *sols* a pound
Fat winter beavers, 3 *livres* a pound
Wildcat skins, 5 *sols* apiece
Deerskins, 30 *sols* by weight
Wolfskins, 50 *sols* each
Large bearskins, 5 *livres* each
Ordinary bearskins, 3 *livres* each

One typical shipment of peltry delivered to Detroit, valued at "6,102 *livre* 12 *sols* 10 *deniers*," contained the following:

	Livres
210 wildcat skins @ 25 *sols*	143.15
30 skins of the same	[amount missing]
1,651 wildcat skins, same price	2,063.15
107 fox and Louisiana skunks @ 40 *sols*	214.
44 skunks @ 50 *sols*	110.
268 wildcats @ 25 *sols*	224.11.8
80 large bears @ 4 *livres*	320.
100 large bears @ 3 *livres*	300.
56 medium-sized bears @ 3 *livres*	168.
12 large cubs @ 4 *sols*	24.
7 packages of deerskins	843.
394 pounds of beavers @ 38 *sols*	748.12

Notably absent are buffalo hides, which were less marketable because of their bulk and the difficulty in processing them. But in 1771 robes taken from the rich Ouachita River Basin sold in the French trade for ten *livres* each.[43] And there were intertribal markets for tanned and quilled buffalo robes and goods made of buffalo parts. In the Southeast, the Creek, Chickasaw, Choctaw, Cherokee, and Natchez wore buffalo robes; north of the Ohio River, the Potawatomi, Winnebago, Illinois, Chippewa, Wabash, Ottawa, Sauk, Fox, Mascouten, Kaskaskia, Miami, Kickapoo, Delaware, and Shawnee wore robes or used items from buffalo.

Merchants also marketed robes among colonists in New France. Listed in the inventory of the estate of Francois Bastien (d. 1763), of Prairie Du Rocher, Illinois, are "3 buffalo robes." Hides appear in the estate of Jacques Bourdon, who, as early as 1704, was living at Kaskaskia:

> 4,443 pounds of beavers
> 84 deerskins
> 12 doeskins
> 6 buffalo hides
> 10 otter skins
> 54 pounds of tallow

On June 4, 1723, D'Artaguiette and crew cast off into the Mississippi to float south, their boats heavy with wheat and corn. From June 29 to July 8, they killed twenty-nine buffalo—totaling perhaps twenty tons of meat—but took only the best cuts. D'Artaguiette's journal only mentions killing buffalo during the return trip.

> June 30: About noon we landed to go after a herd of more than a
> hundred buffaloes, both bulls and cows, of which we killed five
> and wounded more than twenty. We cut out only the tongues.
> July 1: About noon we landed on a sand bar to amuse ourselves
> with hunting. We brought down eight animals. We contented
> ourselves with cutting out their tongues.
> July 2: About noon we . . . went after a herd of nine buffaloes, all
> of which we killed.

"The most worthless Frenchman can kill a buffalo in this region," D'Artaguiette recorded on July 5, 1723. Yet, on July 14, he complained that he and his men "no longer had any hope of killing any buffaloes." D'Artaguiette and his crew surely remembered that herds thinned considerably below the mouth of the Arkansas. But they had failed to prepare for the dearth. The men had recklessly shot buffalo to hack out their tongues and left the mutilated carcasses to bloat in the sun. They were forced to subsist for two weeks on wheat bread and mush before reaching New Orleans on July 30, 1723.

On June 4, 1701, Charles Juchereau de St. Denys, lieutenant general of Montreal, received a *Lettre patentes* to build a tannery at the confluence of the Ohio and Mississippi near what is now Cairo, Illinois. There he built Fort St. Vincent, collecting thirteen thousand buffalo hides in less than two years and shipping them downriver to Mobile. His success was short-lived: Fort St. Vincent was half completed in 1702 when attacks by Fox warriors and a deadly virus swept the area, killing most of the people, including Juchereau. By 1704 the survivors abandoned the tannery.[44]

French officer Bernard de la Harpe left his post on the Gulf by 1721 to ascend the Mississippi. He floated past the mouth of the Arkansas, passing a flotilla of French hunters en route to New Orleans with five thousand pounds of salted wild beef. In 1726 two French boatmen docked at the port with 480 salted tongues.[45] These may be the first recorded instances of white men slaughtering buffalo for profit.

It is estimated that by 1700 about seventy thousand Indians lived in the Lower Mississippi Valley. Near New Orleans, French-Natchez relations turned bitter, and by 1730 the French annihilated the Natchez. And large bands of marines—in a move instigated by Governor Le Moyne de Bienville and led by Diron D'Artaguiette and Captain Alphonse de la Buissonniere—waged war against the British-allied Chickasaw.

In 1708 the colonial population of Louisiana numbered "122 soldiers and sailors, 80 Indian slaves, and 77 settlers, or habitants (24 men, 28 women, and 25 children)." By 1718, their numbers grew to between 350 and 400 people, a population scattered among six administrative posts along the Gulf Coast, including outposts at Mobile, Fort Toulouse, and New Orleans, and consisting mostly of military personnel and employees for the Crown. In June 1723 D'Artaguiette recorded that there were "64 habitants at Kaskaskia, 41 white laborers, 37 married women, and 54 children." Sixteen miles north, at Fort de Chartres, were "39 habitants, 42 white laborers, 28 married women, and 17 children." Fewer people lived at Cahokia than at either Fort de Chartres or Kaskaskia; Kaskaskia had eighty houses and four mills by 1721.[46]

Longevity and low mortality were the exception. Historian Daniel Usner notes, "Of the seven thousand whites who entered the Lower

Mississippi Valley from 1717 to 1721, at least half of them either perished or abandoned the colony before 1726."[47] African slaves suffered similarly. Periodic food shortages made things worse.

New Orleans stores regularly sold wild beef. As late as 1738 hunters were killing from the thinning droves grazing near the mouth of the Yazoo. Settlers ate the best cuts; merchants shipped the rest to Caribbean sugar cane plantations. Records from the 1700s show that there were 4,700 slaves in Louisiana, 65,900 on Martinique, and 40,400 on Guadeloupe. Keeping island slaveholders and their slaves in meat was difficult, but buffalo beef and tallow from New Orleans and Mobile eased shortages. It was a lucrative market: By the 1760s George Morgan and other firms sold to the slavers, competing with French and Spanish hunters killing buffalo in Illinois and along the Cumberland.[48]

On June 15, 1749, just after King George's War (War of the Austrian Succession), Captain Pierre Joseph de Celeron de Bienville's flotilla of thirty-two canoes left Lachine, near Montreal. His party of 234 voyageurs, soldiers, and Abnaki warriors included Father Jean de Bonnecamps, professor of hydrology at the Jesuit college at Quebec. Celeron's mission, as authorized by the king of France and the Marquis de la Galissoniere, governor of New France from September 1747 until 1749, was to travel to the principal tributaries of *La Belle Riviere*—the Ohio River—erect wooden crosses, and bury lead plaques inscribed with the governor's message. In March 1847 shifting waters uncovered one of the eleven-by-seven-inch plates at the mouth of the Kanawha. Its bold message makes clear the imperial designs of these bearers of the heraldic gold on white fleur-de-lis.

> In the year 1749, of the reign of Louis XV, of France, We, Celeron, commandant of a detachment sent by the Marquis de la Galissoniere, Captain-General of New France, in order to re-establish tranquility among some villages of savages of these parts, have buried this plate at the mouth of the river Chi-no-da-hich-e-tha, the 18th of August, near the river Ohio, otherwise beautiful river, as a monument of renewal of possession, which we have taken of the said river Ohio, and of all those which empty themselves into it, and of all the lands of both sides, even to the sources of said rivers; as have enjoyed, or ought to have enjoyed the preceding kings of France, and that they have maintained themselves there, by force of arms and by treaties, especially by those of Riswick, of Utrecht, and of Aix-la-Chapelle.[49]

Celeron's crew hammered more plaques bearing the same defiant declaration on the most conspicuous trees growing along the banks of the rivers. "These plates," concludes author Richard Taylor, "are act and prelude to the French and Indian War."[50] The fleet paddled up the St. Lawrence to Lake Ontario, crossed Lake Erie, then, after a seven-day portage, moved on to Chautauqua Lake in New York. They endured incredible hardships and reached the Allegheny, floating to the Monongahela at Pittsburgh and easing into the Ohio. Celeron returned to Montreal on November 10.

Jean de Bonnecamps's detailed account of the expedition deals mostly with Indians, but he saw buffalo too. Yet there is a difference between his accounts and those of his kinsmen who had gone before him. Canadians told Celeron that he would find buffalo enough to feed his men—"the tongues alone," they declared, "would suffice to support the troops." But it was not until they passed the Great Kanawha that the men saw their first buffalo. "This is not the first time when I have experienced that hyperbole and exaggeration were figures familiar to the Canadians," Bonnecamps complained.[51]

Where Marquette and Hennepin saw herds of hundreds—and by Father Rale's account, thousands—of buffalo, Celeron and Bonnecamps saw scattered droves. As early as 1680, asserts historian Richard White, buffalo "had markedly diminished on the lands near the Great Village of the Kaskaskias."[52] Hunters did not cease to exploit the herds.

On December 26, 1750, Lieutenant Jean-Bernard Bossu and four marine companies boarded a ship bound for New Orleans. To garrison troops stationed in Illinois, the commander of New Orleans dispatched Bossu and some marines to Fort de Chartres. Bossu lived there for six years before returning to France.

Buffalo in the upper Illinois were most plentiful, observed Bossu, at salt licks. Panthers stalked the wild cows from above, leaping from perches of low-lying branches, claws grappling humps, fangs severing jugulars, the big cats slamming the bawling beasts to the dirt in a tawny whirl of thrashing black hooves and scarlet froth.

To meet the demands of the meat trade along the Mississippi, the carnage was immense. Bossu saw how Indian hunters adapted buffalo items to fit European uses. "Their arms," he wrote on November 6, 1751, "consist of a rifle, a buffalo horn for powder strung across the shoulder, and a small skin sack in which to keep bullets, flints, and a wad-extractor." During morning hours, Indians launched canoes into the shallows to skirt the water's edge. They shot buffalo grazing the shore and piled up the beef for the boatloads of Frenchmen. "The Indians carefully cut the tongues and the steaks from the animals they have killed and offer them as gifts to the commander and the officers of the convoy."[53]

On January 1, 1757, while camped on an islet in the midst of the Mississippi downstream from Fort de Chartres, Bossu's men gave him a special New Year's salute. To facetiously take possession of their tiny slip of land, they carved "BOSSU" into the bark of a big tree. Drum rolls hammered. The sergeant took off his hat to shout terms of conquest: "In the name of the King, all you cats, bears, wolves, buffalo, deer, and other animals of this island shall recognize our commander as your governor, and you shall obey and serve him as he commands you." Gunners touched smoldering linstocks to touchholes, blasting a battery of lead from big-bore swivels aimed just over a buffalo herd. Muskets boomed. The buffalo stampeded into the water. The men hoorayed, gave chase, and killed four of the beasts.[54]

By 1758 Bossu went to Fort Toulouse, Alabama. He sailed back to France in 1762, then returned to Louisiana in 1770 for a final year-long North American stint. In 1768 Bossu's letters to the Marquis de l'Estrada de la Cousse describing his second voyage were published and entitled *New Travels to the Western Indies; Containing an Account of the different Peoples who live in the vicinity of the great River Saint-Louis, commonly called the Mississippi; their Religion; their government; their customs, their wars and their trade.* In 1777, after his third tour in New France, his second book, *New Travels in America,* appeared.

In *New Travels* Bossu describes new exploits: Alligators attacked him; he nearly drowned; the Quapaw adopted and tattooed him; he turned sachem; he hunted. Armed, accoutered, and uniformed as a marine, and crowned with a detachable woolen "traveler's hood" attached to his cappo-coat, he carried a skin, wool blanket, rush mat, and native air mattress for bedding and shelter. "I had some skins dressed and neatly sewed for this purpose. I inflated them by blowing air into them through a cane tube."

On the morning of September 27, 1770, nearing the confluence of the Ohio and the Mississippi, Bossu and his men saw an odd sight: On a sandbar jutting off a hundred paces from the woods bordering the western shore were what looked like buffalo. Heifers and yearling bulls capered awkwardly near the water's edge. Calves appeared to suckle cows.

"Quietly lift oars, my friends," said the skipper. "Good booty! Lucky day! Buffaloes! To arms."

The men did as they were told, easing the vessels to the herd. One *boucanneer* doffed his deerskin hood, the badge of a French meat getter. He exhorted the men to shoot only cows. The boats drifted closer.

The buffalo paid the flotilla no mind. The whites made ready. Hammers clicked into full cock.

Suddenly a guide yelled. A trap! All hands grabbed oars.

"Knowing how eager Frenchmen are to pursue buffalo," Bossu wrote after they hastily pulled away and rowed to the east shore, "the Chickasaw had some of their men dress in skins of these animals in order to lure us into the woods where they planned to scalp us or make us prisoners." On other occasions, Chickasaw warriors stamped fake buffalo tracks in the ground to lure the men inland. Bossu's trackers discerned the sham hoofprints. Forewarned, the men did not fall prey to the ambush.

Bossu watched Quapaw hunters on Grand Prairie—a veldt between the White and Arkansas Rivers—slaughter buffalo. Warriors on horses brandished spears tipped with crescent-shaped iron blades and charged, hamstringing the wild cows. Indians on foot pounced on the beasts with clubs and stones. "Sometimes it happens that the bull, having become enraged, attacks the horse, wounding it with its horns, and greatly endangers the rider."[55]

"Jolicoeur" Charles Bonin, a marine touring the upper Ohio during the French and Indian War, watched Indians hunt herds numbering two to three hundred by driving them into nets of woven birch bark. Warriors tied the nets to stakes driven into the ground. Teams of beaters thrashed through the woods to drive buffalo to the corral. Warriors lying in wait hamstrung and stuck and bled those beasts snared in the webs. Bonin remembers: "It must not be thought that a great number of buffalo are taken in the nets; for the nets very often are broken by their strength. When they have made an opening, they dash through it and escape. It is a fact that some are always caught."[56]

The French were settling North America. Voyageurs, coureurs de bois, and traders took Algonquin wives; became mediators, interpreters, and guides; and begat a synethnic progeny known as the Métis. Catholic priests worked to convert Indians to the Church. Trading posts linked Montreal to the Great Lakes and the Mississippi. In the Middle Ground these bonds, coupled with temptation and fear from both sides, secured French-Algonquin alliances.[57]

The fur trade began. The French, Dutch, Spanish, and English were the primary players. Beaver, otter, fox, marten, fisher, and coon pelts counted in six figures annually flooded fur buyers. Deer skins became

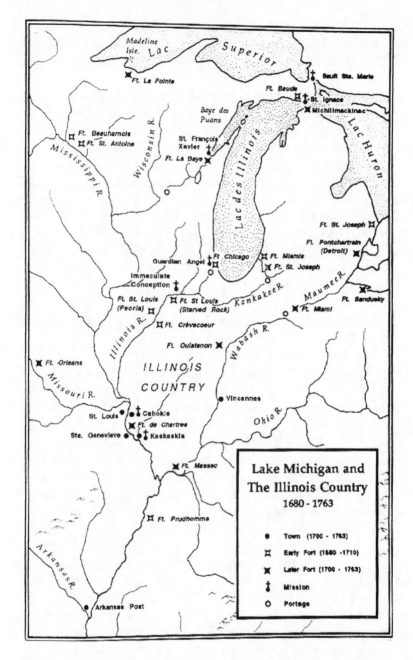

"Lake Michigan and the Illinois country: 1680–1763." (Reprinted from Charles J. Balesi, *The Time of the French in the Heart of North America: 1673–1818.* Map by Tom Willcockson.)

currency in the New World's frontier-exchange economy. Market hunters shot buffalo for the meat, tongue, tallow, and hide trade, but killing the wild cows did little to promote French dreams of self-sustaining colonies. Settlers altered the habitat sustaining herds east of the Mississippi: Fires for hunting and clearing land, plowing, shifts in human demographics, the fur trade, the settlers' new breeds of domestic animals, and newly transplanted Old World grasses, weeds, fruit trees, shrubs—all such factors changed the countryside.

Neither Spain nor France would ultimately possess the American lands they claimed as their own, nor were they alone in their imperialistic quest for empire and wealth. English colonies along the Atlantic coast portended of global tensions to come.

Englishmen and Wild Cattle

THE PERMANENT SETTLEMENT OF ENGLISHMEN IN THE NEW WORLD
began in Jamestown, Virginia, in 1607. The Plymouth Massachusetts
colony followed in 1620. Puritans arrived by 1630 at Massachusetts Bay.
Soon hamlets and towns stretched to the Connecticut River. Quickly
this new wave of whites settled in with kith and kin. By 1763 English
colonies along the Atlantic coast reached from New England to the
southland.

The English brought their families, indentured servants, slaves, and
laborers. "Of all the Europeans colonizing North America," asserts
Francis Jennings, "Englishmen migrated in the greatest numbers."[1] Their
reasons for coming were many: to find wealth, to worship, to escape
debtors' jails, to flee poverty and absolutist law. Whatever their motives,
the newcomers shared a desire to get land.

Journals and diaries reveal their wonder at what they saw. Indian
husbandry induced much of the flora and fauna the whites attributed to
"natural bounty." Controlled burns, mobile villages, seasonal hunting and
fishing regulating cycles of life, trapping, planting—such forms of subsistence prove Indians were gleaning food and peltry that they had managed. English settlers, like the Indians, the French, and the Spanish,
changed the land to fit their needs, bringing new crops, grasses, and livestock, as well as Old World weeds that took hold and flourished. Their
domestic animals overgrazed the range, creating a need for "more intensive colonial deforestation" to open new pastures.[2]

Hunters in Pennsylvania, Virginia, Georgia, and the Carolinas whose
explorations took them far past their fencerows and fields and into the
interior saw scattered buffalo sign. Perhaps the earliest observation by
an Englishman of buffalo skins as trade items occurred in 1584 when
Captain Arthur Barlowe—a scout for Sir Walter Raleigh—saw Indians
trading in "chamois, buffe and deere skins" in North Carolina.[3]

Samuel Argall may have recorded an encounter with buffalo in 1612 when he landed near the headwaters of the Potomac (though some historians place him on the James River). Within fifteen miles of present-day Washington, D.C., he "found a great store of cattle as big as kine . . . which we found to be very good and wholesome meat."[4] In 1624 Henry Fleete was near the same region and reported that the woods "swarmed with deer, buffaloes, bears, turkeys." He found "no great store" of the beasts near the coast. He does not state the herd size of the buffalo he saw.[5]

In May 1673 the Honorable Major General Abraham Wood sent James Needham and Gabriel Arthur to the Cherokee town of Chota (in what is now Monroe County, Tennessee) to establish trade with the Indians. After the men crossed the mountains, Needham saw "many horns like bull's horns [lying] upon their dunghills" near Citico Creek on the Little Tennessee River.[6]

That September, while Arthur lived with the Occaneechi Indians to learn their language, Needham reported back to General Wood. Needham's Occaneechi guide slew him on his return trip to Tennessee, and Arthur became a captive. He was facing death at the stake when some Shawnee freed him and took him to the mouth of the Scioto, where he lived until he found his way back to Fort Henry, Virginia, on June 18, 1674. In a letter describing the disastrous Needham-Arthur expedition and the two men's observations of Indian life, Wood wrote that some of the foods Indians ate included corn, fish, and buffalo.[7]

John Lawson saw buffalo east of the Appalachians. Lawson sailed to the New World in July 1700.[8] Enterprising, brave, ambitious, and educated at either Oxford or Cambridge, young John arrived in New York seeking land and adventure. He sailed to Charleston in mid-August. By December he was ready to journey into the Piedmont on a reconnaissance survey commissioned by the Lords Proprietors of Carolina. Unsure what to expect from Indians, he took five Englishmen and three native guides with him.

The men traveled from the South Carolina coast through the Piedmont and finished their trip on the North Carolina shore. Lawson saw a Tutelo band from the Yadkin Valley, "tall, likely Men, having great Plenty of Buffaloes," he wrote. He does not qualify his observations. Most likely, if these Tutelo were packing large amounts of wild beef, they had been hunting beyond the Yadkin to trespass on Cherokee land where game was plentiful.

Lawson sampled wild beef near Salisbury and decided it was not as good as domestic beef, but "the Calves," he declared, were "cry'd up for excellent Food." He wondered about crossbreeding. "It is conjectured, that these Buffaloes, mixt in Breed with our tame Cattle, would much better the Breed for Largeness and Milk." Lawson reckoned that he traveled one thousand miles from December 28, 1700, to February 23, 1701, visiting tribes along the Santee, Wateree, and Catawba Rivers. He saw hunters knap arrow points from bottles to shoot buffalo with. After killing the beasts, they took the hides back to their villages to make beds.

"Of the Wild Bull's Skin, Buff [leather] is made. The Indians," Lawson recorded, "spin the Hair into Garters, Girdles, Sashes, and the like, it being long and curled, and often of a chestnut or red Colour. These Monsters are found to weigh (as I am informed by a Traveller of Credit) from 1600 to 2400 Weight." He heard rumors of two buffalo killed near what is now Appomattox, Virginia. A London firm published Lawson's journal, *A New Voyage to Carolina,* in 1709. Besides being one of the first books to use the term "Buffelo," his work featured an engraving of a buffalo with this caption:

> The Buffelo is a wild Beast of America. . . . He seldom appears amongst the English Inhabitants, his chief Haunt being in the land of the Messiasippi, which is, for the most part, a plain Country; yet I have known some kill'd on the Hilly Part of Cape-Fair-River, they passing the Ledges of vast Mountains from the said Messiasippi, before they can come near us.[9]

In the fall of 1711, shortly after the release of his book, Lawson, along with Swiss land proprietor Baron Christopher Von Graffenried, two African slaves, and two Indian guides, canoed up the Neuse River to find a river route to Virginia. Two days into their trip, some Tuscarora fired on them, commandeered their canoe, piled the men high with booty, and ran them through the woods to their town on Contentnea Creek, near Snow Hill. The Indians freed the slaves and the baron, but they blackened Lawson's face with bear grease and soot—the sign of death—and killed him.[10] His words lived on. *A New Voyage to Carolina* sold well in Europe and was widely plagiarized.

English attempts in the early 1700s to push into the Southeast heightened tensions among European powers. Thomas Nairne was a central broker in such doings. In 1702 his Yamasee henchmen invaded Florida, looting, torching palmetto-thatched chickees, preying on

Indians as far south as the Everglades. During one raid his slave catchers
seized thirty-five men and women, loaded them with plunder, and
marched them back to South Carolina to sell at Charleston's auction
block. Soldier, cartographer, Indian agent, slaver, and entrepreneur who
dabbled in politics, Nairne had an annual income that surpassed that of
the governor of South Carolina.

In 1708 Nairne described one of his western journeys from
Charleston. Thomas Welch, a trader to the Chickasaw, traveled with him.
They passed through South Carolina, Alabama, and Mississippi, stopping
to visit the Ochesee, Tallapoosa, and Chickasaw. Securing trade, gift
giving, and creating alliances was key in empire building and thwarting
the French and the Spanish. "May it please your Lordship," he wrote on
July 10, 1708, to Charles Spencer, earl of Sunderland, "the Indian trade
for cloth always attracts and maintains the obedience and friendship of
the Indian."[11]

Keen-eyed Nairne observed many facets of native life unseen by
Englishmen living along the coast. In northeast Mississippi, he and Welch
dwelt with the Chickasaw. Chickasaw women thought themselves well
adorned, Nairne wrote, when wrapped about the hips with a stroud of
deep blue or scarlet, their hair oiled with bear grease mixed with cinna-
mon or sassafras and wrapped with a dried eelskin, and their necks, ears,
and wrists garnished with glass beads. If one's husband could not afford
to trade for cloth or jackets, then "drest Buffaloe calf skines suply the
defect." But after having gazed on the European duffels, Chickasaw
women loathed their "painted Buffeloe Calf skins."[12]

Chickasaw hunters stalked buffalo at salt and sulfur licks. "In the
spring and all sumer, these cattle eat [an] abundance of Clay. They find
out such places as are saltish, which they lick up in such quantities as if
some hundreds of thousands of Bricks had been made of them." Buffalo
traces led hither and yon, causing Nairne to remark that "the paths
leading to these holes ar as many and well Trod, as these to the greatest
Cowpens in Carolina."[13]

Nairne reveled in the hunt. Buffalo bulls, he said, were eaten only
from May to July, when they were at their fattest. "In killing Buffeloes
they Aim at the yearlings and the heifers, being the tenderest and indeed
no Beef exceeds them. . . . The tongues of these Creatures are extraordinary fine atasting like marrow, and that causes the death of many
hundreds of them."[14] The warriors ignited fire rings five miles across and
trespassed on Choctaw and Creek land. At night, Nairne's rifle and

pistols—primed, loaded, flints sharply knapped, and locks set on half cock—were at hand in his blanket. His caution was warranted. Times were perilous, especially for men like Nairne.

War erupted east of the Blue Ridge. Abuses from traders and slavers in North Carolina led to the Tuscarora War of 1711. The English forted up. When the Indians faltered, the English took to arms, killing many Tuscarora and capturing four hundred. The tribe fled north to the League of the Iroquois for refuge. In South Carolina and in the ambiguously claimed lands of the French, Spanish, and English, factions of the Creek, Cherokee, Choctaw, Yamasee, and Catawba plotted, chaffing under the same ills. The veneer cracked. A new war began. Squarely at its center were Thomas Nairne and whites of like mind.

In 1715 the Yamasee killed Thomas Welch and trussed Nairne up like one of his slaves. They bound him to a stake to burn him. Nairne's tormentors kept him alive for three days. On the third day they stuck him full of pitch-pine splinters till he bristled like a porcupine, then set him aflame. His death marked the beginning of the end of the Yamasee Nation. The English retaliated and the Yamasee War began. By 1717 most of the warring tribes sued for peace. The English rounded up the remnant Yamasee to sell to slavers bound for the Caribbean.[15]

Trade was king. Competition was fierce among the English, Spanish, Dutch, and French. Deer skins were cash, as were, in the words of the South Carolina Commissioners of the Indian Trade in 1716, other "Goods, Wares, Merchandizes, Liquors, Slaves, Furrs and Skins either carried to, or bartered, or sold to, or bought from any of the said Indians." An invoice sent that July to Colonel Theophilus, factor to the Cherokees, contained the following:

400 Lbs. of fine Gun Powder
2 Cs.: 2 Grs: 00 Lb. of Bullets
1000 Flints
7 brass Kettles, quart
20 Yards Half Thicks
7 Pieces Strouds

Charleston fur buyers counted deer skins and beaver pelts at the same rate of exchange on April 30, 1716:

	Skins
A Gun	35
A Yard Strouds	8
A white Duffield Blanket	16
A Yard of Half Thicks	3
A Hatchet	3
Thirty Bullets	1
A Knife	1
A pair Scissors	1
Twelve Flints	1
An Ax	5
A Pistol	20
A Sword	10
A Shirt	5

On June 27, 1716, Theophilus Hastings sent Lieutenant General James Moore 473 beaver pelts and packs of trade goods. "I can get you no Buffalo Skins as yet," he wrote, "but shall slip no Opportunity." On August 7, 1718, the Indian Commissioners ordered a trader to deliver "one Buffaloe Skin" to Robert Blakely as a reward for the care that he took in delivering a load of wares by pirogue.[16]

Naturalist and artist Mark Catesby saw buffalo in South Carolina during his travels in 1722. Only at dawn and dusk did he see the buffalo emerge in small droves to graze the Piedmont's savannas. In the heat of the day they retired to the forest to bask along rivers. If people were near, Catesby said, buffalo hid in canebrakes, leaving trampled swaths in their wakes, making it easy to hunt them. The first volume of his work, *The Natural History of Carolina, Florida, and Bahama Islands,* was published in 1731. The second volume appeared in 1743, and an appendix was finished in 1747, two years before his death. Portions of his text, Catesby admitted, were condensed from John Lawson's *A New Voyage to Carolina.* Included in Catesby's *Natural History* was his watercolor of a buffalo, which now hangs in the Royal Library in Windsor Castle.[17]

In November 1728, six years after Catesby's travels, Colonel William Byrd II (1674–1744), a Virginian whose Westover estate spanned 179,440 acres, spotted buffalo tracks and dung in western North Carolina. Byrd's location at the time is unknown; he and his surveying team were on a mission to ascertain the "dividing line" between North Carolina and Virginia to validate his claims to his own "Land of Eden." A few days went by before Byrd and his men were able to get close in on a yearling and kill it. They deemed the wild beef "a rarity we had never had the fortune to meet before."[18]

Byrd judged buffalo and domestic cattle to be the same species. "There are two Reasons for this Opinion: the Flesh of both has exactly the same taste, and the mixed Breed betwixt both, they say, will generate." The party was so taken by the flavor of the meat that "Gridiron and Frying-Pan had no more rest all night." A stewed dish of blanched and sliced buffalo tongue mixed with boiled udders was "so good," Byrd wrote with alacrity, "that a Cardinal Legate might have made a comfortable meal upon them during the Carnaval."[19]

In the woods near Halifax, West Virginia, at "a longitude of 78° 40' W and 155 miles from the Atlantic coast," Byrd's men killed a buffalo bull. (Near the site in 1753 some Moravians saw "a large buffalo lick.") Byrd thought it odd that the buffalo was by itself—"it was all alone, tho' buffaloes seldom are. . . . They are Seldom seen so far North as 40° of latitude, delighting much in canes and Reeds, which grow more Southerly." He christened a rivulet "Buffalo Creek, so named from the frequent tokens we discovered of the American behemoth."

Colonel Byrd was impressed with the "Ocean of Milk" given by the cows, and the strength of the brutes led him to wonder whether they could be broken to a harness. Influenced by Indian lore, he theorized that buffalo horn spoons would "Split and fall to Pieces whenever Poison is put into them." Settlers might tan buffalo skin into dark, spongy leather and tame calves for draft. "These, with the other Advantages I mention'd before, wou'd make this sort of Cattle more profitable to the owner, than any other we are acquainted with." Tending buffalo, Byrd warned, might prove taxing—"they would need a world of Provender." His men, short of rum, imitated Catawba hunters by "sucking the water out of the guts"; quaffing the steaming glops of fermenting grass and slime mashed from the greasy hanks of buffalo intestines "made them drunk."[20]

When they were heavy in buffalo meat, Byrd's men ate heartily and snored the night away, which caused them to break camp too late in the morning to make good time. "We cou'd not decamp before 11, the People being so much engaged with their Beef," Byrd complained. "I found it always a Rule that the greater our Plenty, the later we were in fixing out." On another occasion, Byrd wrote that, "when Provisions were Plenty, we always found it Difficult to get out early, being too much Embarrest with a long-winded Breakfast." Before early-morning marches, "every man took care to pack up some Buffalo steaks in his Wallet, besides what he crammed into his Belly." Homeward bound, Byrd stopped at the house of a Mrs. Mumford, who washed, carded, and spun a few hanks of buffalo hair to knit the Colonel a pair of wool stockings, which he declared "would have served an Israelite during his forty years march through the wilderness."[21]

Dr. John Bricknell, the most famous plagiarist of John Lawson, wrote, "The buffalo . . . its chiefest haunts being savannas . . . there were two taken alive in the year 1730 near the Neuse River." Since parts of what Bricknell wrote is a rewrite of Lawson's account, no one is sure whether Bricknell was writing from the Carolina wilds or sitting in his armchair in Edenton, Ireland. Critics called his work an "almost verbal transcript of John Lawson," and a "slavish plagiarism." One author notes, "The Library of Congress card for Bricknell's book says that Lawson "was almost verbally copied, without acknowledgement."[22]

But much of Bricknell's writing is his own. Buffalo horns, he wrote, could be fashioned into "cups, powder-horns, lanterns, and many other necessaries . . . rings from them are said to help the cramp, and the liver the spleen."[23] In 1737 a Dublin house published Dr. Bricknell's imposing to me with its equally imposing title: *The Natural History of North Carolina. With an account of the trade, manners, and customs of the Christian and Indian inhabitants. Illustrated with copper-plates, whereon are curiously engraved the map of the country, several strange beasts, birds, fishes, snakes, insects, trees, and plants & c.*

In 1733 Sir William Berkeley, governor of Virginia, sent Captain Henry Batt to explore the interior of the region. Leaving Appomattox, Batt and his men reached the Appalachians after seven days' travel and found plenty of game, including buffalo. The beasts had so little fear of men that the Englishmen almost could pet them; Captain Batt described them as "gentle and undisturbed."[24]

The same year, James Oglethorpe, former general and member of Parliament, saw buffalo in Georgia, where he founded a colony. Land acquired in trade from the Creeks allowed him to build the city of Augusta. He worked to gain a monopoly on the deer-skin trade with the Lower Creeks, which pitted him against Carolinian traders. Oglethorpe noted that "the wild beasts are deer, elk, bears, wolves, buffaloes." In 1735 Francis Moore, who tended Oglethorpe's stores at the southern settlement of Frederica, had watched Indians hunt buffalo near Darien. There were no buffalo on St. Simon's Island, he wrote, but there were "large herds upon the main." On July 31, 1739, west of the Oconee River in Laurens County, one of the men "killed two buffaloes, of which there are abundance . . . seeing several herds of sixty or upwards."[25]

Near the Ogeechee River, in Screven County, another of Ogle-thorpe's rangers "killed several buffaloes, of which there is a great plenty." One observed that Indian women planted and tilled the soil, while men hunted for deer and buffalo for hides to trade. On August 8, 1739, in Russell County, Alabama, at a Creek village on the Chattahoochee, Ogle-thorpe's men saw warriors "hunt deer, turkeys, geese, buffaloes." At a Creek village in Elmore County, Alabama, another of his hunters observed that the Indians "spend much time in hunting deer, turkeys, and bison."

In 1743 Edward Kimper marched with Oglethorpe from Georgia into northeastern Florida and witnessed Indians sewing buffalo skin moccasins. Henry Fowler, a settler, "counted one hundred buffaloes at one time on a single acre of ground," in what is now Abbeville, Georgia. Eighty miles from Augusta near the Savannah River was the Great Buffalo Lick. Oglethorpe wrote from Glynn County on March 16, 1746, that he and an Indian chief, Tomochichi, would "at his desire go out tomorrow to hunt ye buffalo." In the 1740s Thomas Spalding heard exaggerated reports from Colonel William McIntosh that "he has seen ten thousand buffaloes in a herd between Darien and Sapelo River."

In 1742 John Howard and John Peter Salling led a team of hunters to explore western Virginia. Just past the headwaters of the Ohio, they shot a buffalo bull and halted for a day to make a hide boat. They descended the Ohio in their craft. Near Fort de Chartres, the French captured these "suspicious characters" and shipped them to New Orleans. They were prisoners for three years before returning to Virginia to report to the Board of Trade that they "saw more good land on the Mississippi, and its many large branches, than they judged was in all the English colonies as far as they were inhabited."[26] Such news excited speculators, spurring exploration and western settlement.

In November 1748 Peter Kalm, a Swedish botanist, explored south of Pennsylvania. Near the Blue Ridge, he wrote, poorer North Carolinians ate buffalo "like common beef"; the hide was too porous for shoe leather, but many folks used tanned hides as quilts. In 1752 Bishop A. G. Spangenberg, a Moravian minister looking for a site to start a settlement, was in Alexander County, North Carolina, on the banks of the Little River when he noted that "the banks of the streams are so high that a man could not ride across, had not the buffalo broken them down here and there."[27]

A Choctaw tradition recalls that in Mississippi in the early 1700s there was a great drought. For three years no rain fell. The Tombigbee and the Nowubee dried up and the forests died. The Choctaw legend says that during the parched times the buffalo swam the Mississippi and never returned.[28] But in the Lower Mississippi Basin, as elsewhere, habitat destruction and overhunting took the heaviest toll. And as James Adair's writings reveal, Indians slaughtered the beasts as wantonly as white market hunters.

James Adair was one of the best-known traders in the Southeast. Born in London in 1709, Adair migrated to Charleston in 1735. In less than a year, he was leading teams of packhorses from Carolina's borders to the forks of the Little Tennessee, swapping wares for deer skins among the Catawba and the Cherokee. Adair was one of many traders working the area. Competition was keen. By 1744 he had moved to north Mississippi to set up operations.

Living among the "cheerful brave Chikkasah," Adair found his niche. Through his diplomacy and political maneuvering among the Chickasaw, Choctaw, and Creek, England's borders in the colonies expanded westward. Adair's trade flourished.

Fluent in Chickasaw and much beloved by the tribe, Adair led warriors on forays against the pro-French Shawnee. He passed easily between native and Anglo societies, earning the title "an English Chickasaw." But Adair was an anomaly of frontier life: A student of ancient history, versed in the Bible and Judaism, literate in Hebrew, he rode in the saddle many a mile to swap deer skins for books. By his own reckoning, Adair "lived and traded with the Indians, particularly the Chickasaws, from 1738 until 1768."[29]

Encouraged and assisted by others, most notably Indian traders George Galphin and Lachlan McGillivray, who lived among the southern tribes, Adair began writing his memoirs in 1761. The first edition of his work, *Adair's History of the American Indians,* was published in London in 1775. Well received in its day, Adair's book still is praised. Charles Hudson refers to him as "the extraordinary James Adair, on whose work we rely for much of what we know about the Southeastern Indians." Independent scholar Kathryn E. Holland Braund calls his book "one of the most important sources on southern Indians."[30]

Adair made many notes about buffalo, or "Yanasa," as the Chickasaw called the bulls. He watched Chickasaw hunters kill buffalo, observed women dressed in buffalo hides and men wearing loincloths of buffalo wool, slept on cane beds draped with buffalo robes, and saw sachems dance wearing ceremonial buffalo headdresses.[31]

Some tribes, Adair asserted, claimed bulls as totems, using "the name of a buffalo as a war appellative." Men credited with slain foes were given the title Yanasabe, meaning "buffalo killer." Chiseled in stone alongside panther manitous were petroglyphs of men wearing buffalo horns. War leaders, wrote Adair, had to fight in three "wolfish campaigns" before being allowed "to wear a pair of a young buffalo-bull's horns on his forehead, or to sing the triumphal war song, and to dance with the same animal's tail sticking up behind him."[32] Choctaw artisans made buffalo-hide saddles, which to Adair resembled saddles made by the Indians of the Dutch West Indies.

> The Indians provide themselves with a quantity of white oak boards, and notch them, so as to fit the saddle-trees; which consists of two pieces before, and two behind, crossing each other in notches, about three inches below the top ends of the frame. Then they take a buffalo green hide, covered with its winter curls, and having properly shaped it to the frame, they sew it with large thongs of the same skin, as tight and secure as need be; when it is thoroughly dried, it appears to have all the properties of a cuirass saddle. A trimmed bearskin serves as a pad.[33]

Buffalo meat, Adair said, tasted like tame beef but was sweeter and coarser grained. Therein lay a problem, Adair admitted: "The buffaloes are now become scarce, as the thoughtless and wasteful Indians used to kill great numbers of them, only for the tongues and marrow-bones, leaving the rest of the carcasses to the wild beasts."[34]

In South Carolina, the tale was the same. A descendant of John C. Calhoun wrote, "We know that some of those who first settled the Abbeville district in South Carolina in 1756, found buffalo there." James Glen was in South Carolina in 1761. "The wild beasts," he said, "are . . . deer, elk, buffaloes." In 1763 Dr. John Milligen noted in his *Description of South Carolina* that "buffaloes . . . are not near so numerous as they were a few years ago." Historian David Ramsey wrote in 1808 that in South Carolina before the days of settlement, three or four men with dogs could kill ten to twenty buffalo in a day. But by 1802, reported Governor John Drayton, the buffalo in South Carolina were "entirely exterminated."[35]

It was no different farther south. Naturalist William Bartram wrote from Florida in 1773, "Buffiloe . . . is becoming scarce in East Florida, yet there remain a few in the Point [the peninsula]."[36]

Southeastern buffalo herds were thinning and so were white-tailed deer—a direct result of the skin trade. Indian and white market hunters slaughtered deer from Catawba land to Chickasaw territory; skin traders counted deer skins in the hundreds of thousands annually.[37] The following vouchers show that deer skins were big business between traders and Indians. Beating competing French and Spanish interests in the region was vital; the skin trade was the key to it all. And because of their high-quality, low-priced, readily available wares, Englishmen kept the upper hand.

The first inventory lists English goods bought by the Choctaw in 1750.

"Annual Trade with the Choctaw Indians, circa 1750"[38]
5,000 ells [1 ell = 1.2 meters] of Limbourg, half blue and half red
1,000 white blankets with two points
200 white blankets with three points
500 blankets with stripes
2,500 regular trade shirts, for men, as long in front as in back
150 ordinary trade muskets
4,000 pounds of gunpowder
300 pieces of scarlet colored, woolen ribbon
250 pounds of rough vermilion in small one-pound sacks and in
    barrels of 100 and 50 pounds
150 pounds of red lead (a vermilion or red pigment made specifi-
    cally from mercuric sulfide)
200 pounds of blue and white drinking glasses of assorted sizes
30 gross of woodcutter knives
18,000 musket flints
4 gross of trade scissors
3 gross of flintlocks
3 gross of awls
400 mirrors in cases

The second list shows English wares in relation to the buying power of deer skins in 1767. If one compares this list with the earlier 1716 inventory of goods (on pages 59–60) traded in Charleston, the message becomes clear: To thwart French and Spanish efforts, English traders were willing and able to cut prices.

"Tariff of Trade in the Creek Nation Agreed upon between the Traders and Indians at a Congress Held at Augusta, Georgia, May 27, 1767, In pounds of Dressed Deerskin"[39]

	Skins
Gun	16
Strouds, 2 yards	8
Blanket, plain duffel	8
Knives, 2	1
Scissors	1
Beads, 5 strands barley corn	1
Beads, 3 strands common	1
Flints, 20 common	1
Flints, 15 fine	1

At about the same time that Captain Pierre Joseph de Celeron de Bienville was burying his lead plates and claiming the lands and rivers in the heart of North America for Louis XV, the president of the Virginia Council, Governor Thomas Lee, proclaimed the boundaries of Virginia to be "the Atlantic on the east, North Carolina on the south, the Potomac on the north, and, on the west, the Great South Sea, including California."[40] It mattered little that Englishmen believed California was an island. Exploration and surveying in the interior soon precipitated clashes between the European powers and Indians, culminating in war.

Following in the wake of the conflicts was a tough breed of frontiersmen who saw themselves less as British subjects than as Americans. They cared little about pacts signed in faraway places by kings. These men—and later, these men with their wives and children—led a swelling flood of settlers through the mysterious, heavily canopied forests, beyond the Blue Ridge into the lush canelands and barrens of Tennessee and Kentucky. They were harbingers of death for the buffalo and dispossession for the Indians.

Speculators, Traders, Long Knives, and War in the West

THE RUSH FOR AMERICA WAS ON. COUREURS DE BOIS AND VOYAGEURS in the 1740s grew uneasy at the sight of George Croghan's one-hundred-horse pack train outfitting hunters and Indians in the West. The Ottawa, allied with the French, warned Englishmen to stay out of the land south of the Great Lakes. In 1753 French soldiers seized John Fraser, a trader and gunsmith who lived with the Shawnee at the mouth of the Great Miami. Fraser was warned and released. And he was just one of many.

English scalps began showing up in trade to the French, but the English would not be denied their try at conquest. Clashes between Old World powers, each with native allies, were inevitable. Survival for most tribes pitted them against military titans and global economies that they scarcely understood. But there was one thing the Indians knew: Their land was at stake. Without land, the Indians could not be a people; without furs, skins, and meat, they could not live.

The French planned to build a string of forts from the St. Lawrence and the Great Lakes to the Ohio and the Mississippi. If the French completed their outposts, English western claims would be lost and their colonies would be threatened. The expansionist dreams of New France created a stir among wealthy Englishmen and nobility.

In 1748 twenty merchants, mostly Virginians, formed the Ohio Company. Their goals were simple: to push for western exploration, to trade with the Indians, and to acquire land. The company petitioned King George II for a grant of two hundred thousand acres west of the Alleghenies "to anticipate the French by taking possession of that country southward of the Lakes to which the French had no right nor had then taken possession, except a small block house fort among the Six Nations."[1] George II obliged the Virginians. Englishmen, both at home and abroad, secured stockholders, formed companies, and petitioned for their own estates to subdivide and sell, or lease for quitrents.

In April 1750 a party led by Dr. Thomas Walker passed through a gap in Pine Mountain, which he named for William Augustus, duke of Cumberland. That October, Christopher Gist and his seventeen-year-old slave rode to Kentucky by way of Ohio; after passing through Pound Gap, Virginia, Gist returned to his home in the Yadkin Valley in May 1751.

Walker was a graduate of William and Mary College. Little is known of Gist's schooling, but he wrote in a strong hand and his compass readings are precise. Both were skilled surveyors and woodsmen. The Loyal Land Company of Albemarle County, Virginia, hired Walker on December 12, 1749, "to go westward, in order to discover a proper place for settlement." The Ohio Company employed Gist for 150 pounds sterling "and such further handsome allowance as his service should deserve."[2]

Indians in the Middle Ground called the Virginians "Long Knives" notes Yale historian and author John Mack Faragher, "because of the sabers many carried into battle."[3] The Indians were suspicious of this first trickle of Long Knives and surveyors in the Ohio Valley, fearing settlers would follow.

Gist kept his compass wrapped in rags and stowed in his saddlebags. His mission was one great subterfuge enacted upon Indians: While scouting the illegally held holdings of the Ohio Company, spying on the French, and beseeching Indians to treat with Virginians, Gist gave his word that the English wanted no more from Indians than trade and friendship. Certainly, he told them, the Great Father across the big water had no plans to steal land from his children. The Wyandot, Shawnee, Delaware, Miami, and Mingo took Gist in, lodged him in their villages, fed him from their kettles, and traded him corn and horses.

Had the veil been ripped from Gist's masquerade, he would have met his end. "The People," he wrote, "began to suspect me, and said, I was come to settle the Indian's Lands and they knew I should never go Home again Safe." Fearing for his life, Gist lied about his intentions and managed to complete his mission.[4]

He stayed at Indian towns in central Ohio from December 1750 to February 1751. From there he and his slave rode to Kentucky. The land was "well timbered with large Walnut, Ash, Sugar Trees, Cherry Trees, &c."[5] Streams and rivers full of catfish, sturgeon, shad, and mussels watered meadows of wild rye, clover, and bluegrass. Elk, deer, and buffalo numbered in the hundreds. Bear were plentiful.

In March, as the pair rode across the greening pastures along the Little Miami, Gist "coud sometimes see forty or fifty Buffaloes feeding at once." He saw more buffalo the next day and would have shot one, but he heard a distant crackle of gunfire; fearing Indians, he veered from the path and rode thirty miles in the woods. At dusk he "killed a fine barren Cow-Buffaloe and took out her tongue and a little of her best meat."[6]

On March 12 Gist and his slave ferried across the Ohio from the Scioto. Gist's orders were for him to push to the Falls of the Ohio to skirt the far west fringe of the Ohio Company's grant. But Indian sign was everywhere: hoofprints, tracks, fire pits, and deadfalls. Reports from friendly Shawnee warned him of sixty French-allied Indians camped at the falls. Gist turned back. He had seen enough to tantalize speculators and company stockholders. "In short," he summarized about the land he toured, "it wants nothing but Cultivation to make it a most delightfull Country."[7]

The Ohio Valley seemed virginal to Gist's eyes. Lost upon him was the fact that Indians had utilized the rich region and harvested its resources for millennia. Notions that Indian-managed land needed European-style "Cultivation to make it a most delightfull Country" forever proved to be a bane to native life.

Gist and his slave rode east along the Kentucky, stopping to camp, hunt, and water their horses. The men ate well. "Monday 25.—killed 2 Buffaloes & took out their tongues and encamped."[8] By May 18, 1751, Gist had returned to his home in the Yadkin. He died of smallpox in 1759.

Dr. Thomas Walker's expedition for the Loyal Land Company began a year earlier than Gist's. In 1749 the governor of Virginia granted the company eight hundred thousand acres that spanned southwestern Virginia to southeastern Kentucky. On December 12 the company contracted with Walker, himself a shareholder, to scout the estate to find a site to start a settlement. On March 6, 1750, Walker and five companions—Ambrose Powell, William Tomlinson, John Hughes, Colby Chew, and Henry Lawless—left Walker's home in Castle Hill, Albemarle County. "Each man," he recorded, "had a Horse and we had two to carry the Baggage."[9]

Before going on to Kentucky, on March 15, 1750, Walker and his men stopped at Buford's Gap on Staunton Creek, near Roanoke, to buy corn. They wanted to buy wild meat too, as that region had been renowned for its herds. But Walker was dismayed to learn that the game was gone—killed out. "Hunters had killed the Buffaloes for diversion," he lamented.[10] A half bushel of meal and hominy had to last them until they could hunt.

By late March, the party was tenting beside Reedy Creek, which empties into the south fork of the Holston. On March 30, near Kingsport,

Tennessee, the men caught two buffalo calves. They killed one calf to eat and notched the ears of the other to mark it, then set it free.

Travel was tedious. Seven or eight miles was a good day. Downed trees, steep ridges, and timber rattlers buzzing from their dens slowed them as the riders ascended the Appalachian slopes. Nearing the Cumberland Gap on April 12, Walker discovered "a large Buffaloe Road . . . which we took and found the Ascent and Descent tollerably easie."[11] The next day they rode through the great cleft.

"April 16th. Rai(n)." And on April 17, as Walker logged in his journal, "Still Rain."[12] After the rains ceased, they guided their horses along the shores of the Shawanoe; to again commemorate England's duke, the Butcher of Culloden, Walker changed the river's name to the Cumberland.[13] On April 19 they hit a large salt lick "much used by Buffaloes" and crisscrossed by traces. They followed a spoke emanating from the hub of paths.[14]

They passed near the Bluegrass, missing the meadows by a day. On April 23 they built a base station near what is now Barbourville to house them during their forays. A week later they rode northeast into the rugged hinterlands of eastern Kentucky, where they encountered more rain, hail, and occasionally snow. Blustery winds downed trees and flattened tents. Walker's dogs bayed into the nights, fearful of howling wolves stalking the camp. Warmer days drew rattlesnakes from rock lairs to bask in the sun. Tired, snake-bitten horses and trail-worn men led to more woes. Colby Chew and his mare tumbled off a ridge. A bear mauled Ambrose Powell.

The men potted wild cows, bear, and elk. Walker saw a buffalo herd on the Cumberland numbering about one hundred head.[15] The men stuck to traces for travel.

> May 18th. We went up Naked Creek to the head and had a plain Buffaloe Road most of the way.[16]
> June 4th. I blazed several trees four ways on the outside of the low Grounds by a Buffaloe Road, and marked my Name on Several Beech Trees.[17]

On June 19, while traveling along a trace, they encountered a buffalo not willing to give way, so they shot it.[18] The six men returned to Walker's plantation on July 13. During their six-month sojourn, the company killed "13 Buffaloes, 8 Elks, 53 Bears, 20 Deer, 4 Wild Geese, about 150 Turkeys, besides small game." "We might have killed three times as much meat," Walker added, "if we had wanted it."[19]

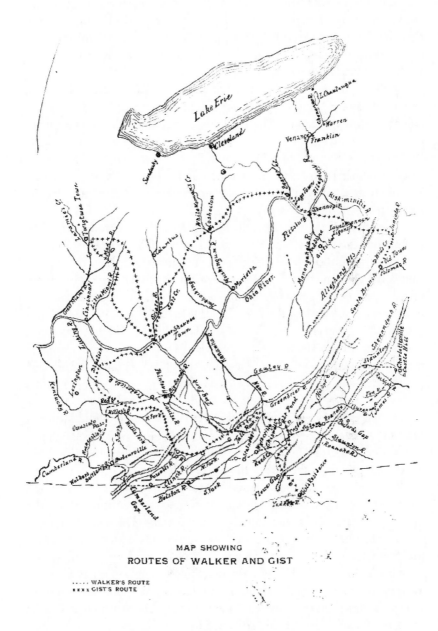

MAP SHOWING
ROUTES OF WALKER AND GIST

····· WALKER'S ROUTE
ⅹⅹⅹⅹ GIST'S ROUTE

The routes of Dr. Thomas Walker and Christopher Gist. (Courtesy the Filson Club)

Walker and Gist explored parts of Kentucky at nearly the same time, yet their journals are not at all alike. Gist, a Marylander-turned-North Carolinian who lived near the home of a teenager named Daniel Boone, crossed the Red, Licking, and Kentucky Rivers and may have gotten near the Salt River Basin; he penetrated Kentucky's heartland, traveling deep into the Bluegrass, and stood on the peak of Pilot's Knob in Powell County to gaze with awe at the plains below him.

Walker plowed through the thickets blanketing the slopes and ravines of eastern Kentucky and slogged through swollen rivers and turbulent streams and creeks. The land was craggy and wild, crawling with rattlesnakes, wolves, bears, and panthers. Gist saw the best of the land; Walker saw the worst. In 1755 Lewis Evans drew a map of Kentucky based on the reports of these two men and those of George Croghan. Published by Benjamin Franklin of Philadelphia, it is thought to be the first map of Kentucky ever made.[20]

Tales from men like Gist and Walker stirred the blood of hunters, speculators, and settlers, who began to see the West as a place of opportunity. Across the mountains it was all there: land, waterways, timber, fur, game. Travelers needed only follow the traces to get to this Promised Land. One frontier preacher, unable to think of a way to describe the splendor of heaven to his flock, declared, "Oh my dear honeys, Heaven is a Kentucky of a place!"[21]

But the Cumberland Gap, the gateway to this new heaven, would be fit only for packhorses and small wagons until 1796. And the Indians that claimed the land would have to be dealt with.

By the early 1700s many northeastern tribes, such as the Nipmuc, Massachusetts, and Pocomtuc, were extinct, or nearly so, from disease and war. Others, like the Leni-Lenape, whom whites called the Delaware, were migrating from the east to the Ohio Valley.

The Shawnee claimed central Ohio as their homeland. But the Shawnee were a wandering Algonquin group scattered throughout the Mississippi basin, never during their earliest history merging into a single society. Shawnee culture reflects early relationships with the Sauk, Fox, Kickapoo, Creek, Delaware, and Iroquois. North and west of the Ohio Shawnee towns dwelt the Wea, Potawatomi, Kickapoo, and Wyandot, a remnant of the Huron who were nearly killed out during the Iroquois wars a century earlier. The Ojibwa and Ottawa erected their wigwams along the shores of Lake Erie and Lake Huron.

European wars between the French and English spilled over into the

New World: King William's War (War of the League of Augsburg), 1689–97; Queen Anne's War (War of the Spanish Succession), 1702–13; and King George's War (War of the Austrian Succession), 1744–48.

By the end of King George's War, Crown law deemed land west of the Appalachians as Indian territory. Near Detroit and Lake St. Clair were a few French towns; Jesuits and Moravians lived near villages; French, English, and Dutch traders and trappers could also be found. Spanish colonies grew in pockets in Florida, along the Gulf, and west of the Mississippi. Still, the land was Indian land.

The French, alarmed at the thought of losing America to English rivals, armed native allies to fight the English. The English armed the Iroquois League to fight the French and French-allied Algonquins. Thus in 1754 began the Seven Years War, known in the American theater as the French and Indian War, the fourth and final conflict between the two mightiest powers on earth over land neither was destined to own. Indians were snared between them.

War stalled migration and brought Americans from different colonies together. Talk heard at campfires was a mix of accents, brogues, and dialects. But often the topic was the same: the fertile lands of the West.

Land was wearing out from overcultivation. Land defined a person's wealth and social standing. But in the East there just did not seem to be enough of it to go around. It was not just foot soldiers who talked of land; Benjamin Franklin, George Washington, Thomas Jefferson, and Patrick Henry pursued dreams of pastoral estates and speculated in land.[22] English aristocrats in London schemed to carve out their own American empires.

The war raged on. A twenty-one-year-old sergeant from North Carolina named Daniel Boone signed up with the militia. In 1755 Boone rode to Maryland to join Major General Edward Braddock and His Majesty's British Regulars in an ill-fated attempt on Fort Duquesne. Boone saw the folly of using European tactics in Indian warfare. And he met John Findley, one of George Croghan's men.

In 1752 Findley had set up a trading post at the Shawnee town of Es-kip-pa-ki-thi-ki (in what is now Clark County near Old Springs), meaning "place of blue licks." This one-acre village enclosed by a log palisade was on the north end of the Warrior's Path at the nexus of a web of traces. According to a French census taken in 1736, about two hundred families lived at Es-kip-pa-ki-thi-ki. Abandoned and torched in 1754, it is thought to have been one of the last Indian settlements in Kentucky.[23]

Findley's campfire talk of Kentucky—a paradise teeming with big game—fired Boone's imagination. In 1851 Nathan Boone, Daniel's youngest child, recounted Findley's tales to frontier historian Lyman Draper: "Of bears and buffaloes, elk and deer, their number was legion; and at many of the salt-licks of the country, they congregated in such prodigious herds, that the sight was truly grand and amazing."[24]

During the French and Indian War, wild beef was part of the diet for western troops. In western Virginia, during his Sandy Creek foray against the Shawnee in 1756, Captain John Procter barely kept his 340 men fed. In Logan County they cut down two buffalo hides that they had hung in a beech tree weeks before. The soldiers singed off the wool and sliced the skin into thongs to boil and eat. They named the site Tug Fork.[25]

The Cherokee traded off their British loyalty for French muskets, rum, and powder and ball and in March 1760 laid siege to Fort Loudoun. Under a truce struck between the Cherokee and British that August, the starving whites fled; they had made only fifteen miles before the Indians attacked, killing twenty-seven men and three women. Retaliation by the king's army and a wave of smallpox left five thousand Cherokee dead. The Indians signed articles on November 19, 1761.[26]

Cherokee elders asked that a British officer be sent to them as a token of trust. Two Virginians, Ensign Henry Timberlake and Sergeant Thomas Sumter, volunteered for the job. After traveling near Three Springs Ford in Hamblen County, Tennessee, Timberlake recorded in December 1761 that "nothing more remarkable occurred, unless I mark for such the amazing quantity of buffaloes, bears, deer, and beavers." Arriving at the Tellico on January 2, 1762, he saw "an incredible number of buffaloes."[27] Timberlake and Sumter paddled a canoe to the Little Tennessee, joined a band of Cherokee men and women, and walked through what is now Greene County to Horse Creek, where a drove of eighteen buffalo stampeded them; they "ran in amongst us, before we discovered them, so that several of us like to have been run over, especially the women, who with some difficulty sheltered themselves behind the trees."[28]

Timberlake's journal is the first authoritative survey of the area. The second is that of Lieutenant John Ross, who in 1764 became the first British officer to explore the Tennessee. On that trip, deer were too skittish to shoot, food was scarce, and travel rough. "Had it not been for the Buffaloe Meat," Major Robert Farmer recorded in his journal on December 16, 1765, "the expedition must have failed, being about five weeks short of Provisions."[29] Cherokee, Creek, and Chickasaw claimed parts of Tennessee. By 1714 a Monsieur du Charleville had built an outpost to trade with the Shawnee and Cherokee; his store was on the Cumberland, seventy yards from French Lick Creek. Hunters from Illinois and

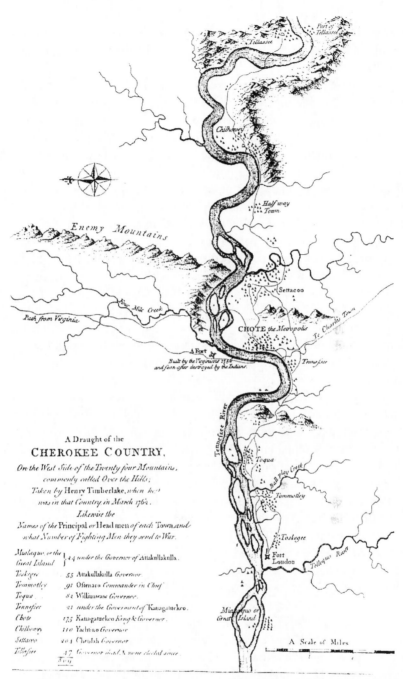

"A Draught of the Cherokee Country," by Henry Timberlake, March 1762.

New Orleans moved into the region.[30] One branch of the Duck, a tributary of the Tennessee, is named Buffalo River for the herds that roamed there.[31]

After nearly a decade of war, treaties signed in Paris in 1763 and the Fort Stanwix Treaty of 1768 pushed British claims to the ends of the Mississippi. French trading posts in the Northwest would be left alone, and life for those in the conquered region would go on as usual. The new King of England, George III, provided sanction for select traders to go west but forbade all other migrations and forays. The Treaty of 1763 would have helped preserve the buffalo east of the Mississippi, but it was impossible to enforce; Americans, who had spent nine years fighting the French, did not heed the proclamation. Hunters, adventurers, and traders soon pushed beyond the Appalachians.

George Croghan was a licensed trader with an eye for land.[32] Since the 1740s he had hired more than fifty men with packhorses to travel the Ohio country to barter with Indians. In 1765 Croghan's party left Fort Pitt via the Ohio. "Here buffaloes, bears, turkeys, with all other kind of wild game in such plenty," he wrote near the mouth of the Little Kanawha, "that we killed out of our boats as much as we wanted. A good hunter, without much fatigue to himself, could here supply one hundred men with meat."[33]

At Big Bone Lick, Kentucky, Croghan saw herds of deer, elk, and buffalo. Leading to the lick was "a large road which the Buffaloes have beaten, spacious enough for two waggons to go abreast." Near Antiquity, Ohio, Croghan watched buffalo swim the Ohio. In June along the Little Wabash he saw a "great plenty."[34] One year later he made a similar trip. Among Croghan's party was the chief engineer of the Western Department of North America, Captain Harry Gordon of the 60th Regiment of the British Forces. Gordon first observed small droves of buffalo about one hundred miles from Fort Pitt (though a few had been shot in the drift between Mingo Town and the Muskingum). "But they are not so common," he added, "untill we pass the Sioto."[35] They camped at Big Bone Lick.

> The beaten Roads from all the Quarters to it easily conducted us; they resemble those to an inland Village where Cattle go to and fro a large common. . . . The Extent of the mudy Part of the Lick is ¾ of an Acre. This mud, being of a Salt Quality, is greedily lick'd by Buffaloe, Elk, and Deer, who come from distant Parts, in great Numbers, for this Purpose.[36]

On June 31, 1766, Gordon sent a dispatch from Fort Massac, Illinois: "The Herds of Buffaloe are hereabouts extraordinary large and frequent to be seen. . . . Hunters from this Post may be sent amongst the Buffaloe, any Quantity of whose Beef they can procure in the proper Season." He saw "great Herds of buffaloe . . . on the beaches of the Islands and River, into which they come for Air and Coolness in the midle of the Day."[37]

Hunters scouring the region ventured south to the Cumberland. In 1766 Jacques Timothy Boucher De Monbruen, a French meat getter from the Illinois country, hunted Middle Tennessee. Joseph Guild, a Tennesseean, knew De Monbruen and described him as a tall "athletic, dark-skinned man, with a large head, broad shoulders and chest, small legs, a high, short foot, and an eagle eye."[38] He wore a blue hunting shirt, leather leggings, and a scarlet waistcoat from his days in the French and Indian War. On his head was a fox-skin cap with the tail hanging down his back.

De Monbruen was a market hunter seeking wild beef, tongues, hides, and tallow. He rendered tallow from bulls in June and July when they were fattest, one bull yielding about seventy-five pounds. His tenders rendered fat from cows in the fall, each cow yielding sixty pounds. De Monbruen favored hunting at Sulfur Springs, a creek on Lick Branch off the Cumberland. In the early 1760s he set out for New Orleans, his keelboat heavy with buffalo hides, smoked tongues, and tallow. In 1780 frontiersman James Robertson, who became known as the father of middle Tennessee, saw De Monbruen's cabin packed with kegs of buffalo tallow.[39] De Monbruen died in Nashville on October 10, 1826, at age ninety-one.

George Taylor of Sheffield, England, traveled across Tennessee in 1768. Taylor's journal, published in Nottingham in 1771, reveals his delight at eating his first wild beef. While he and his men were crossing the Tennessee, a drove of eighteen buffalo bolted toward them. Half drunk on rum and water, and "being merry over our grog," the men shot a cow. "Their flesh is very good. . . . The hunch on their shoulders is esteemed by the Indians the most delicious part of them."[40]

British officers toured the newly conquered West to spy on French settlements. In 1763 orders from New York sent Lieutenant Philip Pittman of the Fifteenth Regiment of Foot to St. Augustine. Pushing on to Mobile, he began a five-month journey ascending the Mississippi to Illinois. He reconnoitered a fort about ten miles past the mouth of the Arkansas, witnessing the heavy trade in wild beef and hides. "These people subsist mostly by hunting, and every season send to New Orleans great quantities of bear's oil, tallow, salted buffaloe meat, and a few skins."

He floated on, past Ste. Genevieve, Missouri, to Fort de Chartres. "The country," he noted, "abounds with buffalo, deer, and wild-fowl, particularly ducks, geese, swans, turkies, and pheasants."[41]

As George Croghan was pushing down the Ohio, the Philadelphia firm of John Baynton, Samuel Wharton, and George Morgan was making ready for an all-out western thrust, complete with a scheme from London's secretary of state for the Southern Department, Lord Shelburne, who proposed starting colonies along the river.[42]

By 1766 the firm had more than seventy-five thousand pounds sterling in the venture. The idea was simple: By shipping goods to Kaskaskia, a burgeoning center of trade that by 1767 had a population nearing one thousand, the firm hoped to supply French citizens and British troops. Wagonloads of trade items soon began the two- to three-month journey from Philadelphia to Fort Pitt, and from there another thirteen hundred miles by boat down the Ohio to Illinois.[43]

The firm hoped to exploit the Indian trade. Bands of Peoria, Kaskaskia, Shawnee, Illinois, Wea, Quapaw, Chippewa, Fox, Osage, Missouri, Potawatomi, and other tribes traded at Fort de Chartres, bringing in tons of fur. Otter, beaver, fox, and mink brought top dollar at London auctions. Ginseng and castors—the beaver's musk glands—were thought to have medicinal value, and sold well too.

Baynton, Wharton, and Morgan were willing to pay cash, but the Indians wanted to barter. Muskets and fusils were the most sought after, though rifles were also in demand. Whiskey, wine, rum, and tafia flowed liberally—at one time the firm's inventory listed over eight thousand gallons of spirits. It was the junior member of this business triumvirate, George Morgan, who took his partners' hopes and goods to Illinois, where he opened the main store at Kaskaskia in 1766 and smaller branches at Cahokia, Illinois, and Vincennes, Indiana. He was confident when he wrote in February 1768:

> Dear Partners:
> I have already sent you a general Order for the Goods which are in demand here & which will afford a great Advance. . . . As to Muscovado & Loaf Sugar, Coffee, Chocolate, Mens, Womens & Childrens best & common Leather Shoes, Tin Ware, Pewter, Silver, Appalachian Handkerchiefs—beaver traps, & Soap, you cannot send too great a Quantity.

Morgan wrote on April 15 that, to take advantage of spring rains that raised the Ohio, "before the Fall of the Waters—We shall be in Want of the following particular articles, viz":

Loaf Sugar	Steel Spurs	Candle Wick
Muscovado	Salt Petre	Candle Moulds
Hyson Tea	Worsted or Cruels	Sheep Skins
Bohea Tea	Short Pipes	Beaver Traps
Chocolate	Blotting Cloaths	Nails
Pepper	Irish Linnens	Scythes
Shoes	Chintz and Callicos	Knives
Tin Ware	White & Red flannel	Forks
Pitch & Cordage	Swanskin	Spades
Pewter Basons &c	Black Cravats	Axes
Brass Candle sticks	Black Bandanas	Cheese
Writing Paper	Small Gilt Trunks	Beeswax
Spike Gimblets	Bed Ticken	Buttons
Tap Bores	Table Cloths	Castile Soap

Equally impressive are Morgan's transactions in 1768. The following is an abridged but typical account:

Powder	Vermilion	Wrist Bands
Balls	Flints	Beads
Tobacco	Ruffled Shirts	Coats
Knives	Breech Clouts	Plain Shirts
Paint	Rings	Jews Harps
Handkerchiefs	Rum	Match Coats
Awls	Shirts	Cutteaus
Leggings	Gartering	Wampum
Brass Kettles	Ribbon	Thread
Silver Crosses	Fuzees	Strouds
Calico Shirts	Narrow Stroud	Petticoats
Silver Brooches	Pipe Tomahawks	Pipes

The firm needed five convoys to float the wares from Fort Pitt to Kaskaskia.[44] Morgan ordered sixty-five more vessels for the 1767 fall trip. Five men per boat was a full crew, and Morgan kept over three hundred boatmen on the Ohio. A keg of salt was aboard each boat so that when they got into buffalo country they could preserve the beef.[45] Buffalo so abounded near present-day Louisville that Morgan wrote his partners on December 16, 1767: "What Plan to propose as the Most feasible for our next Falls Buffaloe Hunt I have not yet hit upon. I think I will take a nap & dream of One."[46]

Fortunately for Morgan, troops at Fort de Chartres needed meat. This new version of the fortress, completed in 1756 at a cost of five million *livres,* was built of wagon-size limestone blocks quarried from the bluffs of Prairie du Rocher. The British called the outpost Fort Cavendish and used it to quarter troops. The flood waters of the Mississippi claimed it in 1772, forcing the Brits to move to Kaskaskia.[47]

At Fort de Chartres, Captain Gordon Forbes hired Morgan's men to hunt buffalo to feed the troops. But many of the hired hands hunted deer and beaver and blasted bear and buffalo for sport. Morgan's men spotted French and Spanish row galleys flying under British colors on the Wabash and Ohio, trading illegally with Indians and killing buffalo for the New Orleans markets.[48] Morgan wrote on December 10, 1767.

> [They] have so thinn'd the Buffaloe & other game that you will not now see the ½₀ Part of the Quantity as formerly & unless some Method be taken to put a Stop to this Practice, it will in a short Time be a difficult Matter to supply Fort Chartres with Meat from thence.[49]

The butchery was not limited to Illinois. From August to the end of September 1767, English hunters in the Cumberland basin killed "up-wards of 700 Buffaloe & rendered their tallow." French meat getters in "twenty large Perrigoues up from New Orleans, killing buffaloe chiefly for tallow," also intruded on Morgan's scheme.[50]

In July 1768 about thirty Cherokee attacked Morgan's hunters in southwest Kentucky. Simon Girty was the sole survivor. Within a score of years Girty would be one of the most feared men in the Ohio Valley, and novelists would call him "the White Savage," yet now it was said that he was "particularly attached to Morgan."[51] In October Major General Thomas Gage sent a dispatch from Kaskaskia to Sir William Johnson in New York saying, "Four Frenchmen had a very narrow escape from a party of Cherokee about twenty leagues from this place."[52]

But hunters put up with the peril. Game was money. On September 15, 1768, George Butricke, adjutant at Fort de Chartres, wrote to Captain Thomas Barnsley in Philadelphia that the lands about the Ohio were "covered with all kinds of Game," the like of which "is not to be seen in any part of the known World."[53]

Army cooks served each company one buffalo yearling a day. Butricke guessed their weight at four hundred to six hundred pounds each and saw herds numbering up to fifty head. But "some people," he wrote, "say in 100s they have seen them. We had such plenty that when a Bull was killed we only took the tongue and left the Rest for the Wolves."

In Illinois tallow sold for eighteen pence per pound. Tallow brought only eight pence per pound at Fort Pitt and was costly to ship upriver. Wild beef, when cured, salted, and packed in hogsheads, could be shipped to white slavers in the West Indies.[54] To cash in on the market, Morgan's men hunted buffalo as far east as the Buffalo River (now called the Green) in Kentucky.

Morgan hired Joseph Hollingshead to oversee his meat packers on the Cumberland and Tennessee Rivers. During winter, tenders packed wild beef—"lightly salted with a bushel and a peck per thousand pounds"—in snug oak casks. "All ours is just as good as the day it was killed," Morgan assured his partners, "and will keep so for seven years with proper attendance."[55] He estimated that forty-four barrels of salted buffalo meat would enter his Kaskaskia storehouse within one month. He shipped cargo between January and February when waters ran high and risk from Indians was low.

On April 5, 1768, Hugh Thompson, one of Morgan's men, floated the Mississippi with "18,000 pounds of [buffalo] beef, 60 Venison Ham, 55 Buffaloe Tongues & Wt of Tallow." It was a ton short of what Morgan had wanted. Morgan wrote to his wife Molly that "there will be no Danger of Starving for I have now two Years Provisions in the House consisting of . . . Buffaloe Tongues, Vennisson & Bears Ham." One hundred deer hams and twenty bear hams hung among two hundred buffalo tongues.[56]

"The Buffaloe Meat I have sent different French Hunters out for," Morgan wrote to John Baynton, his father-in-law and senior member of the firm, on October 30, 1768, "I am to pay for at the same Rate as Mention'd . . . of an Agreement with one Monsieur Dane who supplies me with 20,000 weight." He sold another fifteen thousand pounds of buffalo beef at eight pence per pound and issued "Restrictions laid on the Buffaloe hunting" to slow the meat trade, as the herds were dwindling.[57]

Morgan was vexed, as he floated his tons of bear bacon, tallow, tongues, beef, and hides down the Mississippi, to pass French hunters along the way. Soldiers spotted ten parties of Frenchmen near Memphis "along the eastern shore near the mouth of Hatchie River above Prudhomme

Cliff." In June 1768, John Jennings saw French hunters in the same area slaughtering buffalo.[58] But Morgan was wiping out the buffalo too, so he had no right to complain, unless it was because his profits were being lost.

New Orleans traders worried as shipments of beef and tallow slowed. George Butricke dispatched plans to arm "a very Large Boat . . . to Carry 35 men With six Months provisions &c and a Brass sixpounder Mounted on her forecastle," to patrol the Wabash and Ohio to intercept French and Spanish boats and "prevent them from killing Buffalo, which the people of New Orleans have done in such quantities lately that were they allowed to continue it, they would soon destroy all those animals."[59]

Lieutenant Thomas Hutchins was ordered to man the boat to initiate the plan, but he ignored the buffalo and mapped the rivers, and the "row galley" was again never attempted. Describing the Natchez Trace, Hutchins wrote that the "Buffalo Path that crosses the river appeared to me to have been used equal to ye King's highway." Hutchins first traveled west with Harry Gordon as his assistant engineer in 1766, ended his survey in north Alabama on March 31, 1769, and in 1784 published his memoirs, *A Historical Narrative and Topographical Description of Louisiana*. "The whole country abounds in bears, buffalo, deer, turkeys, etc," he declared.[60] On December 5, 1769, Colonel John Wilkins, successor to Captain Forbes at Fort de Chartres, reported more complaints about French and Spanish hunters: "These people destroy immense Numbers of Buffaloes."[61]

Profits to the firm of Baynton, Wharton, and Morgan were never as high as the Philadelphians thought they should have been. Shipping costs were too steep, and the French did not care for the English or their wares and moved deeper into French territory. Buffalo along the Mississippi and its tributaries from St. Louis southward were vanishing, and competition from the rival firm of Bernard and Gratz cut into the firm's earnings. Within two years the far western enterprise of Baynton, Wharton, and Morgan would be no more.[62]

American market hunters—Long Hunters—from Virginia, Pennsylvania, and North Carolina pushed into Tennessee and Kentucky. Their heyday was short. But their forays into the first Far West helped doom buffalo east of the Mississippi.

Long Hunters, Meat Getters, and Market Hunters

LONG HUNTERS WERE THE FIRST TRUE AMERICAN FRONTIERSMEN TO push beyond the Blue Ridge. Theirs was the first American blood to stain the soil of Kentucky and Tennessee. Elisha Wallen, Uriah Stone, Benjamin Cutbirth, Daniel Boone, Casper Mansker, James Knox, Henry Skaggs, James Dysart, Joseph Drake, Isaac and Abraham Bledsoe—enigmatic names shrouded in mystery and romantic lore. Long Hunters all.

Long Hunters were not, as is often depicted, dashing nimrods clad in fringed buckskins and coonskin caps. They did not, as romanticists insist, trek west to make free the land for God and country, hearth and home. Most did not, contrary to James Fenimore Cooper's Leatherstocking hero, Natty Bumppo, love Indians or the "Indian way." Nor did they see themselves as noble light bearers sallying forth to "blaze the trail"—as declared in glowing mythmaker cant—for the coming of "civilization."

No. Long Hunters broke treaties and laws to trespass and poach on Indian land. Unlike Cooper's "Hawkeye," most hunters—although they adopted Indian skills, trappings of Indian dress, and supplanted the Indians' role as middlemen in the skin trade—despised their native peers as foes and competitors and were prone to shoot them on sight. Long Hunters did not care to "civilize" the West. They headed west to make money in deer skins and fur.

Most were plain, poor men seeking land, relief from debt, a way to feed hungry mouths. Urbane whites and circuit riders often were not sympathetic to their plight. "The Men," remarked English explorer and writer William Byrd of borderland North Carolinians, "impose All the Work upon the poor Women.... They lye and Snore, till the Sun has run one third of his course. . . . Thus they loiter away their Lives, like Solomon's Sluggard, with their arms across, and at the Winding of the Year Scarcely have Bread to Eat."[1] Methodist preacher David Barrow warned his flock that men ensnared in the hunter's life were "always indigent, always ignorant, always idle. Their poverty, their whole condition, is their vice."[2]

Few got rich from hunting. Many wound up landless or in debt. "I never knew anyone to make anything, or to do well hunting," said ex-market hunter James Wade to Reverend John D. Shane. The love of the chase, he said, became "a ruling and absorbing passion.... They need little capital, and a few peltry or furs is all they obtain." Wade swore that he never would have amounted to much had he not sold his rifle, which forced him to farm and lead a more domestic life.[3]

Yet market hunting did offer some men a way out of a hardscrabble life. If it became "a ruling and absorbing passion" for hunters such as Wallen, Stone, Knox, and Mansker, it meant that they took their jobs seriously. Barring calamity, a hunter might earn more than a thousand dollars a year—a big sum for the day. But Wade's bleak portrayal, though he did not hunt during the classic Long Hunter era, which lasted from the early 1760s to the 1770s, is in part a true one. It was for Daniel Boone, the archetypal Long Hunter and frontiersman.

Romance, moralizing aspersions, and Manifest Destiny aside, who were the Long Hunters? How did they and those like them operate in the skin trade? What effect did such intruders have on the buffalo roaming from the Bluegrass to the Cumberland, from the Green to the Wabash?[4]

Long Hunters were the freest Anglo-Americans to live before the Revolution. The stark edge of life and death inured the tough, individualistic frontier folk to toil, hardship, heat, cold, rain, snow, ice. Long Hunters had to be blacksmiths enough to shoe horses; forge froes, frizzens, gun springs, and knives; and repair guns and beaver traps. They could haft axes and tomahawks, and knap flints from fist-size pieces of chert to fit the cocks of their rifle-guns, dubbed "widow makers" by red-coated Brits who bore the sting of their fire. Such men were skilled in hunting, trapping, stalking, hiding, reading sign, building shelters, surviving. They were their own doctors, veterinarians, boat builders, coopers, militiamen, cooks, cord wainers, gunsmiths, skinners, and tanners. And more.

They were packhorse men. Their work demanded that they follow game trails deep into the forests to hunt deer. Deer skins were currency in the East and in Europe; in 1753 North Carolina merchants exported over thirty thousand hides.[5] Hunters sought the deer's skin in summer and early fall, when coats were reddish. After the first frosts, coats take a deeper root in the skin as blood vessels in the dermis swell to feed the new growth of hair. Leather made from deer skins taken in the hard of winter cracked along vein lines. Skins tanned from summer-killed deer did not.[6]

Camp tenders put deer skins in order by scraping off hair and grain "as a currier dresses leather," then they yanked the skins over a staking board to break down the hide's fibers to make the skins easier to pack. Tenders wrapped these "half-dressed hides" in bear hides in lots of fifty and bound the bundles with buffalo tugs—"made by cutting hides round and round into long strips and twisting them"—and loaded the bales onto horses. Half-dressed deer skins averaged two and a half pounds each and sold for forty cents a pound—roughly a dollar a hide.

Shooting twenty or thirty deer a day made for long hours of skinning. James Kenny, who journeyed to Pittsburgh in 1761, said hunters kept unskinned deer safe from buzzards by leaving a hat or garment on the beast. Or the hunter could "Bark or blase 3 or four Trees round it & then wets some Powder in their Hand . . . then dips their finger in it & Sprinkles on ye Blazes, which in ye Night will look like Sparks of fire all around, & no Vermin would touch ye Carcase."[7]

"By Christmas deer are not worth hunting for," stated Daniel Bryan, nephew of Daniel Boone.[8] Then hunters turned to trapping beaver, mink, fox, racoon, and otter. James Wade's steel traps were "8 inches across the jaws . . . costing from six dollars to eight dollars apiece."[9] Hunters shot bears to render their fat into tallow for butter and cooking, one bear yielding about twenty-five pounds of lard. Smoked bear meat, called bear bacon, was always in demand in the backcountry.

Hunters placed little value on buffalo or elk hides, which, like bear hides, were too bulky to transport. But there was value in buffalo meat: In 1761 wild beef and tallow sold at Fort Pitt for three dollars a pound.[10] Wild beef was in the best order in the autumn, after the buffalo had feasted on grasses, clover, and pea vine.

Long Hunters made buffalo hide boats, a skill acquired from Indians. Daniel Boone's description of such a craft is not very detailed (typical of Boone, said to be "quiet, of few words and to the point"), but it is a rare glimpse of how hunters made hide boats.[11] On a hunt in the Kanawha Valley with his son Nathan, Boone shot nine buffalo. To float the meat to market, he hacked down two slim hickories, bent them into hoops to bind with tugs, and "fastened the edges of the buffalo hide to it, making it bag down like the half of an egg, then ribbed it with poles, like a basket— longer than wide."[12] High winds could swamp these craft, which could float eight hundred pounds; hunters on horseback or on foot lashed hide boats together for stability to tow in the shallows. In 1851 Nathan Boone, serving as a captain in the U. S. Army in Missouri, elaborated on how his father made hide boats:

> Get poles a little larger than a man's wrist and split them and bend them over ... for the ribs of a boat, making the boat 8 or 10 feet long according to the size of the skin, and four or five, or six feet wide. . . . . Lay the skin (of the buffalo) down with the hair next [to] the ribs and stretch it down to the whaling or rib which forms the gunwale of the boat, trim off the edges and cut loops through it and lash it along.[13]

Hunters contrived rafts of cane or logs and canoes of elm bark. One poplar dugout used on the Cumberland measured fifty-six feet long and three feet across; it drew three feet of water and needed seven grindstones for ballast.[14]

In 1794, during Tennessee's Nickojack War, Casper Mansker made two hide boats from domestic cattle skins and a buffalo hide hut. A typical shelter was a half-face—a three-sided, bark-topped log lean-to with an open front to keep men and peltry out of rain and snow.[15] Half-faces built to last a season were tall enough in the front for a man to stand. William Sudduth's half-face shed was "8 feet wide and 10 feet deep, covered over with puncheons and built up on three sides with logs."[16] Daniel Boone's family lived in a half-face for a season; a visitor who slept there said that grease from the bear bacon hanging overhead dripped on his face in the night.[17] John Baker's half-face was built of red oak logs and was big enough to keep "his family in one end and a barrel of whiskey in the other."[18]

For a quick shelter, hunters stripped off sheets of elm and ash bark and shingled them onto lean-to frames bound with withes or tugs. "The whole slope of the roof from the front to the back was slabs, skins, or ... the bark of hickory or ash trees."[19] Moss, grass, and leaves chinked in the cracks of the hut made walls airtight. Rain showers were just put up with; the canopy high overhead kept one dry for an hour or more. Hunters sought shelter in caves, which they called "rock-castles," or in limestone sinkholes, abandoned camps, or the nook of a big tree. During the winter of 1780–81, Thomas Sharpe Spencer, a tall, robust woodsman, lived in a hollow sycamore at French Lick, now called Nashville.

One hunter used a "buffalo hide . . . stretched across poles overhead for a covering from the damps and rains." During a blizzard in February 1778, Daniel Boone holed up in a buffalo hide hut on the banks of the Lower Blue Licks; the next day, the 7th, some Shawnee gave chase, seized him, and captured his party of twenty-six salt boilers. Kentucky scouts Laban and Spencer Records once killed an elk and set up its hide as a lean-to to wait out a storm. In the winter of 1780, Daniel Trabue and some other hunters on the Green hunkered down for a few days in "a camp covered with buffeloe hids." Casper Mansker said that during a hunt on the Cumberland, he stayed in a "skin house"—possibly a shelter made from buffalo hides, but more likely a small cabin used as a base camp.[20] White hunters on good terms with Indians often found respite in Indian towns.

At night when wolves drew close and Indians were not about, hunters might kindle four small fires, spread their bearskins, buffalo robes, and wool blankets, and sleep in the midst of the fires. "Skins," said Kentucky hunter Hugh Bell, "with the hair side up would be placed upon the ground before the fire, to be used as a . . . bed at night and sometimes with another hide for a covering."[21] The men packed slivers of slippery elm bark to pound and boil into a poultice "in case of wounds."[22] Blankets worn high on the back stayed out of the way and helped protect from sniping bullets. Hunters built tree scaffolds ten to twelve feet off the ground to keep goods safe from bears and to sleep on. Some hunters carried a deer hoof or turkey foot to make tracks in the dirt to throw off Indian trackers.

Meals were plain. Wild meat and jerk were standard fare. Hunters parched corn to pound into meal and mix with sugar, hickory nuts, chestnuts, dried beans, peas, or dried persimmon. In the fall they gathered hickory nuts. To get the nut meat, they crushed the nuts and swirled them in a pan of water till the hulls sank and the meats floated to the top to be skimmed off and dried.

Boone toted a haversack stuffed with jerk and johnnycakes.[23] To jerk meat, hunters cut four forked saplings three to six feet tall and stuck them in the ground. Then they placed poles lengthwise in the forks and sticks across the poles three to four inches apart. They sliced the meat with the grain into strips half an inch thick, weighing up to a pound each, laid the strips on the rack, and kindled a fire underneath. Blankets placed overhead "as protection against the night dews" also kept buzzards from flying off with the meat. Smoking might take two days.[24] Nicholas Cresswell built his jerk racks low to the ground.

The meat is first cut from the bones in thin slices like beef steaks, then four forked sticks are stuck in the ground in a square form and small sticks are laid on these forks in the form of a gridiron about three feet from the ground. The meat is laid on this and a slow fire put under it, and turned until it is done.[25]

Some hunters loved beaver tail, greasy flaps of gristle and fat; others loathed them. Beaver tail, said Hugh Bell, must be "wrapped up in a coat of wetted oak leaves, and put into a bed of coals and covered up overnight."[26] John McQueen said panther meat "ate a good deal like mutton." Nathan Boone said panther had "a sweet and cattish taste." Thomas Walker craved rattlesnakes. In lean times hunters ate anything: slabs of dried buffalo hide, raw turtle, even dog meat dripping with maggots. John Fitch choked down dung-tainted tripe and deemed it "very mellow."[27] Once Boone's men were so hungry that they ate their moccasin soles.[28]

Wheat bread was rare; corn bread was common. Turkey breast was a fair bread substitute, but hunters grumbled when salt was scarce. They boiled coffee in kettles and blew the fire with a piece of hollow cane.[29] When the coffee gurgled over and hissed in the flames, tenders removed the kettle and doused a shot of water in the brew to settle the grounds.

Reading, singing, and whistling helped pass the hours. Bibles were the favored reading material. Boone carried a copy of *Gulliver's Travels*. James Dysart, a Long Hunter during the classic era, once said, "I am never lonesome when I have a good book in my hand."[30]

Hunters blended European and Indian attire. Deer-skin leggings were common, as were those made from loose wool, which, besides being warm, helped deflect pit viper fangs. Hugh Bell wore a coat made from a bear skin; he slit the skin down the middle from chin to tail, slit the hind legs, then turned the pelt inside out; "the forelegs thus answer for arms, and the head for a cap."[31]

While laid up in a cave on the Rockcastle to wait out a storm, Thomas Walker's men "dressed an Elk skin to make Indian Shoes—most of ours being quite worn out." As the river swelled, the men "concluded to stay and put our Elk skin in order for shoes and make them."[32] For the six woodsmen, it would have been easy to flesh the hide, soak it until the hair slipped, half dress it, then yank the skin over a rock until it was soft enough to sew. Hides tanned with white-oak and sumac bark could be had nearer the settlements or by trade. "Indian-drest" hides—buckskins dressed with brains—were available from Indians, stores, or traders.[33]

Frontier women sewed garments of linen, wool, linsey-woolsey (a blend of wool and linen), leather, cotton, raw silk, or other textiles. Woodsmen, scouts, and Indians wore hooded wool cappo-coats (capotes) of mid-thigh length. Kentuckian John Hanks (1767–1840) explains: "My mother made some cappo-coats . . . to take along and sell among the Indians. Made them of blue broadcloth with a cap or hood to draw over the head, otherwise like a matchcoat."[34]

Hats tended to be low crowned, wide brimmed, and made of felt, but some men wore fur caps or hats made from buffalo wool. At times Spencer and Laban Records did not wear hats, and once frontiersman Simon Kenton mistook the long-haired, bare-headed Records brothers cloaked in dark hunting shirts for Indians. In 1785, during a hunt on the Green River, John Stovall sewed himself a hat from a goose skin fixed with thongs for chin straps, wearing it feather side out. Another Kentuckian, George Michael Bedinger, said Stovall looked "ludicrous"; but Bedinger, who wore a cocked hat, "camlet" jacket, green baize shirt, buckskin frock, and leather breeches laced with leather ties from thigh to knee, then stitched with thread to his ankles, conceded that he did not look much better.[35]

Stockings were common. For added insulation, hunters crammed their moccasins and shoes with white-oak or beech leaves, deer hair, or buffalo wool. But moccasins were only "a decent way of going barefoot" in damps, as men suffered when their feet stayed moist, the flesh rotting and peeling off.[36] The cure for "scalded feet" was salve boiled from pounded slippery elm bark. For prevention, the men slept with their feet to the fire and hung their moccasins on sticks to dry. If Indians were near, woodsmen tied their moccasins to their knees and set their guns on forked stobs, to keep them off the ground and the priming dry.

In snow and ice, hunters wore buffalo-skin moccasins. Daniel Trabue explained, "We made socks to go over our shews with Buffelo skins putting the wool inside and we had woollen gloves." On one winter hunt, Trabue and a companion "put on 2 pairs of gloves and buffeloe socks on over our shews."[37] Buffalo socks, "the hair side turned in," Hugh Bell elaborated, "would not easily saturate; at night they were taken off and thrown to one side and away from the fire that they might freeze . . . for the buffalo moccasins were all the better for being frozen."[38]

Philip Bruner, a Canadian who once lived in Illinois wore shoepacs, described as "a kind of moccasin, made of undressed, unfinished leather . . . tanned with oak bark until the hair would rub off." When the bottoms wore out, he "sewed on a sole of the same material with a leather whang." But in wet weather, Bruner complained, even shoepacs did not keep his feet dry.[39]

On Thursday, June 8, 1775, at Harrod's Landing, Nicholas Cresswell, an English traveler in Kentucky, saw four hunters in a canoe floating down the Kentucky. Three were dressed in breechcloths, leggings, and dirty linen shirts that did not hide their naked thighs. On a mission to Point Pleasant in October 1776, a scout named Robert Patterson wore a "hunting shirt and britch clout and flannel leggings." In the 1790s young men wore breechcloths to "brush arbor" services. Their appearance, Reverend Joseph Doddridge complained, "did not add much to the devotion of the young ladies."[40]

"Hunting shirts"—a distinguishing badge of a hunter—were made of linen or buckskin or, if made to be traded to Indians, of red and blue calico. Hunting shirts reached to mid-thigh and were belted with a beaded or plain finger-woven wool sash, tied in back or on the side in a bowknot or cinched tight with a leather belt buckled in front. One traveler saw Daniel Boone in a linen hunting shirt; Boone's shirt and moccasins both were dyed the color of leaves.[41] Some hunting shirts were pullovers; some were open fronted, caped, and embroidered with silk thread; others were plain.

Guns carried by market hunters were as distinct as the men cradling them.[42] Casper Mansker and Bill Linn used smoothbores for the versatility of shooting shot, ball, or buck-and-ball loads. For fun Linn would let snakes crawl down the barrel of his British musket, then blast them against trees. Daniel Boone killed an Indian at the Battle of Blue Licks with a long fowler loaded with three or four undersize balls and sixteen to eighteen buckshot.[43] Other hunters may have liked the stout Jäeger, with its short barrel and big bore. Most favored rifles ranging from .45 to .52 caliber made by the gunsmiths of Pennsylvania and North Carolina. The finest arm of the era was the long-barreled Kentucky rifle, as it was later called.

Long Hunters outfitted themselves and left for a hunt with horses in tow and dogs stringing behind. Most long hunts were seasonal; some lasted over a year. It was a hazardous, lonely calling. And many a hunter bade adieu to loved ones and headed beyond the Blue Ridge, never to be seen again.

Richard and Hancock Taylor and Abraham Haptonstall were typical of such men. Leaving Virginia in the spring of 1769, they pushed down the Ohio to the Mississippi then up to Fort de Chartres. A year later, they floated downriver to Natchez and New Orleans. They returned home by schooner in 1771.[44]

Adventuresome lads. And they were not alone.

In June 1769 twenty Long Hunters from the New River region of Virginia and western North Carolina gathered in North Carolina to make plans to hunt west of the Appalachians. One of their number, Uriah Stone, had seen the game herds in 1766 when he and Colonel James Smith traveled through Kentucky and Tennessee.[45] In 1766 Stone hunted and trapped on what is now the Stone's River. His fortune was lost when French trappers stole his bateau and its cargo of furs and skins and floated them down to New Orleans. Stone returned to the settlements broke, but he confirmed the tales of bountiful game others had only heard about.

Now Stone and a band of Long Hunters were ready to try again. The men rode off during the second week of June with a string of packhorses laden with supplies and provisions enough to see them to the hunting grounds. Included were Casper Mansker, Abraham and Isaac Bledsoe, Joseph Drake, Obadiah Terrall, John Baker, Henry Smith, Ned Cowan, John Rains, and others.

They passed down the Holston into Powell's Valley, through the Cumberland Gap to the Cumberland River, and down to Wayne County, Kentucky, where they set up a skin depot—a base camp to cache peltry and supplies—and divided into groups of three or four, each party agreeing to return to the main camp every five weeks with skins. Mansker's band went north of the Cumberland, headed west and struck the Big Barren, and crossed the ridge dividing the Barren and the Cumberland. They rode south to Station Camp Creek and struck a buffalo trace in what is now Sumner County, Tennessee.

Mansker and Isaac Bledsoe left to explore the trace. Mansker rode west, Bledsoe east. Buffalo sign abounded. When Bledsoe came within two miles of the broad salt lick later named for him, his horse dashed into a galloping buffalo herd. He told Mansker that the lick was "covered with a moving mass of buffaloes, which he not only estimated by the hundreds, but by the thousands."[46] He shot two deer, but the swirling horde stomped them into the mire. Catching his scent, the beasts thundered away, leaving Bledsoe glad he had not been run over.

Ten of the men returned to the settlements in April 1770 with horse loads of furs, deer skins, bear bacon, and tallow. The rest of the party stayed west to hunt. At French Lick, Mansker, Stone, Bledsoe, and the others saw "an immense herd of buffaloes and other animals and killed several buffaloes for their hides with which to cover their boats."[47] They sold their hides at Natchez and returned to North Carolina that summer by ship.

Surveyors, explorers, Long Hunters, and Long Knives signaled a bold new era of encroachment on Indian land. The effect on game herds was striking. Most of the buffalo had been killed out in Virginia by the 1730s. By 1770 few, if any, were left in the Carolinas or northern or eastern Georgia. The buffalo had been destroyed east of the Appalachians. Herds had diminished in the Southeast.[48]

News of the West—with its abundant herds and endless miles of fertile land—fell on eager ears. Land-hungry men like William Bean, John Sevier, and the mixed-blood Huguenot Bennett Belue began settling in east Tennessee. They were not the only exploiters of the Cumberland basin; Frenchmen paddled down the Mississippi to shoot buffalo, as did the Spanish. Indians continued to hunt the beasts as they had for generations.[49]

Meanwhile, back east, Mansker, Colonel James Knox, and forty Long Hunters were making plans for a fall hunt.

In early fall of 1770, the group of Long Hunters left North Carolina to hunt beyond the Blue Ridge. Joseph Drake, Henry Skaggs, and James Knox were elected leaders. Passing through the Cumberland Gap, they reached Laurel County, Kentucky, built a base camp and rode off in small bands to hunt.[50]

James Dysart followed a trace a few miles south of Dix River in Lincoln County, noting that the dirt around Knob Licks was "strongly impregnated with particles of salt." While on top of one of the knobs, Dysart and his companions saw more than a thousand animals—mostly buffalo. As they drew near, their scent spooked the beasts, which scattered them and gave the hunters a chance to enter the lick. The buffalo "had so eaten away the soil," Dysart said, "that they could in places go entirely underground."[51] Drake and Skaggs, meanwhile, pushed southwest to the Green River to the Skin House branch of Caney Fork of Russell Creek. There they made camp and laid up stores of "deer, elk and buffalo."[52]

The Long Hunters heaped up deer skins and ate buffalo tongue and marrow bones. As Hugh Bell explained, "First scorch the tongue a little, then peel off the outside coating, then stick [it] upon a spit made of spice brush with the lower end inserted in the ground."[53] Hunters tossed shank bones on coals to cook one end at a time, and then cracked them open with the flat end of a hatchet to get at the hot marrow. Knox ate thirty-six for Christmas. Ben Harris ate so much marrow that one comrade remarked he "foundered and never got over it." August Ross ate as much marrow as he could choke down, then gobbled six goose eggs. He sat all night on his side of the canoe, John Hanks remembered, "feeding the fishes." "One bone is as much as a man ought to eat, be he as hungry as he may," Armstead Block warned.[54]

Arguments over who shot the most game led to jealousy between Charles Ewing and Henry Skaggs. Disgruntled, Ewing and twenty-five hunters returned east in late 1770. The remaining men hoarded their ammunition and pushed on. In February, seven men elected to stay at the depot fleshing and stretching furs and graining skins while the rest hunted and trapped. The hunters would rendezvous at the camp in March to start their ride eastward. Mansker, Knox, Charles and Richard Skaggs, James Dysart, William Miller, and one or two others split into two groups. One party headed north to the Ohio, the other went west to the Green.

The hunters returned in March to a dismal sight. Indians had raided the skin camp, stealing supplies and leaving the depot wrecked and utterly deserted. Piles of deer skins and fur lay exposed to rain and sun. Cut in the bark of a beech was a message: "2,500 Deerskins Lost, Ruination By God." Captain Will Emery, a mixed-blood Cherokee, was blamed for the act. (Later, in 1771, Emery caught Daniel Boone twice when Boone and his men were trespassing in Kentucky.)[55]

That the whites received a stinging rebuke for poaching on Indian land did not dissuade them; the hunters divided their supplies and powder and ball to try again. They hunted the tributaries of the Green, Big Barren, and Little Barren. As they shot out the deer and trapped out the beaver, the men journeyed southward to what are now Gallatin and Nashville.[56] Near Bledsoe's Creek, the cane, unlike a year before, now grew so dense the men feared they were on the wrong trace. When they rode to the lick they saw why: The buffalo that had once stomped down the cane and fed on it were gone. "One could walk for several hundred yards around the lick and in the lick on buffalo skulls and bones . . . the whole flat around the lick was bleached buffalo bones."[57]

Frontiersman Timothy De Monbruen and his team of meat getters hunted this area hard; it may have been his men who had so devastated the herds. Buffalo roamed the lower Cumberland over the next decade, but herds that Bledsoe once "estimated . . . by the thousands" were gone forever.

The Long Hunters went back to North Carolina and Virginia in the fall of 1771. In the coming years, they would return to the Cumberland to harvest bear, deer skins, tallow, tongues, jerk, and fur. Mansker settled in the region. Others followed. During the winter of 1776, hunters from Carters Valley, in Hawkins County, killed some buffalo within fifteen miles of that settlement. De Monbruen was at Deacon's Pond (near Palmyra, in Montgomery County) in February 1777, when he came upon a party of six white men and one woman. They had left Kentucky by boat, launching at the mouth of the Rockcastle and floating down the Cumberland, and had seen small buffalo droves. Yet within a score of years, the herds would be gone in central Tennessee.[58]

The role of Long Hunters as pathfinders in the expansion of this nation cannot be denied. "While the entrance of long hunters did not open the trans-Appalachian frontier," observes Princeton historian Stephen Aron, "their presence expanded contacts between Europeans and Indians in the Ohio Valley." In their quest for peltry, they killed out and drove out from before them game herds. Indians saw the threat white market hunters posed, yet, as Aron notes, "there was no consensus about how to deal with the intruders." Violence was one response; conciliation was another.[59] Speculators and colonizers came in the Long Hunters' paths. Then came Anglo-American settlement, which radically altered the cycle of life in the West.

Skirmishes erupted. Cherokee and Chickasaw fought the new hordes of whites in Tennessee and along the Cumberland and Mississippi; Creek and Chickasaw fought them in the Southeast; Shawnee, Wyandot, Miami, and other tribes fought them in Kentucky and north of the Ohio. But still the people came. John Lipscomb, the first Tennessee traveler to write about his visit to the fledgling settlement of Nashville, "met a great number of people moving constant," he wrote on August 30, 1784, "some to the Cumberland and some to Caintucke."[60]

Kentucky I

"STAND AT THE CUMBERLAND GAP," SAID FREDERICK JACKSON TURNER in 1893, "and watch the procession of civilization, marching single file— the buffalo following the trail to the salt springs, the Indian, the fur-trader and hunter, the cattle-raiser, the farmer—and the frontier has passed by."[1] In Turner's famous treatise, *The Significance of the Frontier in American History,* the teams of Long Hunters trailing through the Cumberland Gap were Anglo fists in the ever-shifting line called "the West": Their duty— lo, their foreordained right—was to subdue the land and "conquer the wilderness." Indian "savages," where they appear at all in Turner's elegy, are sad obstacles to "the procession of civilization."

Turner declared that what happened in Kentucky in the 1770s continued to happen until about 1890, a date signifying the official "closing" of the frontier. "Stand at the South Pass in the Rockies a century later and see the same procession with wider intervals between," he concluded.

New Western historians have dismissed much of Turner's thesis for at least two reasons: his imperialistic view of Indians, and his neglect of the impact of ecology and environmentalism. Even so, asserts Stephen Aron, "what Frederick Jackson Turner said about the frontier still matters. . . . One of Turner's central pillars still stands: the idea that westering history more or less repeated itself, that what happened at the Cumberland Gap in the eighteenth century shaped what happened at South Pass in the nineteenth."[2]

For the Shawnee, what happened at the Cumberland Gap cast a pall upon their world. Shawnee warriors, like those of Mingo, Delaware, Kickapoo, and Great Lake groups, crossed the Speleawee-thepee, the river whites called Ohio, into Kanta-ke to hunt. They established villages, with the exception of Es-kip-pa-ki-thi-ki, north of the Beautiful River, until the dark days brought on by the pale spawn of the evil Great Serpent,

97

Matchemanitou. Indians from the Great Lakes to south of the Cumberland resented the flow of whites into Kentucky, but it was the Shawnee
who became their staunchest foes.[3]

Thus the "opening" of Kentucky to Anglo-Americans was a pivotal
era in the history of the West, both in the failure of Indians and whites to
reach peaceful accommodation in their mutual exploitation of the Ohio
Valley, and, as an archetypal showcase of buffalo slaughter in the East.

Kanta-ke. The Shawnee called it "the land of great meadows." One
hundred years before the coming of white settlers, Shawnee lived in the
Illinois country, in Ohio, along the Ohio River, in Maryland, and along
the banks of the Savannah. In 1715 a band of Shawnee moved south to
the Chattahooche, which divides Georgia and Alabama. Other bands migrated to Pennsylvania to be near their Delaware kinsmen living in the
fertile hub encompassing the native towns of Logstown, Chartier's Old
Town, and Paxtang. Because of the flood of whites settling along the
Tidewater and pouring into lands east of the Alleghenies, by the mid-
1700s most Shawnee had fled back to southern Ohio to the land of their
fathers, where they, along with other tribes of the Ohio Valley, made their
stand before American relocation policies led to their last dispersion.[4]

In 1775 a Chickamagua Cherokee, Tyi.yu Gansi.ni., or Dragging
Canoe, warned Daniel Boone that "there was a dark cloud over that
country," which started the tale that Kentucky was known as the Dark
and Bloody Ground.[5] But to frontiersmen Kentucky became the new
Eden.

In 1761 Elisha Wallen, a tall, strongly built Long Hunter in his early
thirties, led a score of like-minded men from the Smith River in Virginia
to the Holston Valley. Jack and William Blevins, William Pittman, Henry
Skaggs, Charles Cox, William Neuman, and William Harrison rode with
Wallen. They skirted the Clinch and set up camp on Wallen's Creek near
the Cumberland Gap and slew game prodigiously for nearly two years.
Wallen and his men returned to the region in 1763 for their fall hunt, this
time pushing through the Gap and on into southeastern Kentucky, hunting and trapping along the Rockcastle, going as far as Crab Orchard. On
both hunts the Virginians had reaped far beyond their expectations.
Frontier Virginian John Redd, who knew Wallen well, said that "he
always returned home from his hunts with his horses heavily laden with
skins and furs."[6]

Early in 1769 Major John M. McColloch left Pittsburgh "accompanied by several white men and a Negro" and floated down the Ohio to

Kentucky. Captured by Indians near the Wabash and held prisoner for five months, they returned home after enduring severe hardships.[7] Elisha Wallen and John McColloch were typical of those Americans who heard the tales about Kentucky and risked their lives to see for themselves if the stories were true.

George Washington heard of Kanta-ke from Christopher Gist and studied plats of the Cumberland plateau drawn by John Connolly during his voyage up the river in 1768. Washington descended the Ohio to the Kanawha Valley in 1769 to see the claims he had purchased. On November 2 he and his men "went a hunting; killed 5 buffaloes and wounded some others."[8] A dedicated speculator, Washington sent an agent to Ireland and England to recruit emigrants to settle his land. In 1770 in western Virginia, he met Kiashuta, an Indian scout who had served him in the French and Indian War. Pleased at seeing his commander, Kiashuta presented him with a flank of wild beef. Near Ravenswood, West Virginia, Washington wrote, "On this creek, many buffaloes used to be, according to the Indians." "This country," he declared at Point Pleasant, "abounds in buffalo and wild game."[9]

Delaware scouts told Washington of buffalo herds in Kentucky and at the confluence of the Scioto and Ohio numbering in the thousands. The possibility of domesticating wild cattle for draft intrigued him, and in 1775 he wrote to a friend, "Buy all the buffalo calves you can get and make them as gentle as possible . . . as I am very anxious to raise a breed of them." He also toyed with the idea of marketing "cloth made of buffalo hair."[10]

Washington's journals of his trip through the Kanawha Valley also reflect the "growing impatience of the western Indians at the gradual encroachment of the whites on the lands south of the Ohio River." It was a portent of dark things to come.

In 1773 John Murray, earl of Dunmore, the governor of Virginia, granted permission (though he later denied it) to Captain Thomas Bullitt, a veteran of the French and Indian War, to survey Kentucky as far west as the Falls of the Ohio. Bullitt called for volunteers; about forty men signed on. James Harrod was one of them. Tall, dark, and lean, his face wrapped in a coal black beard, Harrod is one of the phantoms of the frontier. No one is sure when he was born (possibly between 1742 and 1746) or when, how, or where he died. But historians agree that Harrod played a strong role in the settlement of Kentucky.[11]

As Captain Bullitt was getting ready to go west in 1773, a smaller party of Virginians, which included the McAfee brothers from Botetourt

County, made similar plans. The surveyors met at the mouth of the Kanawha, joined forces, and elected Bullitt as their leader. Bullitt, perhaps with Harrod, pushed on to the Falls and laid out grids at a site to be called Louisville. The McAfees followed a trace to the Kentucky to look for good land.

In June 1774 the men felled trees for one of the West's first settlements, Harrod's Town, and hunted as far north as Big Bone Lick; in 1785 the Virginia legislature registered Harrod's Town as Harrodsburg. Hancock Taylor, James Strother, and Abraham Haptonstall followed the Kentucky to the Bluegrass. Near Midway, Haptonstall helped Taylor survey land for Colonel Hugh Mercer, a Virginian. "I knew of a place of great resort of buffaloes on the side of a hill about two miles above Lee's Town," Haptonstall wrote. "It had the appearance of a stamping ground."[12] Indians killed Taylor and Strother in July. Overlooking the stamping ground and the amazing swirl of game at the lick from a bluff near Harrod's Town, one writer described it:

> 10,000 or more buffalo . . . [and] other animals . . . all moving about in one vast throng, rubbing against each other, the stronger frequently preying on the weaker. The ground . . . was a perfect barren waste, worn out and torn up by the stamping and pawing of the animals.[13]

That the men saw "10,000 or more buffalo," besides panthers, wolves, and bears, is probably an exaggeration. Yet the maelstrom of beasts fighting to keep up in the churning stampede must have been a sight.

Isaac Hite, deputy surveyor for Colonel William Preston, and Preston's thirty-five men were in the canelands too, scouting out land for the eastern elite; assistant surveyor John Floyd staked a claim for Patrick Henry in 1774. Numbered among the surveyors and their crews were land jobbers and outliers. A land jobber secured land for a buyer in the east; an outlier roamed the countryside staking claims by erecting tiny, roofless, "pigsty" cabins. Thomas Hanson, a chain carrier, was near Big Bone Lick on May 17, 1774, with "Mr. Floyd and Mr. Hite and five men," where they saw "about 300 buffaloes collected together."[14]

Back in Virginia that June, an alliance of Shawnee, Mingo, and Cherokee took up the hatchet in a glut of blood vengeance called Lord Dunmore's War. On June 26 Clinch Valley militia leaders dispatched Daniel Boone and Michael Stoner to Kentucky to warn the Virginians. Stoner was a tough, stout man with a thick German accent. He was a crack shot and one of Boone's most enduring companions. In Kentucky, they found the surveyors, Boone reported, "well drove in by Indians."[15]

Nathan Boone recalled to historian Lyman Draper a tale his father told him about the 1774 trip. Boone and Stoner were exploring near the Lower Blue Licks when they spotted a lone buffalo cow half hidden in a deep, well-gnawed rut, munching away at the briny dirt.

"Sthop, Gabtain, and we will have shum fun," said Stoner. He eased up and poked his hat through a hole in the thin wall of the rut right under the big cow's nose. The cow wheeled and charged, bursting through the dirt wall in a rage. Stoner howled and took off.

"Schoot her, Gabtain! Schoot her, Gabtain!" he bawled. But Boone fell on his back with laughter at Stoner's retreat.[16]

Lord Dunmore's War ended after the Indians' defeat at Point Pleasant, West Virginia, on October 10, 1774. Shawnee elders reluctantly agreed to stop hunting on their land south of the Ohio, thus clearing the way for another western thrust by the Americans. Cornstalk, principal chief of the Maquachake division, warned Americans that he held less sway among younger warriors and was unable to control them. Nor could he dictate terms to other Shawnee divisions or tribes.

Daniel Boone is one of the legendary figures of American history. Born in Berks County, Pennsylvania, on October 22, 1734, he was the sixth child of Squire and Sarah Morgan Boone and spent his childhood on the Pennsylvania frontier.

Myths abound. Boone was not, as is often claimed, the first white man to explore Kentucky. Not an Indian hater, Boone deplored depictions of him as an Indian killer. And he despised coonskin caps, calling them "uncivilized." But as a woodsman, pathfinder, and perennial Long Hunter, Boone stands as the prototypical American frontiersman.[17] He was one of the earliest market hunters to exploit the game herds in Kentucky and write about it; his memoirs, a collaborative effort with John Filson published in 1784, reveal much about Kentucky flora and fauna.

By the early 1760s, Boone, living in the Yadkin Valley of North Carolina, began hunting over the Blue Ridge into east Tennessee. Often buying traps and gunpowder on credit, he lived in debt and stayed entangled in lawsuits, "chiefly [for] small debts of five pounds and under contracted for powder and shot."[18] Richard Henderson, a lawyer in Salisbury, North Carolina, liked Boone and at times defended him. And Richard Henderson wanted land.

Boone was no different. He had a family to support and was plunging into debt. For the next few years, he pushed westward to hunt. Benjamin Cutbirth, the husband of Boone's niece Sarah Wilcoxen, told him of the rich lands to the west. Cutbirth had explored to the Mississippi with a band of Long Hunters in 1767, hoping to set up trade with New Orleans in "lumber, pelts and furs, bear bacon and bear oil, buffalo jerk and tallow, and dried venison hams."[19]

That year Daniel and his younger brother Squire followed a branch of the Big Sandy to the eastern edge of Kentucky, but the fabled meadowlands eluded them. Before he and Squire returned to the Yadkin, Boone killed his first buffalo near Young's Old Salt Works, about ten miles west of Prestonsburg.[20] In the fall of 1768, a visit from John Findley, who remembered Boone from Braddock's army fourteen years earlier, dramatically altered his life. Findley was blunt: Did Boone want to see Kentucky?

Broke and mired in debt, Boone knew a successful hunt could end his financial woes. With Findley, Boone's brother-in-law John Stewart, and three men hired as camp tenders, Boone's party left North Carolina on May 1, 1769. Squire would join them in the fall after the crops were harvested. "We proceeded successfully," Boone recalled to biographer John Filson in 1783, "after a long and fatiguing journey through a mountainous wilderness." On June 7, from atop Pilot Knob on the Red River, Boone and his men "saw with pleasure the beautiful level of Kentucke."

> The buffaloes were more frequent than I have seen cattle in the settlements, browsing on the leaves of the cane . . . fearless, because ignorant, of the violence of man. Sometimes we saw hundreds in a drove, and the numbers about the salt springs were amazing.[21]

They built a station camp and in seven months packed the shelter with furs and deer skins. Boone and his men lived on the fat of the land, feasting on venison, tongues, marrow, and hump meat. But in late December, Shawnee warriors seized the trespassers and confiscated their gear, thirteen horses, bales of fur, and nine hundred deer skins.[22] Captain Will Emery, the leader, warned Boone to stay out of their land and leave their "cattle" alone. To see them safely back east, the Shawnee gave the poachers two pairs of moccasins apiece, patch leather, a French fusil, powder, and ball. Emery left Boone with a last rebuke: Go home and stay there.

From a European perspective, Boone and his band had committed a capital offense. Under the English "Bloody Code" and the enforcement of eighteenth-century Old World game laws, poachers got the death penalty. Emery was much more lenient on the whites than an English lord would have been.

Boone's crime was as serious from a native viewpoint: He and his men were thieves. The Shawnee and other Woodland groups depended on deer skins for trade. Every deer slain by a long rifle deprived an Indian of a skin. Every poached buffalo was hundreds of pounds of meat and a robe denied to a native family. For many backcountry whites, treaties and Crown law were meaningless. Yet for Indians, those solemn oaths were their only hope in managing their territory and its dwindling resources. The Shawnee did not rob Boone and his men. Rather, through giving the whites gifts critical to their survival, the Shawnee sought accommodation as a means to make peace with the interlopers.[23]

Boone did not care either way. His men had been stripped of their wares and a season of hard work. Undaunted, they began anew. Squire joined them, bringing horses, guns, powder and ball, traps, supplies, and provisions. Soon fresh deer skins and furs were piled high in their new half-face huts. But when John Stewart vanished in January 1770, Findley and others, unnerved by it all, fled to North Carolina. Five years later Boone found Stewart's skeleton in a hollow tree, his left arm bone broken from a musket ball—killed by Indians.

On May 1, 1770, Squire took their peltry back to North Carolina. Boone stayed to explore, left without "bread, salt, and sugar, without company of my fellow creatures, or even a horse or a dog."[24] Although much has been written about these idyllic wandering days of Boone, he may have been scouting land for Richard Henderson. If so, then he was also scouting land for himself.

Once, caught in the midst of a buffalo herd, Boone stood for two hours with his back against a tree as the mass of woolly brutes rumbled by along both sides. Nudging them on with his rifle barrel, Boone saw that the younger cows and the calves came first, followed by the yearlings and two-year-olds. Old cows and bulls guarded the flanks and the rear. Crippled and infirm buffalo hobbled behind, aware, no doubt, of the wolves trailing behind them. Another time he spied a buffalo bucking to shake a panther from its bleeding back. He shot the big cat.[25]

Boone rendezvoused with Squire on July 27, 1770. They hunted and trapped and in March 1771 traveled west. For a week or two, the pair hunted with Casper Mansker and the Long Hunters on the Green. The

Boones started for home, only to have their peltry seized by Cherokee warriors a few miles past the Cumberland Gap. After having been gone for two years, Boone returned to North Carolina penniless.

In September 1773 Boone tried again, this time taking his wife and five other families. As the caravan wound to Kentucky, more families joined and they split into three groups. On October 10, in western Virginia, some Shawnee and Cherokee set upon the last bunch, killing Boone's sixteen-year-old son, James, and four others. The settlers persuaded Boone to turn back.

Boone's stories of Kanta-ke turned Richard Henderson and his cronies into land moguls. On March 17, 1775, at Sycamore Shoals on the Watauga River, near Elizabethton, Tennessee, the Cherokee allegedly "sold" their Kentucky claims between the Cumberland, Tennessee, and Kentucky Rivers—a twenty-seven-thousand-square-mile tract spanning seventeen to twenty million acres—to Henderson, Nathaniel Hart, and the Transylvania Company for several wagonloads of trade goods and livestock worth about "two thousands pounds of lawful money with Great Britain."[26]

The Treaty of Sycamore Shoals was a case of mutual duplicity: It is not clear whether the Cherokee held full title to all the land they "sold," as the extent of the western borders of their territory was debatable; and the illegal Transylvania Company was negotiating with Indians without the consent of the Crown for a vast territory protected by the Proclamation of 1763, the Treaty of Fort Stanwix (1768), and Virginia law. Divided tribal leaders may have viewed the fraudulent Sycamore Shoals land grab as a necessary expedient—the politics of Indian survival under Anglo pressure. Company shareholders and Cherokee representatives Attakullakulla, Oconostota, and Savanukah the Raven of Chota reached uneasy terms and signed the deeds, and the Indians accepted the trade goods. North Carolinians passed whiskey jugs and hailed the day as a triumph.[27]

But some Cherokee leaders, their people now cut off from their Kentucky hunting lands and the Ohio River by a slip of paper, condemned the treaty. Oconostota, who later recanted his role in the treaty, protested to Richard Henderson, "You, Carolina Dick, have deceived your people." Another chief lamented, "We told you that those lands were not ours, that our claim extended not beyond the Cumberland Mountains." Speakers at council fires denounced Henderson as a liar. Another Indian, Old Tassel, declared that the lawyer had forged Oconostota's mark. Governor Josiah Martin of North Carolina branded the Company "land Pyrates."[28]

Dragging Canoe, a negotiator for the Chickamauga and son of Attakullakulla, stood aloof and angry during the proceedings. At the close of the day he stamped his foot, glowering with exasperation, and pointed west, warning Henderson that Kanta-ke was still their hunting ground and the buffalo were still their cattle.[29]

Thirty miles away at Long Island on the Holston River, Daniel Boone, on Henderson's payroll, had already hired thirty roadcutters.[30] Enticed by the lure of land, they would blaze a trail—the Wilderness Road—from the Holston through the Cumberland Gap to a site where Boonesborough would be built. Boone's oldest daughter, Susannah, and an African slave woman fed and tended to the woodcutters and thus became two of the first American women to enter the West. Henderson and company followed Boone, remaining during the entire trip about two weeks behind the woodcutters.

Boone's epic trek largely followed traces. The Wilderness Road began as part of the Warrior's Path at the Block House. Built in 1775, the Block House was near the north fork of the Holston. From there, the road led to the Clinch River; north of the ford, the hardest traveling began. Up and over Wallen's Ridge, the Wilderness Road threaded on for five or six miles into Powell's Valley, crossed Station Creek near Jonesville, Virginia, and ran forty miles north through the Cumberland Gap. Miles later the trace split at Hazel Patch in Laurel County, Kentucky; the east fork again became the Warrior's Path at Stinking Creek and made a northeastern sweep up to Ohio past the west bank of the Scioto, and the west fork meandered on as the Wilderness Road.[31]

Eight miles past the Gap, an old station camp lay abandoned on Stinking Creek, named for the rotting deer carcasses hunters rolled into the stream. In 1779 Lieutenant-Governor Henry Hamilton of Detroit described Stinking Creek as "a remarkable buffalo salt lick."[32] Here the Wilderness Road joined Skaggs' Trace, a path used by the Skaggs brothers, who hunted with Mansker and Knox in 1769. At Crab Orchard, the Wilderness Road branched; one fork went to Logan's Fort (now Stanford), ran past Harrod's Town up to Bullitt's Lick, then north to Louisville, and the other fork, Harrod's Old Trace, ran north, then west to the falls. In Shelby County, Harrod's Old Trace crossed Bullskin Creek at the mouth of Little Bullskin, so named in 1776 by John Floyd, who camped there under a buffalo hide hut.

Skaggs' Trace left the Warrior's Path at Flat Lick in Knox County and ran to the Dix River in Lincoln County, then angled northwest. It

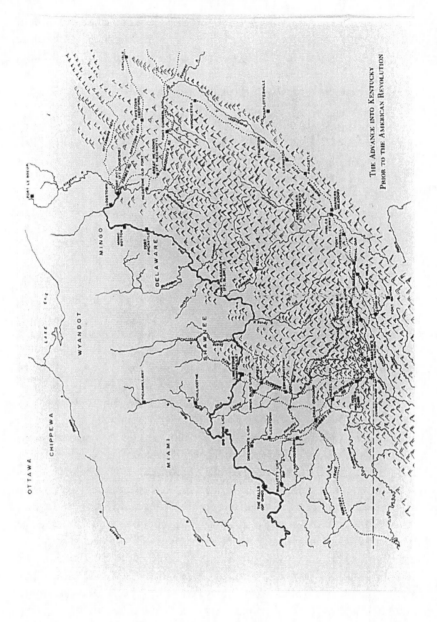

"The Advance into Kentucky Prior to the American Revolution."
(Reprinted from Otis K. Rice, *Frontier Kentucky,* copyright 1975 by the
University Press of Kentucky, by permission of the publishers.)

meandered past London to the headwaters of Hazel Patch Creek, went on to a ford in the Rockcastle, and ended at Stanford. Perhaps more people entered Kentucky's heartland by way of Skaggs' Trace than by Boone's Trace, another road in the Bluegrass.

Boone and his ax men went through the Cumberland Gap via the Warrior's Path and pushed on to Skaggs' Trace until they got to Hazel Patch. There Boone blazed Boone's Trace leading to the Kentucky River; it went north to the Madison County line and cut past what is now Berea to a stamping ground called Boone's Blue Lick.

Richard Henderson and his men, following in Boone's wake, got lost along the path.[33] That Boone's Trace was a poorly-marked buffalo path is confirmed by testimony given in early nineteenth-century court depositions regarding overlapping land claims. "The first time I traveled Boone's Trace," William Bush testified in 1808 in the case of *John Fowler vs. David Lynch,* "it was a great big buffalo road." David Lynch deposed on May 27, 1814, "I believe the Buffaloes made the road, and that Boone marked and traveled the same road."[34] In another case, Samuel Estill was asked:

> Question: Was Boone's Trace so plain that any person could travel it without a pilot?
> Answer: Boone's Trace was a marked trace but it was pretty difficult to follow through the thick cane, though I have followed it.[35]

When the woodcutters got to Boone's Blue Lick, Boone sensed trouble. He had gone to the lick to hunt buffalo, but the herds were gone. Had they been spooked? Boone wondered. They camped on Boone's Trace at the Hays and Hart Forks of Silver Creek in Madison County.

The night of March 24 no one posted a guard. At dawn, Indians attacked, killing two and wounding Felix Walker. The whites hastily built a hut and breastwork, calling the outpost Twitty's Fort for one of the dead, Captain William Twitty. Henderson's band, with the main body of settlers, followed in Boone's wake and reached Twitty's Fort on April 19. William Calk wrote in his diary, "Smart frost this morning they kill 3 bofelos about 11 oclock we come to where the Indians fired on Boons company."[36]

Boone's men buried the bodies, rigged up a horse litter for Walker, and pushed on, following Otter Creek to the Kentucky. And there, in April, the woodcutters began felling trees to build their fort.[37]

When Boone's party got to the site of Boonesborough, they camped and boiled a kettle of meat, which drew a wolf pack. Howling most of the night, the wolves kept the men awake until nearly dawn, yet Boone was up at daylight, rifle in hand. Gazing at a buffalo herd grazing the lush, shimmering, waist-high sea of bluegrass, white clover, buffalo grass, and reeds, the jubilant Boone exclaimed, "Look yonder—we are richer than Jacob, he had his cattle on a thousand hills; we have them on ten thousand."[38] Felix Walker pulled himself up in his stretcher in time to see "buffaloes of all sizes, supposed to be between two and three hundred ... some running, some walking, others loping slowly and carelessly, with young calves playing, skipping and bounding through the plain."[39]

Boone's legendary fifteen-day, two-hundred-mile exodus was not without loss. But most saw the journey through, and on May 20, 1775, at the clump of crude huts called Boonesborough, Henderson's short-lived feudal empire, Transylvania, meaning "beyond the woods," was established.

Transylvania Company woodcutters and settlers lived in half-face shelters, bark lean-tos, and osnaburg tents until the log palisades went up and the fort took shape. They girdled and burned the trees, carving the woods into crude, arable stump-filled lots. Boonesborough was not Kentucky's first white settlement, but it was probably the first fort, and it became the Commonwealth's first chartered town.[40]

Meanwhile, to the southwest, James Harrod and his surveyors and some settlers had returned to the remnants of Harrod's Town on March 14, 1775. By summer Harrod's Town boasted a seventy-acre cornfield and "eight or ten cabins without doors."[41]

Due north, Simon Kenton was helping to divide Limestone (now Maysville) into plots to sell to immigrants floating down the Ohio on flatboats or coming to Kentucky via the traces. In another Kentucky court case involving disputed land claims, Kenton deposed on June 5, 1824, that "in 1775, 1776, May 1780, and in 1784, he was well-acquainted" with the buffalo trails that led into the Bluegrass. The Middle Trace went from the Lower Blue Licks to the head of Lawrence Creek in Washington, four miles south of Maysville. From Cabin Creek to the Lower Blue Licks ran the Upper War Road. "Roads at the Blue Licks were forty yards wide, and that for a good distance," said Joshua McQueen, who came to Kentucky in 1775. Settlers called the other trace the Lower War Road.[42]

At Boonesborough, each of Boone's woodcutters received ten pounds, ten shillings for "work making roads to Caintucke"; the sum bought 420 acres of prime Bluegrass.[43] Nathan Reid met Boone years later and reminisced with the old hunter about the early days at Boonesborough. "What a country it was," exclaimed Boone. He spent his time seeking out the best land or hunting buffalo and deer, "of which there were vast herds." Hump meat, Boone said, "consists of a streak of fat and a streak of lean, and when properly cooked, would be considered delicious by a city epicure."[44]

From the beginning, the settlers at Boonesborough slaughtered buffalo. Hunters hired themselves out to provision those who wanted to claim or clear land or those who did not want to hunt. Some men, though, were too proud to hire anyone, no matter how inept they were, "but from conceit, from having a hunting shirt, tomahawk, and gun, thought it was an insult to offer another man to hunt for them, especially as pay was to be made." Others "loved it much better than work."

Buffalo moved twenty to thirty miles away, making it risky for hunters to hunt them and then ride back to Boonesborough and other forts with their meat-laden packhorses in tow. An exasperated Richard Henderson wrote in his journal on May 9, 1775:

> We found it very difficult at first and indeed yet, to stop the great waste in killing meat. Many men were ignorant of the woods, and not skilled in hunting . . . would shoot, cripple and scare the game without being able to get much. . . . Others of wicked and wanton dispositions, would kill three, four, five or ½ dozen buffaloes, and not take half a horse load from them all.[45]

Henderson tried to stop such "evils . . . but found it not practical, many complaining that they were too poor to hire hunters." By May 17 the people had "no meat but fat bear, and a little spoiled buffalo," and during the first convention of the "Colony of Transylvania" held on May 20—the first American legislative assembly west of the Appalachians—Boone introduced a bill to halt the "wanton destruction of game." Highlighted in the document was mention of the diminishing numbers of "wild cattle." Boone's bill became law.[46]

Men continued to slaughter buffalo in secrecy. On Tuesday, July 11, 1775, Henderson complained of "a great scarcity of meat" and began interrogating hunters about kills.[47] Fear of public censure, he wrote, "saved the lives of many buffalo," but Henderson could not do much with what he judged to be "a set of scoundrels who scarcely believe in God or fear a Devil."

Buffalo pushed through rail fences, collapsed cabins by rubbing against them to scratch, and stomped through fields. Simon Kenton saw "two acres of corn" destroyed by them in 1776.[48] "Buffaloes," said James Wade after looking at his demolished corn patch, "take great delight in rolling in it and roll and mash eight or ten hills at a time."[49] So the settlers shot them—at times for beef, at times to thin their ranks to plant crops, at times because they were something to shoot.

Such waste made no sense. Until they could count on steady harvests and surplus livestock, Kentuckians depended heavily on buffalo. William Poague's family brought the first known spinning wheel to the Bluegrass in 1775, "from which coarse yarns were made from buffalo wool; and it was not too long before a few rude looms were improvised that served for weaving a rough cloth suitable for the men's winter wear."[50] Women spun warp threads—those that run lengthwise in the loom—from nettles gathered in the spring, after melting snow and rain rotted the prickly stems so that they could be split into fibers. Then they wove woof threads—those that cross the warp—from buffalo wool. Wool was in the best order in February, when the hair was sheared off the hides and spun into yarn.[51] William Clinkenbeard and four other hunters once shot twenty-four buffalo for their wool. "Yearlings and two year olds always had the best wool on," he said. Sinews alongside the buffalo's spine are "very strong and when dried [were] very easily divided into small fibers" to sew moccasins. Riders sat on "buffalo rugs" placed over saddles. One chair upholstered with buffalo hide lasted more than fifty years. Pioneers stuffed tallow in "bodkoos" (buffalo hide bags), slept on robes, and bound books in buffalo leather. One backwoods fiddler even made for himself a set of buffalo gut strings.[52]

Two weeks after Henderson founded Boonesborough, James Nourse, Edmund Taylor, George Rice, Tom Ruby, Ben Johnston, Nicholas Cresswell, and George Nolan beached their thirty-foot walnut dugouts, *Charming Sally* and *Charming Polly,* at the wide maw of a trace falling into Elkhorn Creek. They followed it to the present-day site of Lexington. (Part of the trace is now U.S. 62 and the Old Frankfort Pike.) The men had left Fort Pitt on April 29, 1775, seeking land and adventure. Nourse and Cresswell kept daily logs. Their journals may be the first recorded glimpses of the central Bluegrass.[53]

As the sun rose on May 30, 1775, Nourse came out of his blanket and took off his greatcoat, tying it to his pack. Near the riverbank the men shot three buffalo—"a Cow, a Yearling, and a Calf"—and feasted on the best cuts. After a midmorning rest, Nourse and some of the men hit the trace at a hard walk. The trace, Nourse said, was steep and rocky, but "as well trod as a Market-town path."

The men saw five buffalo herds during the first twelve miles of their walk. But the winds blew their scent to the grazing beasts, which snorted and scampered off before the hunters could close in for a shot. In the late afternoon, the men stumbled over a dozing buffalo calf that Edmund Rice blasted pointblank. The calf's heart, liver, kidneys, sweetbread, and about ten pounds of meat were soon impaled over a fire.[54]

Rain. Nourse put on his greatcoat to pass the night under a tree.

The next morning they returned to the Elkhorn. More rain. Nourse and Cresswell had their tent pitched in five minutes. The rest of the men were "out about an hour in worst of the rain making a bark tent."[55]

Thursday, June 1. En route to Harrod's Town via the trace, the travelers spied an old bull held at bay by their dogs. They shot the brute, but its meat was tough as a pine knot, so they took none of it, not even its tongue. The men pushed on to Harrod's Town—some fifteen miles away—where they ate buffalo stew, endive, and lettuce.

Harrod's Town, population forty-one, was a bustling hive of squalor—dirty people living in filthy cabins, bark huts, and half-face shelters. Nourse cut saplings and put up his tent, fitting it with a bark floor and mats back and front. On June 14 he feasted on "boiled beef and buffalo, bacon and young cabbage plants, Fritters and hominy, and wheat bread." Days later, Nourse and his men trekked northeast to Boonesborough, where he staked a land claim.[56] Marking land claims was often based on buffalo traces, as seen in his survey, written on June 25, 1775:

> Cross some highish land to a Buffalo path . . . continue the buffalo path still keeping the whole way north where the buffalo path fails continue course till you meet with paths . . . they will lead you to a very plain buffalo path. . . . Continue the plainest buffalo path to the westward of North I believe it will lead to the lower corner, as it appears to be at the largest Buffalo crossing.[57]

Nourse's band stayed in the Bluegrass until late June, hunting buffalo with James Harrod and sharing the beef with the people of Harrod's Town and Boonesborough. "Killed a fatt buffalo and bro't the best of it to Boonsburg," he wrote on June 25.[58] But the heat of the sun soon tainted the meat, forcing the settlers to get by on corn mush mixed with wheat flour and tallow. One hunter shot a bull, lame from two bullets bored in its flank and shoulder, and rode into the fort with its tongue and one side of back meat. The wounded side, he said, oozed putrefaction.

Nourse and the others (except Nicholas Cresswell) decided to return to Fort Pitt on foot so that they might stake land claims. "A finer country can not be conceived," Nourse wrote of the central Bluegrass. "Springs are the only thing that it can be said to be deficient in."[59]

The company found Boone's Trace hard to follow:

> Wednesday, June 28: traveled and missed our way, got up a steep mountain beat all around the ridge. . . . Traveled without being able to keep any course till night.[60]

Lost. Darkness closed in. They camped. No wind. Swarms of mosquitoes. The men stoked a bonfire to keep bugs down and ward off chills. Fearing Indians, Nourse doused the flames. Dawn.

> Thursday, June 29: Settled that we should steer something to the south and west—which we did brought us to large lick—kept down the buffalo path. . . . At nine o'clock got into the right path . . . there was an Indian mark on a tree.[61]

They took a trace to Boone's Blue Lick, shoved through a canebrake, hunkering, rifles ready "to kill to barbacue on our journey. Disappointed—found no buffalo there."[62] Near the Rockcastle they shot a wild cow, slit her udders to drink her milk, then roasted her. "Very good Barbacued the Beef," declared Nourse.[63]

Cresswell had joined Nourse at Fort Pitt on April 29. They floated their dugouts down the Ohio and then on to the Kentucky River and Elkhorn, camping without fire, which might attract Indians, and eating bread knotty with weevils. Cresswell's diary supplements Nourse's.[64]

Cresswell shot his first buffalo on May 17, near the Scioto. "It was a large Bull, from his breast to the top of his shoulder measuring 3 feet, from his nose to his tail 9 feet 6 inches. . . . I am certain he would have weighed a thousand [pounds]," though he guessed their weight "when fat" at "14 to 15 hundred pounds." Hump meat, he asserted, "makes the best steaks in the world." Stuffing their budgets with buffalo jerk, the weary men trudged to Big Bone Lick. "All hands well tired and D——d cross."[65]

On May 23 Cresswell saw a spiraling net of deep, wide traces leading this way and that to licks.[66] The next day they surrounded a buffalo drove crossing the river, killed two heifers for their tongues, and captured two calves to notch their ears, then let them go. A surround was risky. The key was the wind direction: "If you are windward, they run long before they see you."[67]

May 24 was a night to remember. They camped at a lead trace at the junction of a wide crossing along the Ohio's banks. After dragging the bows of their dugouts clear of the lapping waves and dining on wild beef, they put their guns in order and curled into their blankets. Ben Johnston bedded down in one of the dugouts. Hours later Johnston's screams woke the men to the sight of a buffalo pack trotting through their camp, plunging down the bank, and splashing into the river. Between the buffalo and the water were the dugouts—no great obstacles for the beasts, which hurdled the one with Johnston, then smashed through the second craft moored half out of the river. The boat was splintered and cracked, with splits fourteen feet long running the length of the hull and the stern now stomped under the water. Thursday, May 25, was spent repairing the vessel, "calking her with the bark of the white Elm, pounded to a paste."

Eight miles from the mouth of the Miami, the men spied two bulls in the river and launched a canoe to cut them off. Halfway over they intercepted one bull; a man in the bow grabbed its tail. For half an hour the animal towed the canoe up and down the Ohio. The men blasted the buffalo eight times, but the bull staggered ashore and lurched off gushing blood.[68] Such sport became common.

> Thursday, May 25: Some of the company shot a Buffalo Bull, saw several cross the River while we were at work.
> Sunday, May 28: Saw a great many Buffaloes cross the River above us, all hands went ashore to surround them. I . . . shot a fine young Heifer, some of the rest shot a Cow and Calf.[69]

The men took only the best cuts. The waste annoyed Cresswell: "Our stupid company will not stay to jerk any, tho' we are in want of provisions." The killing went on.

> Thursday, June 1: Saw a gang of Buffaloes cross the River. Shot a Bull.
> Friday, June 2: Shot at some Buffaloes, but killed none.
> Sunday, June 11: This morning killed a Buffalo Cow crossing the River.

Friday, June 16: Killed another Buffalo on the Banks of the
River.[70]

At Drennon's Lick, a huge lick merging into the Elkhorn a few
miles from the confluence of Drennon's Creek and the Kentucky,
Nicholas saw "an immense number of Buffaloes." Traces there were "as
large as most public roads in a populous country. They eat great quantities of a sort of reddish Clay found near Brackish springs. I have seen
amazing large holes . . . cut by them." Salt deposits forming crusty suds
along edges of brackish pools gave off a stench that drew game for miles.
"This is the largest lick I ever saw. I suppose it is 50 acres of land trodden
by Buffaloes, but there is not a blade of grass upon it. Incredible numbers
come here to the Salt springs." The men blazed away at a herd of two
hundred buffalo from a range of twenty yards, wounding many but
killing none.[71]

While Cresswell was at Big Bone Lick (Boone County) on June 17,
he recorded that Indians believed that the massive 'elephant bone'
remains—which were actually, mastodon, mammoth, and sloth bones—
scattered. . . . around the lick were those of extinct giant white buffalo.[72]
At Big Bone they saw buffalo but could not kill any. Days later, the company was reduced to eating "a little stinking jerked beef crawling with
maggots." Rainwater seeping into the beef barrel caused the jerk to rot;
the smell got so bad that Joe Brashears threw the oak cask overboard in a
rage. "Now we have not a morsel to eat," moaned Cresswell.[73]

It was their fault. In one killing spree they shot ten buffalo in five
days—perhaps seven tons of wild beef. Yet, on the sixth day they
intended "to kill some meat—our provision is nearly out."

Cresswell's adventures continued. For a few weeks he lived with
some Delaware camped at the forks of the Muskingum, taking a
Mohawk mistress and going native, wearing leggings, a breechcloth,
moccasins, and a calico shirt trimmed with silver. In 1777 young Cresswell sailed back to his father's farm in England. Debauched and debili-
tated from long bouts of drinking and carousing, broke but not broken,
he returned home with a tomahawk, an Indian feathercap (gastoweh),
Indian snowshoes, and a buffalo horn mounted in silver.

By the 1770s surveyors, settlers, speculators, hunters, and adventurers
were invading Kentucky. By 1796 more than twenty thousand people
traveled the Wilderness Road by way of Cumberland Gap.

American buffalo, published 1552 in *Historia de las Indias,* by Francisco Lopez de Gomara.

American buffalo, featured in André Thevet's *Les Singularites de la France Antarctique,* Antwerp 1558.

"Boeuf de la Nouvelle France," c. 1683. Copied from a drawing by Father Louis Hennepin.

Buffalo, c. 1724, by Mark Catesby. *(The Royal Collection, Her Majesty Queen Elizabeth II)*

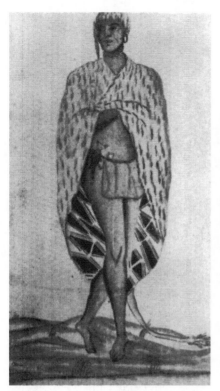

"A Savage in Winter Dress," by A. de Batz, c. early 1700s. An Indian from near New Orleans in a buffalo robe painted in designs of red and black. *(Bureau of American Ethnology)*

"Bison Hunt," by A. de Batz. Natchez tribe. *(Bureau of American Ethnology)*

"Indians Going A-hunting," by Philip Georg Friedrich von Reck, c. 1730. Figure on left is wearing a painted buffalo skin; middle figure has a gun, kettle, tumpline, and duffel blanket; figure on right is dressed in European trade shirt and cloth leggings. *(Royal Library, Copenhagen: NKS 565, 4to.)*

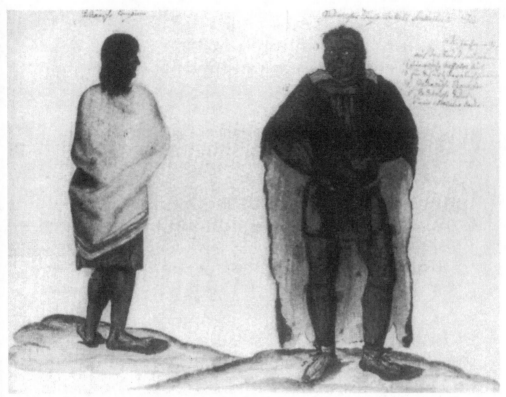

"The Indian King and Queen of Uchi, Senkaitschi," by Philip Georg Friedrich von Reck, c. 1730. Woman is wearing white duffel blanket trimmed in red, and blue stroud shirt; warrior is dressed in buffalo robe, blue stroud leggings, and a red breechcloth, and has chest and face tattoos. *(Royal Library, Copenhagen: NKS 565, 4to.)*

"An Indian Camp as They Make Them When They Are Hunting," by Philip Georg Friedrich von Reck, c. 1730. Creek hunting camp with bark-topped shelters, deer skins, kettles, women, and dogs. *(Royal Library, Copenhagen: NKS 565, 4to.)*

"Buffalo Hunt," from Jean-Bernard Bossu's *New Travels in North America: 1770–1771.*
This romanticized scene of Indians hamstringing buffalo was rendered by a European
artist.

Watercolor by Fleury Generelly depicting a hunter's camp in the lower Mississippi Valley, c. 1820. Note 1) half-face lean-to; 2) cradle of blue stroud; 3) log for pounding corn;
4) hide rack. On the far right is a rack to make jerk; to its left near the shelter is a beam-
ing log used for dehairing hides. The hunter is wearing a blue cloth turban and a black
breechcloth. *(Courtesy Tulane University Library, New Orleans, Louisiana Collection)*

"Daniel Boone looks out upon Kentucky and a great herd of buffalo." Published in 1895 in Z. F. Smith's *History of Kentucky.*

Buffalo trace followed by Kentuckians at the Battle of Blue Licks, August 19, 1782. *(Courtesy the Filson Club)*

Receipt from James Harrod to John Martin, Flanders Callaway, and Daniel Boone for buffalo beef totaling 5,238 pounds. Richard Henderson, Richard Callaway, and David Gass sold 2,276 pounds of pork, c. 1775. *(Draper Manuscripts, Courtesy the State Historical Society of Wisconsin, Madison)*

"Col. Daniel Boon.," by Chester Harding and James Otto Lewis. This engraving, released two weeks after Boone's death on September 26, 1820, is the only true full-length likeness of Boone extant. *(Courtesy Pathfinder Press. Original housed in the Missouri Historical Society)*

Stabbing buffalo was a feat admired by some frontiersmen. Such bravado nearly cost the life of more than one man.

Buffalo turban with tail, c. mid to late 1700s, Winnebago. Turban consists of two pieces of buffalo hide sewn in front and tied in back, adorned with eighteenth-century brass shoe buckle. *(From the Loren Herrington Collection. Photo by Fleury Studios, Troy, Michigan.)*

Buffalo armband, Great Lakes, c. mid to late 1700s. Consists of a ten-inch piece of buffalo hide with two tie thongs inside. Tail and long hair hangs in rear. *(From the Loren Herrington Collection. Photo by Fleury Studios, Troy, Michigan.)*

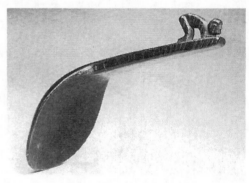

Feast spoon, c. mid to late 1700s. About 11½ by 6¾ inches at widest point. Carved from a black ash burl. Effigy represents Winnebago buffalo dancer imitating and appeasing buffalo during the Maple Sugar Feast. *(From the Loren Herrington Collection. Photo by Fleury Studios, Troy, Michigan.)*

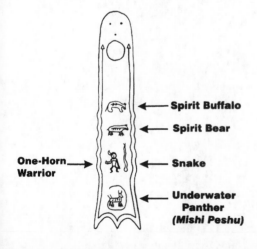

Spirit Buffalo

Spirit Bear

One-Horn Warrior

Snake

Underwater Panther (Mishi Peshu)

Elk antler roach spreader, Winnebago (c. mid to late 1700s). Measures 5¾ inches long by ¾ inch wide and is thought to be the only such piece in existence. Note spirit buffalo effigy. Pictographic warrior is wearing a one-horned buffalo turban. Great Lake Indians, according to the late Loren Herrington, "made them that way . . . just one horn from that one side." Such turbans signified valor in war. *(From the Loren Herrington Collection. Drawing by Michael J. Taylor)*

Fighting erupted between settlers and Indians north of the Ohio. And back east a storm was brewing between colonists and the greatest military might on earth, the British. The king was incensed at the audacity of the rebels in attacking His Majesty's Regulars at Lexington and Concord, Massachusetts, on April 19, 1775. Equally outrageous was talk of independence. George III was determined to force his erring subjects back into the fold, even if it meant arming Indians against them. The era of Kentucky's border wars was near. So too was the Revolution.

Kentucky II

April 19, 1775. Lexington, Massachusetts. One shot—perhaps a misfire or the crack of a pistol. Instantly volley fire shrouded the court green in a haze of sulfur and soot. By 3:00 p.m. a frenzied march from Concord became a sixteen-mile gauntlet of death. The spring day ended dreadfully: The British had 250 killed and wounded; the Americans, 146. War was declared and ripped into the West. British commanders at Niagara, Michilimackinac, and Detroit armed native allies with muskets, powder, and ball.

Raids intensified. At Harrod's Town, Hugh McGary, whose stepson had been killed by Indians, shot a Shawnee wearing his dead boy's hunting shirt, chopped up the corpse, and fed the hunks to his dogs.[1] Warriors hunkered along traces to pick off settlers. "We went several times in the woods exploreing the country and hunting, but as the indeans was in the habit of watching the roads they had to be very caucious and not to go any road in Day light," remembered Daniel Trabue.[2]

Gunpowder sold at Boonesborough for $2.66 a pound in 1775, and one-pound lead bars cost 17 cents each.[3] Some friendly Cherokee killed a buffalo yearling and quartered it for the new arrivals at Boonesborough— Daniel Boone's wife, Rebecca Bryan, and their daughter Jemima, who came to join Boone's oldest daughter, Susannah. Frontier life was hard for the men but even harder on the women, who had to till the fields, split kindling, chop wood, lug noggins of water on yokes across their shoulders, hunt, and fight alongside the men, as well as bear the children, cook, sew, and keep hearth and home to give the crude settlements a civilized sense of an ordered, meaningful life.

On July 7, 1776, a party of Shawnee and Cherokee kidnapped Jemima Boone and Fanny and Betsy Callaway. After three days the warriors eased up, thinking they had pulled off the coup. As they paused to shoot a buffalo and feast on tongue and hump, Daniel Boone and a few men stormed them with guns blazing and rescued the girls.[4]

A Mingo named Pluggy attacked Harrod's Town on Christmas morning; four days later Pluggy's band fired on McClelland's Station.[5] Settlers at McClelland's fled to Boonesborough on New Year's Day 1777. Kentuckians abandoned Hinkston's Station and seven other outposts to fort up at Harrod's Town and Logan's Station. Others left for good. The Wilderness Road swelled with families fleeing to North Carolina. "We were afraid on account of Indians but frequently followed buffalo paths that were plain," said settler George Phelps.[6]

Keeping the settlers fed was a struggle. Nicholas Proctor of Estill's Station said they rode fifteen to twenty miles to hunt.[7] George Bedinger, a hunter for Boonesborough in 1777, told how they evaded Indians. Four or five men slipped singly out of the fort at dusk to rendezvous miles later at a secret camp. Rising before dawn, they split into groups of two or three and pushed on, avoiding hilltops, ridges, and traces, signaling by blowing across the tops of their powder measures. Spencer Records said he and his brother, Laban, had to leave the fort at night, ride twenty or thirty miles, hobble their horses and camp without fire in the darkest spot they could find. Cold or heat, plus hordes of mosquitoes, gnats, and blackflies, made such hunts miserable.[8]

If the men saw buffalo, they waited until dusk before shooting. Then, as darkness began to cloak the land, one or two stood guard as the rest of the men used "buffler" knives and tomahawks to sever hide and gristle and bone out the meat, which they wrapped in buffalo hide bags brought from the fort or made on the spot and laced with tugs.[9] It was hard, dangerous work. "The bone on the back," said Daniel Bryan, nephew of Daniel Boone, "was sometimes twenty-one inches high. The brisket . . . would stand up higher than a table. Two men couldn't turn a big bull if he had fallen on his side."[10]

Hunters stuffed each bag with about 100 pounds of meat, tied them off, and swung them across the saddle. Three hundred to four hundred pounds was a good load. Hunters might hang the bags in trees to retrieve, but panthers or buzzards could devour the cache or Indians who spied the bags might ambush returning hunters. If the "Yellow Boys" were near, hunters gutted the buffalo, split the carcass lengthwise, and "put it on the horse, back foremost: after balancing it, cracked the backbone, so that it may hang down on each side."[11] Hunters on foot hoppussed the bags back to the fort.

At Fort Randolph, Virginia, in the fall of 1777, frontier blackguards murdered Cornstalk, principal chief of the Shawnee, under a flag of truce. On February 7, 1778, a war party seeking revenge captured Daniel Boone near the Lower Blue Licks and forced him to surrender nearly thirty salt boilers. The Shawnee sold fourteen of these men to Lieutenant-Governor Henry Hamilton at Detroit and adopted the rest. Several captives escaped across the Ohio River back to Kentucky, but most lived as white Indians in the Middle Ground. Soldiers shackled those Kentuckians sold at Detroit to ship them to Canada to rot away in floating prison barges. Of these, some died in dungeons; the fate of a few is unknown. And though the British freed all hostages at the end of the American Revolution, six years passed before the ordeal fully ended.[12]

Boone escaped in June. Boonesborough was in disrepair. Buffalo were distant. "We found a poor distressed, ½ naked, ½ starved, people; daily surrounded by the savage. The people were dirty, lousy, ragged, and half starved when I came through," wrote Josiah Collins, a traveler, who arrived in early 1778. Yet they held on during a nine-day siege in September.[13] At Harrod's Town, too, times were hard: "Dirt and filth of the fort, putrefied flesh, dead dogs, horse, cow, and hog excrements" fouled the springs.[14] Typhoid and dysentery ravaged communities. Women daily tossed soiled bed ticks from cabins for chickens to peck clean of filth and lice.

Indians and whites crossed the Ohio to harass each other's forts and villages, collect scalps, and steal booty, horses, corn, and wild meat. In 1778 Lieutenant John Bowman asked Simon Kenton to take some men to spy on the Shawnee towns and recover horses. Kenton invited Daniel Trabue along, and the men "made prepararation to go, got some nise halters made with grained raw Buffelow hides . . . Deer lether lagons, parched corn Meal, and some Jirk. With 2 pair Mockinsons to each man, etc., our Guns and ammonition in the best Order, the next morning we was to start."[15]

Hunger was rampant. "Hunters were afraid to go out to get buffalo," one pioneer recalled. In 1778, the militia men of Captain John Martin, an early resident of Boonesborough, left the fort to float their canoes up the Kentucky to kill buffalo for the settlers. When the meat ran out, one of the men in desperation shot a steer belonging to Colonel Richard Callaway. Outraged, Callaway tried to have the soldier court-martialed and swore he would shoot the next man who killed one of his stock.[16]

Martin's men were a ragged bunch. "The militia in those times," remembered Sarah Graham, who arrived with her family in the 1780s, "had no other shirts than buckskin hunting shirts; and wore moccasins, and bear skin hats." These frontier militiamen kept at hand a bag of parched

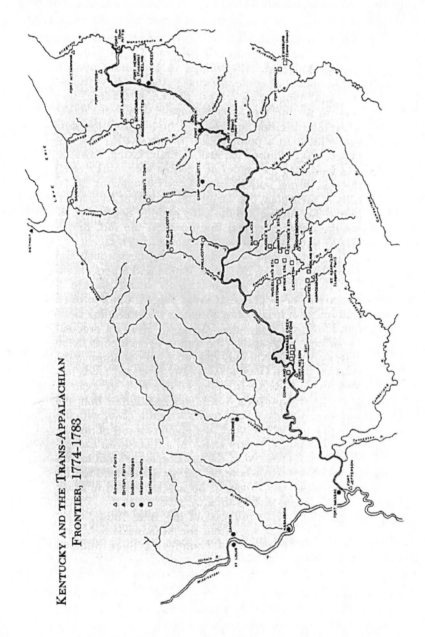

"Kentucky and the Trans-Appalachian Frontier, 1774–1783."
(Reprinted from Otis K. Rice, *Frontier Kentucky,* copyright 1975 by the
University Press of Kentucky, by permission of the publishers.)

corn, some jerk, and a horse. By 1787 Colonel Levi Todd's mandates were law: Officers and privates must own a musket with a forty-four-inch barrel able to fire a one-ounce ball, fitted "with a good bayonet and iron ramrod ... a cartridge box ... to secure 20 cartridges ... a good knapsack and canteen, and one pound of gunpowder and 4 pounds of lead." Men with rifles used them in place of muskets; one man, Ephraim Sadowsky, had an unusual "double-loading gun."[17]

Feeding the militia involved "a great deal of hard and dangersous labour," said Daniel Trabue, quartermaster sergeant at Logan's Station in 1778. "Employing hunters, pressing cattle, buying corn, etc., etc., a great deal of provisions needed as many of Col. Clark's men were frequently passing and drawing provisions from our fort." From July 13 to October 6 of that year, Trabue procured for Logan's Station "84 bushels of corn, 724 pounds of pork, 2,779 pounds of 'tame beef,' and 2,820 pounds of buffalo beef."[18]

In the winter of 1778, George Rogers Clark crippled British power by seizing Cahokia and Kaskaskia; in 1779 he struck Vincennes and captured Lieutenant-Governor Henry Hamilton. On his march, he saw "numbers of buffalo on Cot Plains near the Wabash."[19] He bought supplies on credit or with his own money and sought reimbursement from the Western Commissioners of Virginia for the purchase of wild beef.

> May 1779: Paid Mr. [Jacob du] Plassy for 29 lb. of Buffaloe beef
> May 1779: Paid Cerre [for] 405 lb. Buffaloe Beef
> December 8, 1779 to June 24, 1780: There is due Edward Hogan Five pounds Seven Shillings & two pence for 643 lbs. of Buff. Beef.
> April 20 to May 12, 1782: There is due to Joseph Archer twelve pounds ten Shillings & four pence for Buffalo Beef & Bear Meat furnished Captain [Robert] George's troops.
> October 23 to November 23, 1782: There is due to Edward Parker fifty one pounds two Shillings & eleven pence half penny for Buffaloe beef.
> ["]   : There is due Sergeant Elms Six pounds eleven Shillings & Eight pence for Buffalo Beef.
> ["]   : There is due to William Thompson Eighteen pounds Twelve Shillings & Six pence for Buffalo Beef.
> March 1783: David Morris claim as assistant [Quarter Master General] and conductor of military stores no. 5, and his Vouchers for 300 lb. of Buffalo Beef.[20]

In 1780 British Major Arent De Peyster dispatched Captain Henry Bird to Kentucky with two field cannon and a large force of Regulars and Indians. In June, Ruddle's and Martin's Stations surrendered to Bird. Warriors torched the forts, tomahawked twenty unarmed men, women, and children, and marched the rest to Detroit.

In January 1780 Governor Thomas Jefferson of Virginia authorized George Rogers Clark to build Fort Jefferson at the confluence of the Ohio and Mississippi to stop the flow of British arms to Indians and secure the western borders. Wild meat kept the garrison alive. John Donne, Clark's Deputy Commissary, recorded on November 23, 1780, "Received of the Kaskaskia savages ... five thousand and thirteen pounds of buffalo beef, seven hundred and forty-five pounds of venison and fifty-eight pounds of bear meat."[21] On March 17, 1781, Donne purchased "one thousand six hundred and fifty-two pounds of buffalo beef and one hundred and eighty-eight pounds of bear meat."[22] A week later Captain Robert George swapped a hunter "one pound of coarse thread" for thirty pounds of salted buffalo beef.[23]

Leonard Helm wrote from Fort Jefferson to Colonel George Slaughter on October 29, 1780:

> Dear Colonel:
> Sitting here by Captain [Robert] George's fire with a piece of lightwood and two ribs of an old buffalo which is all the meat we have seen this day.... Excuse haste as the lightwoods just out and mouth watering for part of the two ribs.[24]

The Hard Winter of 1779–80 was bitterly cold. Buffalo turned poor early; turkeys froze roosting in trees; settlers suffered. The freezes that began in early November did not let up until March.[25] At the Dutch Station near Beargrass Creek, people died of starvation. Other settlers singed wool off buffalo hides to roast the skins to eat.[26] The "severity of this winter caused great difficulty in Kentucky," Daniel Boone said, "the inhabitants lived chiefly on the flesh of buffaloes."[27] Spencer Records and John Finch shot six buffalo with six shots in November near Estill's Station. On Christmas day, William Clinkenbeard roasted sixty-eight marrow bones for the family meal.

That December, Joshua Archer sold wild beef to the inhabitants forted up at Fort Jefferson.[28] But after thirteen months and twenty days, the Americans abandoned the outpost due to fierce sniping from the Chickasaw. Daniel Bryan brought in thirty-one horse loads of buffalo at

Martin's and Ruddle's Stations—not counting the many hundred-pound meat bags slung over his pack horse.[29] George Rogers Clark hired Evan Hinton to "lay in a . . . large quantity of buffalo meat for the public service." Hinton, George Holman, and Richard Rue drove a four-horse team to Louisville to get salt. Indians captured them near Boone's Station, stole their horses, and dumped their salt on the ground.[30]

By the end of 1780 a wagon load of buffalo meat, hides, and tallow sold for $100 of inflated Continental currency. Most could not buy it. William Clinkenbeard quit hunting to learn surveying; buffalo were scarce, he complained, and he made good money as a chain-carrier.[31] Livestock died, forcing settlers to live on meat hacked from frozen cow and horse carcasses. Even the buffalo starved, unable to eat the sleet covered cane.[32] Rivers and creeks iced over, forcing buffalo to forage with cattle.[33] When settlers boiled off maple sap, "the poor miserable buffalo would come to drink the sugar water and they could hardly drive them off, they were so poor" and people shot them from cabins.[34] After the Hard Winter, Simon Kenton declared, "Kentucky's game herds were never so great—thousands of deer and buffalo perished."[35]

Unscrupulous merchants sold corn for $165 a bushel. Many people, said Daniel Trabue, "would be Taken sick and did actuly Die for the want of solid food." Settlers trudged to Louisville to sit and wait for flatboats bringing seed corn down the Ohio from the Monongahela Valley to plant in the spring. Meanwhile, the Revolutionary War raged on.[36]

Indian attacks at the Falls of the Ohio grew hotter as atrocities from the Shawnee—"those execrable Hell hounds," as Colonel John Floyd deemed them—worsened. Floyd, surveyor and leader of the Jefferson County militia, desperately worked to keep forts at the falls and at Beargrass Creek supplied.[37] "Whole families are destroyed," he wrote to George Rogers Clark on April 16, 1781. "Our dependence to support our families is upon getting wild meat and this is procured with great difficulty and danger."

Salt stores were low. Meat spoiled. "There is not at this time," wrote Floyd, "more than fifty thousand pounds of beef in this county, Fayette and Lincoln; upwards of one hundred thousand weight of that laid up in this county being entirely rotten and lost." Such austerity led hunters to kill with greater zeal. "I hired seven men," wrote Floyd, "went to Lee's Cabin with horses loaded with salt . . . killed and saved 54 buffaloes, 4 elk, 2 wild hogs." Floyd's hunters smoked and salted the meat, rendered the fat, and built a flotilla of canoes to float the provisions to the settlers. But on the trip back to Beargrass Creek, the canoes swamped and tons of meat and tallow ended up on the river bottom.

Lord Cornwallis's surrender to George Washington at Yorktown, Virginia, in October 1781 had little impact on the West: The British held Canada and Detroit, and by keeping the Indians armed, clothed, and fed, it was not hard to maintain Loyalist sympathies. That winter tribal leaders met at Old Chillicothe (now Xenia, Ohio) to form an alliance. The leaders were Shawnee, yet other tribes—the Wyandot, the Wolf clan of the Delaware, the Mingo, and the Potawatomi—pledged to root out the whites. One of those inciting them was Patriot-turned-Tory Simon Girty. Girty's talk at the Shawnee town of Wapakoneta fueled the war flames.

> Brothers: The Long Knives have overrun your country, and usurped your hunting grounds. They have destroyed the cane, trodden down the clover, killed the deer and the buffaloes.[38]

Girty implored his brothers and sisters to rise up and drive the white men from their lands lest they lose the hunting grounds of their fathers. Women, he declared, should sew garments of war for their men, moccasins of buffalo, leggings of wolf skin. Americans despised Girty. "Girty was a dirty dog," said John Crawford.[39]

Kentuckians called 1782 the Year of Blood. Wyandot raids on Strode's, Estill's, and Hoy's Stations that March ended in a shootout at Mt. Sterling that became known as Estill's Defeat. On August 17 Indians stormed Bryan's Station and shot four men dead. Two days later, in a brilliant tactical maneuver by Indians and Butler's Rangers that was contrived in part by Girty, George III's native allies ambushed a force of 182 Americans at Blue Licks, killing seventy-seven. George Rogers Clark and 1,050 Kentuckians rode swiftly along "buffalo traces, which were as plain as roads" to take vengeance. Following Alanant-o-wamiowee, marked on John Filson's 1784 map of Kentucky as "Gen'l Clark's War Road," the whites attacked the Indians near Cincinnati and torched three Shawnee towns and their fields.[40]

Many consider the bloodshed at Blue Licks on August 19, 1782, the last battle of the Revolution, though it was far from being the last Indian fight in Kentucky. But the inability of the British and the Indians to rout the Kentuckians and push them back over the Appalachians signaled the beginning of American dominance in the new West.

The beginnings of Harrod's Town and Boonesborough were pivotal events in the western theater of the Revolution. During the conflict, settlers carved other stations—St. Asaph's (Logan's Fort), Boiling Springs, McClellan's, Hinkston's, and Martin's—out of the Kentucky woodlands.

Tales of fertile land lured the pioneers. "What a Buzzel is amongst people about Kentuck?" Reverend John Brown of Virginia asked a friend. "To hear people speak of it one would think it was a new Paradise."[41] Newcomers complained that men from Boiling Springs, Harrod's new settlement near Harrod's Town, had staked out every good acre and every spring within eight hundred miles.[42]

Tanning—like salt production, labor-intensive farming, animal husbandry, and food storage—is evidence of a more stable mode of life. Westering Americans first tanned hides by chemical means at Boone's Station in the winter of 1779. For buckskin breeches, moccasins, and coats, tanners warmed water in thirty-gallon malt kettles, then stirred in alum, salt, ashes, and skins. After the hair slipped free, they scraped hides free of clots and gristle with a drawknife. As the hides dried, workers pulled and stretched them, sometimes over a board and sometimes by hand, until dry. From this, Peter Houston, one of the original settlers at Boone's Station, said, "leather trousers and jackets were made; principally for the men, but some of the women were under the necessity of wearing them."[43]

To make heavyweight moccasin leather, Houston smeared alum, salt, and ashes on buffalo robes to slip the wool, then tanned the skin. To tan robes with the wool on for quilts or saddle rugs, he "covered the flesh side with the solution made the consistency of paste and after a few days, all of the flesh was removed and the hides pulled and rubbed until dry." Tanners dug wide pits for white-oak or sumac bark tanning, which took weeks.[44] In 1790 Reverend John Evans Finlay recorded how Kentucky settlers bark-tanned cow hides:

1) Take off the horns from the hides, then soak the blood out of them in ye water pool.

2) Then put ye hides into ye lime pit . . . carefully observe when the hair comes off, will be in a week or less—during this time draw them out twice a day letting them stay out 20 or 30 minutes to air.

3) Then unhair them, and put them into bast—bast them twice a week in cold weather and three times in warm. [word illegible] twice a day. Ye bast is a mixture of water and hen dung—You will know by the water when the lime is quite out of the hides then they are sufficiently basted, out of the bast rub hides with a rounding edge iron over a hollow tree out of ye bast.

4) Then handle them in a strong [mixture?] of bast in box or pit
of bark—and 4 calf skins in a handler. . . . Leather is laid down in
a clean pit—a layer of clean dry bark and a hide [and so on] and
then pour on water and in four or five weeks raise and lay down
as before.[45]

Months later, workers removed the skins from the vats to beam and
oil. Two men could tan five hundred skins a year. But tanning was risky.
By day tanners might get shot; at night Indians raided the pits to take
back what they felt was theirs. During the siege of Bryan's Station, a defender shot James Girty, adopted brother to the Shawnee and younger
brother of Simon Girty, as he was stealing hides "from the tan vats"; the
skin stopped the ball, but the impact knocked Girty flat. At Boonesborough, a hail of lead from the fort sent some Shawnee stealing hides
from the tanyards scampering for cover. Hide stealing was common, and
both frontier whites and the warriors who raided their tanning vats wore
Anglo-tanned buckskin.[46]

The role of salt in the expansion of Anglo-American settlement can
hardly be overstated. Salt preserved meat so that it could be stored for
hard times. A fort without a store of salted meat was vulnerable in times
of siege. Salt springs near the Great Kanawha and the Holston, along the
Cumberland, and in Ohio and Kentucky were key factors in allowing
settlers to cross the Appalachians with the knowledge that they could
feed themselves.[47] Of great importance were the licks near Louisville, a
growing town vital to Americans.

George Rogers Clark seized upon the strategic value of Corn Island,
located in the Ohio above Louisville, and occupied it by May 1778 to
quarter and train troops for his Illinois forays. About that time, sixteen
men left the Falls of the Ohio, following a trace through the Knobs to
Bullitt County. Near the Salt River, they built Brashear's Station, also
called Froman's Station (for Isaac Froman) or the Salt River Garrison.[48]
Salinity was highest at Bullitt's Lick, which one observer likened to "the
hub of a great system of buffalo roads leading to it like the spokes of a
wheel." With game, land, and salt abundant, salt boiling at Bullitt's
launched into full steam in the summer of 1779.[49]

For years the only industry in Kentucky was the salt works at Bullitt's
Lick. Workers sent salt by pack train and flatboat to the Cumberland,
Mississippi, and up the Illinois, and by 1846 Kentucky was producing
more than one hundred tons of salt per year. Originally, soldiers built the
works because George Rogers Clark needed salt for his men. Wood-

cutters stretched the Wilderness Trail from Harrod's Town to the Falls of the Ohio, which became its far western terminus. Traveling Clark's lifeline was hazardous: Kentuckians John Floyd, Walker Daniel, and Bill Linn all lost their lives to Indians along the war road.[50]

William Fleming visited Bullitt's Lick in the fall of 1779. It was, Fleming noted, a dangerous region: The Falls area was a favorite hunting ground, buffalo were thick, and Shawnee towns were not far north. To protect salt boilers at Bullitt's Lick, soldiers built Mud Garrison on the bank of the Salt River by erecting two rows of palisades parallel to each other and dumping mud between the rows.[51]

Abraham Fields lived at Colonel James Moore's station, established in 1783 at the Fish Pools, a pocket of springs "about 8½ miles southeast of the Falls of the Ohio and the then small settlement of Louisville." From 1785 to 1787 Fields was a market hunter. "There was no man better acquainted with those woods during that time than myself," he said.[52] But Fields hunted mostly deer and bear, only occasionally hunting buffalo near the Falls or upriver at Big Bone Lick or Limestone. By then, settlers migrating west could no longer depend on game. "If you think of making a tour to this part of America," Thomas Perkins, a settler in Lincoln County, wrote to General Joseph Palmer on July 24, 1785, "you will find ... nothing to be looked for but bread and meat; and perhaps that will be obtained with difficulty. The best way is to carry provisions."[53]

One meat getter, William Sudduth, said that from April to December 1785 he killed sixty wild cows near Strode's Station. Ben Guthrie was surveying with Daniel Boone in 1784 in Fleming County when they spooked a herd into crossing the Licking River. A letter from Maysville, dated February 21, 1786, notes that "the buffalo are very plenty about this place."[54] Yet "plenty," in this case, is relative.

Even with the accurate, hard-hitting long rifles that meat getters like Sudduth used to kill buffalo, bullets still missed their mark. Then things got "tetchy." Hunters would spit lead balls down barrels without wads, prime, and fire, repeating the process until the beast hit the ground dead.

John McMillen was hunting in 1776 with John Gass at Harrod's Lick, on the north side of Stoner's Fork on the Licking River, when McMillen wounded a bull. McMillen tracked the animal's blood into some weeds and bushes, where he bumped into the enraged beast; it charged, breaking his gun and goring him. Gass took McMillen, more dead than alive from loss of blood, to Boonesborough, but he recovered.[55]

In 1777 near Nashville, William Bowen tracked a wounded buffalo into a cane thicket. The buffalo stomped Bowen into the dirt, where he lay for seven days until his companions found him. The next morning he died of gangrene.[56] Near Clarksville, Tennessee, William Baker wounded a bull, cornering it in a brake. The bull charged and Baker sprinted away, but the buffalo tossed him high and stormed off. Although his thigh was gashed to the bone, Baker lived.[57]

James Harrod's wife, Ann, once shot a buffalo. "I never could do much with a gun," she later said. "I did manage to kill a cow and a bear, or the girls would have never have got done laughing at me."[58] At Lexington during the early days of settlement, when women "would take tea together they had nothing but tea and dried buffaloe meat."[59]

Hunting dogs, Daniel Trabue wrote, were "very beneficial in killing bears and Buffaloos. . . . They Generally took several Dogs to the woods." Trabue preferred bulldogs; Peter Houston, like many others, kept spaniels. Mixed-breed hounds reminiscent of the Plott were common, as were wolfish-looking mutts. Joel Sappington, a Kentucky hunter, had a good buffalo dog, as did Nathan Boone. Once Simon Kenton's dogs raced across a frozen river to a buffalo crossing the ice and clamped down on its ears. Hooves flailed, then dogs and buffalo broke through the ice and drowned. Kenton regretted the loss, as his dogs "used to always sleep one on each side of him to guard him at night when he camped alone in the wilderness."[60]

Thrill seekers sometimes killed buffalo by hand. A soldier serving in Colonel John Bowman's campaign of 1779 spied a buffalo on a rise below him. "Desirous of performing some valiant exploit," the man leaped on its back and stabbed the beast to death. "This hero of a hunter was greatly complimented by the troops," said George Bedinger, who witnessed the feat.[61] Another man, Tom Hood, dropped out of a tree onto the back of a buffalo hemmed in by his dogs and was badly shaken before he cut the animal's hamstrings. "Tom was simple and daring," an observer said, "and sought this kind of notoriety."[62]

The earliest recollection Nathan Boone "treasured in his memory" was that of a buffalo drove near Limestone charging a team driven by his father. Spooked by the noise of the oncoming cavalcade, the buffalo bolted from a brake, collided with a horse and knocked it down, and then stormed off into the woods. Years later, on the East Fork of the Little Sandy, Nathan tried to stab a buffalo and hit a rib, snapping his blade in half. The wounded bull treed him, but he "was glad to have escaped as he did and thought it best to let the buffalo go."[63]

Such foolishness did have its heady moments. In Trigg County, Kentucky, Isaac Peterson and Hugh Bell were hunting on the Little River. Each shot a buffalo. Hugh found Isaac's bull and sat down on it for a moment to catch his breath, then left to dress his kill. Upon his return, the bull was gone. Hugh clambered up a tree and spied the bleeding animal lying a few yards off in the thick, tall grass. He hollered to Isaac, who said he "would go and stick it."

Isaac crept warily to the heaving beast. Just as he was about to give the fatal stab, the buffalo bounded to its feet, and Isaac scampered up a dead, limbless tree. He climbed six or eight feet before he began to slide back down to the bull, which all the while "kept up a warfare on the tree." Again he hunched up the tree and again he slid down, howling at Hugh to shoot. But Hugh was laughing so hard he could not hold his gun steady enough to aim. But after Isaac's third ascent, seeing his companion weaken and the flesh from his face, chest and stomach rubbed raw, Hugh shot the raging bull.[64]

Another time, Hugh Bell was hunting with his brother William in the barrens of central Kentucky, when they saw two buffalo. Hugh shot one and William ran after the other. The buffalo turned and charged. William leaped on his horse and galloped around a ten-acre sinkhole close by. William made two laps as the buffalo gained ground. Hugh rode up and dropped the animal twenty steps from William's horse. They reckoned the bull mistook it for its mate.[65]

One could not always choose which tree to scale when faced with the wagging black horns of an angry one thousand eight hundred pound buffalo. Bill Rayburn once wounded a buffalo, which wheeled and ripped a six-inch gash in his side. Dropping his gun, Rayburn spied a thorny honey locust tree and rushed up it before the irate bull could make a second pass. Bleeding, impaled by thorns, and in awful pain, Rayburn was eventually rescued by hunters from his prickly perch. That night William Clinkenbeard's wife "picked a great many thorns out of him."[66]

Buffalo are unpredictable. In the winter of 1780 Reuben Searcy and William Clinkenbeard were hunting in Kentucky. Clinkenbeard wounded a buffalo, which had veered off into a brake. Searcy tracked the beast down. As he shouldered his rifle, the animal charged. Searcy bolted for a tree but tripped and fell, rolling over and over. The buffalo ran up to Searcy, stopped and looked at him, then ran away.[67]

That same year, Old Man John Strode shot down a wild cow nursing a calf and led the calf home to run with his cattle. For two or three years, the little bull frolicked with the cows and was petted and loved. But the buffalo grew and one day "got cross" with his owner. The women were afraid to go into the pasture to milk the cows, so Strode wound up selling his pet buffalo to a Virginian.[68]

Peter Harper, a "half-Indian," was hunting with Enos Terry and William Clinkenbeard in the wintry Bluegrass wilds in 1779, when Harper leveled his gun and at a range of ten steps blasted a buffalo point-blank in the forehead. The bullet glanced off and landed at Harper's feet, flat as a penny. The men chased the buffalo into a creek and tried stoning it to death, as they were out of powder and ball, but the buffalo ran the men off.

"Kill the leader and you might kill three or four more," Clinkenbeard said. His brother once shot a buffalo, knocking it to its knees. He tried to finish it off with his hunting knife, but the beast chased him behind a tree. He stabbed out the animal's eyes, and someone else shot the creature.[69]

George Bedinger helped supply forts in Kentucky with wild meat. On a hunt with Lewis Fields on the Green River in the fall of 1784, he and Fields suffered all sorts of mishaps. During a warm spell, a four-foot cottonmouth struck Fields in the leg and the pair had to lie low for weeks. Bedinger hunted sparingly, as they had only four charges of powder and ball. Hunger drove them to push hard to the settlements when Fields could walk. In a valley, they spied a few buffalo. Fields picked his target. Bedinger told Fields to aim between the buffalo's horn and ear, where the skull is the thinnest. Fields crept from tree to tree until he closed in. He raised up and fired. The buffalo hit the ground. "Thank God," exclaimed Fields. But as Bedinger ran up, the stunned buffalo charged him. Bedinger paused long enough to snap off a shot, then ran for his life, but the buffalo dashed away to join the herd. Fields fired another round, to no avail.

The following year, Bedinger shot "an enormous buffalo, the largest he ever saw." The beast was so big, he boasted, that it barked a tree as it fell to the earth.[70]

Isaac Cunningham encountered a bull snared in a tangle of vines growing near his Lexington home. Cunningham grabbed the bull's scrotum and castrated the beast, which limped off in a huff. John McKinney came upon a yearling wedged between tree stumps and similarly "altered it," helped it up, and led it home. After it added some size, McKinney butchered the half-grown bullock. James Wade spied a buffalo drinking from a creek running near an ash hopper. "I wanted to have it said that I had caught a buffalo, and went and crept under this hopper and caught one by the hind foot."[71]

John Hanks and his family migrated to Limestone, Kentucky, in 1786 and there met Daniel Boone at his tavern. Hanks told Boone that he had a hankering to go shoot a buffalo, but he lacked a good gun. Hanks recalled the moment to John Shane: "We went out a hunting and Boone lent me his rifle in place of my own and saying, as I carried it on my shoulder, if I saw any buffaloes it would twist around towards them."[72]

Daniel Trabue's recollections are rich in colloquialisms, such as "jumed" (meaning "zoomed") and other expressions of the day. Here he recalls a hunt on the Green River in 1778 with a quarrelsome Irishman, who became the camp buffoon after his retreat from a buffalo he had smacked between the eyes with a tomahawk.

One of the men we had with us was a young Irishman who was constant contending and Disputeing with the other young men that was from old Virginia about words and customs, etc. So some time that morning I shot a Buffelo bull and he fell down. We all went up to him. Some of the men had never seen one before this one. I soon Discovered I had shot this buffelo too high and I told some of the boys to shoot him again.

This young Irishman said, "No"; he would kill him and Jumed at him with his tomerhock and [began] strikeing him in the forehead.

I told him it would not Do, he could not hurt him, the wool and mud and skin and skull was all so thick it would not Do. But he kept up his licks, a nocking away.

The buffelo jumped up. The man run, the buffelo after him. It was opin woods, no bushes, and the way this young Irishman run was rather Desending ground and every Jumped he cried out, "O lard! O lard! O lard! O lard!"

The buffelo was close to his heels. The man Jumed behind a beech tree. The bufflo fell down, his head against the tree, the tuckeyho boys laughing, "Ha! Ha! Ha!"

One of them went up and shot the buffelo again and killed him. The Irishman exclaimed againt them, saying this was no laughing Matter but that these boys or young [men] (he said) was such fools they would laugh if the buffelo had killed him.

These young men would Mimmick him, "O lard! O lard!" etc. and breack out in big laughter.

The Irishmen said he would go no further with such fools.
... I advised him to take a load of this buffelo meet as it was very
fat and he was welcome to it, to which he agreed as we did not
need it. We took a little of it and bid him a Due [adieu].[73]

On another day, Trabue and a Mr. Smith shot eleven buffalo at one
stand. "We concluded to shoot the leaders—to wit, the Old cows—and
then the younger ones would not leave them.... So we killed the whole
Gang which was 11." Hunters slew so many buffalo at Blue Licks that the
stench drew wolves for miles. It became law, said James Wade, a Kentucky
meat getter, about the problem, "that no man should kill a Buffaloe but
John Beasley. He co'd tell the fattest and best."[74]

Aside from Boone's law passed at Boonesborough for preserving
wild cattle, few gave thought to the carnage. Yet, like the Indians, until
crops could be cultivated and livestock raised, Kentuckians depended on
game. Word spread quickly in the East that the abundant herds in the
West could keep a man and his family alive until they could farm enough
to afford milk cows, beef cattle, and pigs. And so the people kept coming.

During the mid-1790s there would be buffalo droves of twenty head
or less in the Bluegrass, the Barrens, and west Kentucky (the Jackson
Purchase). Joshua McQueen came from Pennsylvania and hunted near
Boonesborough. "The buffalo were so that you could not have driven
them out," said McQueen. But "many a buffalo, was killed by the whites
and only a little of the rump taken out, or a thigh bone for the marrow.
... Many a man killed a buffalo just for the sake of saying so."[75]

"They did destroy them and waste them then, at a mighty rate,"
William Clinkenbeard recalled. "If one wasn't young and fat, it was left,
and they went on and killed another." "Likewise the cane," Clinkenbeard
said about the canebrakes, which were beginning to disappear too. "I
thought they never would get it out of this country, when I came, but
now it is scarce and a curiosity." At McGee's Station, John McGuire
swapped a man one hundred buffalo hides for a mare.[76]

In 1784 John Filson published a small book, *The Discovery, Settlement
and Present State of Kentucke.* It was Kentucky's first written history, and its
appendix, "The Adventures of Col. Daniel Boon," brought Boone to the
popular press in America, England, France, and Germany and helped
make him an international hero. *Kentucke,* along with John Trumball's
heavily edited, plagiarized version of Filson's book, inspired people to
move beyond the Blue Ridge to find their place in the sun.[77] Verbose and

"Map of Kentucke," by John Filson, 1784. Scrutiny of the map will reveal buffalo traces, forts, canebrakes, rivers, and salt licks.

bombastic, but a good piece of public relations, *Kentucke* presents a florid glimpse of the sylvan glades and endless game herds one was sure to see in the new West. "The amazing herds of buffalo," Filson declared, "by their size and number, fill the traveler with amazement and terror." A traveler to Kentucky, Filson continued, would be equally amazed at the sight of the buffalo traces—"the prodigious roads."[78]

John Filson was a publicist. As such, his *Kentucke* was a transmontane paradise. Kentucky summer, he wrote, did not have "the sandy heats of which Virginia and Carolina experience," and the winter, "which at most only lasts three months," was not severe. "People are safe in bad houses. . . . Snow seldom falls deep or lasts long." People who read Filson's book and, believing his falderal, would move to Kentucky and soon learn that Kentucky summers were hot, winters were cold, and there were no "amazing herds of buffalo."[79]

Such sights were gone. Kentucky was fast becoming a checkerboard of towns, farms, and pastures, resulting in a tangle of land claims. And because of that plus overhunting, game herds were rapidly dwindling.

After the Revolutionary War, the eastern floodgates opened, and waves of Americans poured through the Cumberland Gap, a route that "more than three hundred thousand settlers would follow . . . to Kentucky and beyond." William Clinkenbeard saw the stream of migrants in 1782: "They passed us pretty nigh every day. . . . Everybody coming to Kentucky. Could hardly get along the road for them."[80]

East of the Mississippi the buffalo were doomed. Yet at the same time, early-nineteenth-century "naturalists," publicists, and yarn spinners purported that "vast herds" of buffalo, numbering as many as twelve thousand head, roamed the hills and woodlands of Pennsylvania.

Pennsylvania's "Vast Herds"

ACCORDING TO A FEW OFTEN-QUOTED REPORTS, PENNSYLVANIA WAS once home to huge buffalo herds that supposedly roamed as far east as the Susquehanna River. In his 1772 *Notes of Travel From the North Branch of the Susquehanna to Beaver, Pa.,* Reverend John Ettwein reported that Clearfield County was so named because "the buffaloes formerly cleared large tracts of undergrowth so as to give the appearance of cleared fields."[1]

Keystone lore asserts that buffalo ranged from Buffalo, New York, southward through the Pennsylvania counties of Erie, Crawford, Mercer, and Venango. Before the Revolutionary War, settlers allegedly renamed French Creek—flowing through western Pennsylvania—La Boeuf Rivière, because of vast numbers of buffalo there. Legend has it too that as pioneers poured over hilltops and ridges, most buffalo had fled Somerset County (which borders West Virginia) by 1755. A remnant of the herds lingered behind, cut off from their old haunts by settlers. For years the wild cattle hid in ravines and rockfalls gouged out in the Alleghenies.

On Peter Kalm's map—Kalm was the Swedish botanist who in 1771 confused Canada with Illinois—the buffalo's western boundary is marked by a marsh between the Allegheny River and the west branch of the Susquehanna; today this region is between Oil Creek and Clarion Creek. Thousands of buffalo allegedly roamed there until men spotted them.[2] Hunters organized great hunts each fall, dooming the buffalo.

During the hunts, yarned old-timers, the "bufflers" in southern Pennsylvania escaped to Maryland and West Virginia. In the spring, hunters shot the buffalo for meat; in the fall, they shot them for robes. The saga of the Pennsylvania buffalo became part of regional lore. And in time the chimerical wild cattle became flesh and bone, horn and hoof, and thundered into the pages of "true" history.

Jacob Quiggle (1821–1911), ex-commissioner of Clinton County and grandson of famed hunter and Revolutionary War officer Philip Quigley (1745–?), had never met his forebear, but Jacob's mother told him of Grandfather Quigley's exploits. Jacob listened wide-eyed, committing the wondrous tales to memory. In August 1911 at a Clinton County clambake, Jacob, age eighty-nine and in his last year, passed on to a tippling social lion, Henry W. Shoemaker, the buffalo lore he had heard fourscore years earlier.

Shoemaker had a good ear for a story, a gift for embellishment, and was no slouch with a pen. Nor did he lack funds or a publisher. A well-heeled ex-ambassador to Bulgaria, he was a regional newspaper mogul and self-published writer who specialized in werewolves and bawdy love tales. Upon hearing the reminiscences of Quiggle, Shoemaker knew that he had struck literary paydirt—Pennsylvania buffalo!

Jacob talked. Henry scribbled notes.

Jacob said that Pennsylvania buffalo had differed noticeably from Plains buffalo. Grandpa Quigley had called them wood bison—larger, darker, having no hump, with streamlined haunches. A paragon of bovine evolution, the legendary, long-vanished Pennsylvania bison "was a beautifully proportioned beast," said Jacob, and, "was an agile runner and climber, carried no superfluous flesh, was adapted in every way for life in a rough, mountainous country. . . . The horns, which in mature specimens were very long, grew upwards, like the horns of Ayrshire cattle."[3]

During Quigley's day, supposedly, there were two distinct herds of these majestically horned kine—the northern and the southern herd. Grandpa Quigley had hunted the northern herd. Months later, based on Jacob Quiggle's story and yarns of equal merit, Shoemaker reported in his popular book, *A Pennsylvania Bison Hunt,* that in 1773 the northern buffalo herd had numbered twelve thousand strong.[4]

Of Shoemaker's nine buffalo tales, several were plagiarized from Thomas Ashe's *Travels in America,* published in 1808 and severely criticized and laughed at by contemporary naturalists for its hyperbole. In 1938 historian J. W. Harpster cautioned readers about the reliability of Ashe's *Travels:* "The information concerning Western Pennsylvania contained in this work is to be questioned, considering charges of plagiarism and inaccuracy against the author." In 1989 publisher Stephanie Zebrowski called *Travels* an "adventure novella."[5]

Certainly Ashe, a British traveler, did not lack imagination. In *Travels,* readers encounter twelve-foot rattlesnakes, birds hibernating in hollow trees by hanging from their bills, and Indians seven feet tall. The author discovers "Grecian hieroglyphics" in a cave and translates them. In one poignant tale, a gut-shot black bear sporting five-inch tusks staggers against a tree, scoops up a wad of "clean leaves," and then, "with the utmost precaution," stuffs them in the bullet hole to staunch the bleeding.[6]

The influence of Ashe's tales is noticeably pervasive in Shoemaker's book, and Shoemaker launched his mentor's bombast to dizzying heights. Buffalo herd counts of twelve thousand were Shoemaker's guesses, not estimates from those he interviewed. *A Pennsylvania Bison Hunt* is filled with hyperbole like "countless numbers," "vanished millions," and buffalo more "prevalent in Pennsylvania than all the vast herds of wild animals which were found by the pioneers in South and South Central Africa."[7] And there is no evidence to support Shoemaker's assertion that buffalo migrate in winter and spring like golden plover.

Another story by Shoemaker, and one that was first recorded by Ashe, supposedly took place in Erie County, near Clarion. There an unnamed old man in an unknown year built a cabin at an unidentified trace near an undiscovered salt lick that allegedly drew huge buffalo herds. In Ashe's version the buffalo numbered two thousand; Shoemaker raised the number to ten thousand.[8] When the buffalo came, they delighted in the cabin, rubbing their backs and sides against it, butting and polishing their horns on its logs, pushing and shoving until the hut caved in. After barely escaping death in the falling timbers, the stampeding buffalo nearly trampled the old man as he ran for his life. He would have his day, he decided. Within the next two years, the old man and a few friends shot about seven hundred buffalo and sold the hides for two shillings each. The third and fourth years they did the same, killing and skinning the animals, leaving behind bloated, naked hulks. The fifth year the buffalo no longer came.

Ashe said he met Pennsylvanians who boasted of killing two thousand or more buffalo; no names or addresses are given. He reported that farmers torched the canefields where the buffalo ate by night and hid by day so that the beasts could be shot, the ground cleared, and the soil tilled.[9]

The last so-called "great Pennsylvania buffalo hunt" took place in Union County on December 31, 1799. Shoemaker's account, a wild epic of myth, mayhem, and hyperbole, is given here as he said it was told to him in the early 1900s by Flavel Bergstresser, a descendant of Martin Bergstresser, who, it was said, "helped to wipe out the last herd of wild bison in the Keystone State."

By the close of the eighteenth-century the last herd of Pennsylvania bison, numbering nearly four hundred animals of all ages
had taken refuge in the wilds of the Seven Mountains. The
settlements in Middle Creek Valley prevented them from
wintering there as of yore and the persistent slaughter in the
West Branch Valley made it unsafe for them to try to escape to
the north. Hemmed in on all sides, they survived a while by hiding on the highest and most inaccessible mountains, or in the
deepest and darkest ravines. The winter of 1799–1800 was particularly severe, and life on the bleak mountain tops became
unbearable to the starving brutes. They must penetrate into the
valleys, where grass could be dug out from under the snow, or
perish of hunger. Led by a giant coal black bull called "Old
Logan," after the Mingo chieftain of that name, the herd started
in single file one winter's morning for the clear and comfortable
stretches of the Valley of Middle Creek. While passing through
the woods at the edge of a clearing belonging to a young man
named Samuel McClellan, they were attacked by that nimrod,
who killed four fine cows. Previously, while still on the mountain, a count of the herd had been made, and it numbered three
hundred and forty-five animals. Passing from the McClellan
property the herd fell afoul of the barnyard and haystack of
Martin Bergstresser, a settler who had recently arrived from
Berks County. His first season's hay crop, a good-sized pile, stood
beside his recently completed log barn. This hay was needed to
feed for the winter to a number of cows and sheep, and a team of
horses. The cattle and sheep were sidling close to the stack,
when they scented the approaching buffaloes. With "Old
Logan" at their head, the famished bison herd broke through the
stump fence, crushing the helpless domestic animals beneath
their mighty rush, and were soon complacently pulling to pieces
the hay-pile. Bergstresser, who was in a nearby field cutting
wood, heard the commotion, and rushed to the scene. Aided by
his daughter Katie, a girl of eighteen, and Samuel McClellan,
who joined the party, four buffaloes were slain. The deaths of
their comrades and the attacks of the settlers' dogs terrified the
buffaloes and they swept out of the barnyard and up the frozen
bed of the creek. When they were gone, awful was the desolation left behind. The barn was still standing, but the fences,
spring house, and haystack were gone, as if swept away by a

flood. Six cows, four calves, and thirty-five sheep lay crushed and dead among the ruins. The horses which were inside the barn remained unharmed.

McClellan started homeward after the departure of the buffaloes, but when he got within sight of his clearing he uttered a cry of surprise and horror. Three hundred or more bison were snorting and trotting around the lot where his cabin stood, obscuring the structure by their huge dark bodies. The pioneer rushed bravely through the roaring, crazy, surging mass, only to find "Old Logan," his eyes bloodshot and flaming, standing in front of the cabin door. He fired at the monster, wounding him which so further infuriated the giant bull, that he plunged headlong through the door of the cabin. The herd, accustomed at all times to follow their leader, forced their way after him as best they could through the narrow opening. Vainly did McClellan fire his musket, and when the ammunition was exhausted, he drove his bear knife into the beasts' flanks to try and stop them in their mad course. Inside were the pioneer's wife and three little children, the oldest five years, and he dreaded to think of their awful fate. He could not stop the buffaloes, which continued filing through the doorway until they were jammed in the cabin as tightly as wooden animals in a toy Noah's ark. No sound came from the victims inside; all he could hear was the snorting and bumping of the giant beasts in the cramped quarters. The sound of the crazy stampede brought Martin Bergstresser and three other neighbors on the spot, all carrying guns. It was decided to tear down the cabin, as the only possible means of saving the lives of the McClellan family. When the cabin had been battered down, the bison, headed by "Old Logan," swarmed from the ruins like giant black bees from a hive. McClellan had the pleasure of shooting "Old Logan" as he emerged, but it was small satisfaction. When the men entered the cabin, they were shocked to find the bodies of the pioneer's wife and three children dead and crushed deep into the mud of the earthen floor by the cruel hoofs. Of the furniture, nothing remained larger than a handspike. The news of this terrible tragedy spread all over the valley, and it was suggested on all sides that the murderous bison be completely exterminated. The idea took concrete form when Bergstresser and McClellan started on horseback, one riding towards the river and the other towards the headwaters of Middle Creek, to invite the settlers to join the hunt. Meanwhile, there was another blizzard but every man invited accepted with alacrity. About fifty hunters assembled at the Bergstresser home, and marched like an invading army in the direction of the mountains. . . . Many dogs, some partly wolf, accompanied the hunters. They were out two days before discovering their quarry, as the fresh snow had covered all the buffalo paths. The brutes were all huddled together up to their necks in snow in a great hollow space known as the "Sink" formed by Boonestiel's Tongue in the heart of the White Mountains, near the present town of Weikert, Union County, and the hunters looking down on them from the high plateau above, now known as the Big Flats, estimated their number at three hundred. When they got among the animals they found them numb from cold and hunger, but had they been physically able they could not have moved, so deeply were they "crusted" in the drifts. The work of slaughter quickly began. Some used guns, but the most killed them by cutting their throats with long bear knives. The snow was too deep to attempt skinning them, but many tongues were saved, and these the backwoodsmen shoved into the huge pockets of their deerskin coats until they could hold no more. After the last buffalo had been dispatched, the triumphant hunters climbed back to the summit of Council Kup where they lit a huge bonfire which was to be a signal to the women and children in the valleys below that the last herd of Pennsylvania bison was no more, and that the McClellan family had been avenged.[10]

Their bloody act done, as the tale ends, the slayers marched back to town brandishing knives, axes, guns, and gory trophies, lifting their voices joyfully in German hymns. Behind them were more than three hundred dead buffalo propped up in a red slush of snow and ice. A few hunters returned to the killing field months later to salvage the skins, but the freezes and thaws had ruined the hides. The carcasses rotted. Wind and varmints scattered the bones. Folks snatched skulls and horns as souvenirs. The meadow where the massacre took place was called Buffalo Field, said to lie to the east of Troxelville. In spite of several vigorous twentieth-century investigations, however, no evidence validating the famed kill site has ever been discovered.

According to Shoemaker, even after Old Logan and his renegade buffalo band got bogged down in the snow and wiped out, a few strays were still left. No one is sure who killed the stragglers off, but the honor of the thing, it is debated, rests with one of two men. Some argue that panther killer Jacob Weikert shot the last surviving buffalo near Lewistown. But most concede the fame to Colonel John Kelly.

John Kelly must have been quite a man. Shoemaker lauded him, saying that Kelly not only looked like George Washington and was the best dancer in Buffalo Valley, but also "made an ideal pioneer. He never knew such a thing as fatigue or discouragement." But it was not just his manly countenance or his flashy buck-and-wing that made him a man among men and caused women to swoon and lapse into vapors. No. He was a decorated war hero for his valor at the Battle of Princeton.

No painting or sketch of this "mighty buffalo hunter" exists, said Shoemaker, because the colonel's humility did not allow for such ostentation. But it was rumored that an unknown German artist met Kelly and, unable to restrain his understandable excitement at this once-in-a-lifetime chance, sketched the Great One's noble features while he was not looking. The reputed sketch of Kelly, declared by Shoemaker to "be of priceless value," has yet to be found.[11]

Colonel Kelly was a good hand at Indian killing. "He had one hundred 'nicks' on his trusty rifle," bragged Shoemaker, "indicating the number of red men whom he made 'bite the dust.'" After the Revolutionary War, Kelly, the slayer of redcoats and red men, went home to Union County, Pennsylvania, where he turned his talents and his trusty rifle from hunting Indians to hunting big game. Soon he shot more than one hundred buffalo. His fame spread. But his greatest day was still a few years off.

It was in the fall of 1800, after a freshly fallen snow, that a neighbor of Kelly's, Michael McClister, was out wolf hunting and spied three buffalo—a bull, a cow, and a calf—which, according to the tale, were the sole remnants of the Pennsylvania herds. McClister raised his gun and fired. The calf fell. The bull and cow bolted off as McClister rammed home another ball.

Word leaked out. On January 19, 1801, at the junction of two dirt roads, Colonel John Kelly, tall in the saddle on his old charger Brandywine, which had served him during his war years, and armed with his trusty rifle with its one hundred nicks, shot the "mammoth buffalo bull which completely blocked the narrow cross-road." (No one is sure of the fate of the cow.) He hacked off the head and nailed it to a pine to stink and glare at startled travelers. To mark this proud day, admirers dubbed the hallowed ground Buffalo Crossroads. In 1820 high winds toppled the pine, so a family member yanked the skull off the tree and took it home. Years later, a housekeeper got tired of dusting around the legendary trophy and burned it in a trash heap.

There is no evidence for any of this windy lore. And Buffalo Crossroads received its name before the 1801 incident: In 1773 at the site, townspeople established "The Buffalo Cross Roads Church."[12]

Colonel Kelly died on February 19, 1832, at a venerable fourscore and eight. The family erected an obelisk on his grave at New Cemetery, in Lewisburg, Pennsylvania. Kelly's plot became "a favorite shrine for lovers of history and sport, and for years it was pointed out to visitors."[13]

Were there ever American buffalo in Pennsylvania? The historical record neither proves nor disproves the notion. Most of such "fake-lore" begins with Thomas Ashe and ends with Henry W. Shoemaker. But other accounts of buffalo in Pennsylvania do exist.

Gabriel Thomas lived in William Penn's colony for fifteen years. In 1698, at Penn's behest, Thomas wrote a tract to encourage English emigration to America and settlement in Pennsylvania, titled *An Historical and Geographical Account of the Province and Country of Pennsylvania; and of West-New-Jersey in America,* and dedicated to Governor Penn as a guarantee of its veracity: "Thou wilt find here a true and genuine description of that (once) obscure, tho' (now) glorious place." In the bountiful paradise of Penn's woods, Thomas wrote, he had seen myriad fish and fowl, and "vast numbers of other wild creatures, as elks, buffaloes, and etc."

Thomas assured readers his words were not "fiction, flam, whim, or any sinister design" meant to fool the guileless or curry favor with the king. Moreover, he affirmed, "I was an eyewitness to it all." If one takes Thomas at his word, he must have seen buffalo in southwestern Pennsylvania, though he did not specify the "vast numbers" or say where he saw them.[14]

More clues: A ledger entry of Thomas Penn dated October 16, 1733, noted that Penn paid William Linvil £15 "for a bull buffalo" but made no mention of where the bull came from. Delaware Indians kidnapped Hugh Gibson, and he lived in Pennsylvania as a captive from 1756 to 1759. In his memoirs, given in 1826, he recalled a warrior named Buffalo Horn. Pittsburgh trader James Kenny logged in his journal entry of July 18, 1761, "Came an Indian call'd John and another young fellow who had a pair of little buffalo horns fixed to his cap." All three references are credible, but none of them, as noted in 1969 by one historian, "establishes the presence of buffaloes in Pennsylvania."[15]

An unnamed British officer during General Edward Braddock's doomed campaign against Fort Duquesne recorded on July 3, 1755, "Lick Creek. . . . takes its Name from a lick being there, where Deer, Buffaloes & Bears come to lick ye Salt out of ye Swamp."[16] "Lick Creek" is thought to have been slightly southeast of present-day Uniontown. The soldier himself did not see buffalo; sources told him about them and he wrote what he heard. Nor does the soldier mention eating buffalo; his company ate "three quarters of a pound of flour and half a pound of bacon each day per man," supplemented with venison, bear meat, and timber rattlesnakes.[17]

In November 1758 Captain Harry Gordon, a British Army engineer, neared the site of Braddock's Defeat and sent his scouts into the brush to hunt. He reported that game was "exceeding plenty of all kinds hereabouts, consisting of buffaloes, elks, deer—bear, and innumerable quantity of wild turkeys." He did not record how many buffalo his men saw. Gordon noted that he and his men ate mostly turkeys: "We were so satiated that the hunters would kill no more." In 1763 near Fort Cumberland, a band of English woods runners led by Captain Luke Collins tracked some warriors to the Cheat River, a branch of the Monongahela, and attacked them while "they were barbecuing a buffalo."[18]

And so it goes. Recorded sightings of Pennsylvania buffalo are few. The evidence seems to be against large numbers of buffalo in Pennsylvania; most travelers, traders, and explorers did not mention seeing wild cows, or note their absence. George Croghan, George Morgan, and Moravian missionaries David Zeisberger and John Heckewelder saw buffalo along the Ohio and its branches, but rarely in Pennsylvania. In 1749, Captain Pierre Joseph de Celeron de Bienville's expedition hunted near Pittsburgh, but only after his party made it to the Great Kanawha did they "begin to see the Illinois cattle." Celeron's hunters had to pursue the beasts far into the woods as "they were in such small numbers that our men could hardly kill a score of them."[19]

Two of the first writers to offer supposed proof of buffalo in southern and southwestern Pennsylvania were Dr. James A. Allen and Samuel N. Rhoads. Unfortunately, both men uncritically accepted Ashe's lore. Allen's accurate (for its day) treatise on Pennsylvania mammals becomes flawed concerning buffalo; indeed, his "Memoir on the American Bison" (1876) is little more than an academic rewrite of Ashe's *Travels in America.*

In 1903 Rhoads asserted in *The Mammals of Pennsylvania and New Jersey* that Allen's buffalo essays were "the best data on this subject."

Rhoads listed twenty Pennsylvania counties in which people found what were touted to be buffalo remains, but these claims do not bear scrutiny. A listing of representative examples as cited by Rhoads will suffice.

> Cumberland County: In the Patent Office Records of 1851, a Prof. Baird recorded finding bones of bison in caves near Carlisle, but on inquiry from Dr. J. A. Rhoads, Baird stated he could not be sure whether they were of *B. bison* without reexamination.
> Luzerne County: The first and third lower molars of a bison mounted together on a card are in the collection of the Academy of Natural Sciences in Philadelphia. These were labeled by Dr. J. Leidy as coming "with the fossil teeth [of horse, musk ox, and other animals] from [Pittston] Luzerne Co. . . . I have compared these with teeth of recent bison and find them specifically identical."
> Mercer County: A bison horn was found in this county in 1795, according to B. S. Stokley in Memoirs of the Historical Society of Pennsylvania, vol. 4, p. 77.
> Mercer County: A scapula and pelvis of a recent bison (so identified by Prof. E. D. Cope) were discovered in Indian refuse heaps near Trenton. They are now in the Peabody Archaeological Museum, Cambridge, Massachusetts (Abbott, 1900).

None of these bits of bone, horn, and teeth are now accepted as being from *B. bison*. Most are thought to be from *B. latifrons, B. antiquus,* or domestic cows. Even Rhoads remained skeptical of the existence of the Pennsylvania buffalo.

> Regarding the question of the existence of *B. bison* in the valleys of eastern Pennsylvania since the advent of the white man in America, it is probable that it had been effectively driven from the Delaware Valley long before that date. Indeed, from the scarcity of its remains and the absence of reliable tradition of its presence in this locality, it is unlikely that this species was ever more than a straggler in the regions east of the Susquehanna River drainage.[20]

Recent scholarship agrees with Rhoads's conclusion. In 1963, after a careful examination of the evidence, Carnegie Museum archaeologist John E. Guilday said he believed the relics to be "an intrusion of cattle bones" into an "aboriginal context." Unearthing buffalo bones in south-western Pennsylvania, he noted, "would be a distinct anomaly."[21] Thus there is neither historical nor archaeological proof that "vast herds" of buffalo were in Pennsylvania, and the negative evidence against their existence cannot be ignored.

Still, believers in the Pennsylvania buffalo tales look to Fort Le Boeuf, erected in 1753 just south of the eastern edge of Lake Erie, on the headwaters of French Creek. Fort Le Boeuf—along with Forts Presque Isle, Venango, and Duquesne—was one link in a long defensive chain of frontier outposts that Governor Duquesne of New France had ordered built to keep the English out of the Ohio Valley. In 1763 Great Lake Indians torched Fort Le Boeuf (and eight other forts seized by the victorious British) during Pontiac's Rebellion. Writers have theorized that the name Le Boeuf, which means "the ox," proves that wild oxen grazed in the vicinity.

Europeans in North America often named forts, streams, towns, and landmarks for famous people or martyrs. Church fathers named Sault au Recollect, flowing near Montreal, for Nicholas Viel, a Recollect priest whom Indians killed on that spot. Marquette, Michigan, was named for Père Jacques Marquette, a Jesuit Missionary and explorer. It is probable that Fort Le Boeuf (also called Aux Boeufs or Breboeuf) is a title in memory of Father Jean de Breboeuf (also spelled Brebeuf or Boeuf), a Renaissance holy man worthy of his calling. As a missionary to the Petun-Huron, he had established missions among the Great Lake Indians by the 1620s. Breboeuf worked hard to convert his native kinsmen, modestly commenting on the irony of his last name: He was, he declared, an ox for the cause of Christ fit to bear burdens. In March 1649 Iroquois warriors captured him at Saint-Ignace, on the straits of Michilimackinac. His captors did not heed the Gospel call, and on March 16 hideously tortured Breboeuf to death, hacked up the corpse, and boiled and ate it.

"Thus died Jean de Brebeuf," eulogized historian Frances Parkman, "the founder of the Huron mission, its truest hero, and its greatest martyr." Adding a macabre twist to an already gruesome story, a disciple fished Brebeuf's skull out of the kettle of human broth and a Quebec nunnery housed the skull until the late 1800s. In 1880 Dr. William Egle, author of *An Illustrated History of the Commonwealth of Pennsylvania, Civil, Political, and Military from Its Earliest Settlement to the Present Time,* wrote:

> Very early in the seventeenth century, we find the Neutrie [Neutral] Nation of the Eries spoken of by the French Priests,

and we know that Jean Brebeuf and Joseph Marie Chaumont were on the south side of Lake Erie.

Thus Frenchmen named the fort they built on eastern Lake Erie Le Boeuf to honor the Jesuit martyr Father Jean de Brebeuf, not to commemorate buffalo.[22]

Examples of buffalo-related ceremonies are absent from contemporaneous observations of rituals performed by the Shawnee and Delaware living in the region prior to their migration to Ohio after white intrusion. Nor has documented proof (or, for that matter, native oral traditions) yet surfaced of Indians in Pennsylvania hunting buffalo or trading robes or wild beef. Had buffalo frequented Pennsylvania, the animals would have played a role in native culture and economy.

Some writers contend that the rugged Alleghenies would have prevented buffalo from wandering into the Pennsylvania interior. "Beyond the Allegheny Front, which marks the western boundary of the mountains proper," says Pittsburgh historian E. H. Buck, "lie miles of rugged plateau with two additional ridges thrust up through it in southern Pennsylvania."[23] Even if they were able to cross the mountains, it is doubtful that herds of wild cows would have found sufficient graze.

A last point to ponder is the possibility of misidentification of the animals by early explorers or misinterpretation of documents by scholars. French hunters, as noted, gave the buffalo a variety of names and at times used the same terms to describe elk, moose, and musk oxen. Thus, terms like *boeuf* or even *vaches sauvages* ("wild cattle") may not be trusted to consistently mean "buffalo."

Writing on September 2, 1654, near Onondaga, New York, Father Simon Le Moine observed that "while proceeding across vast prairies, we see in different places large herds of wild cattle; their horns resemble in many respects the antlers of a stag." Father Claude Dablon logged a similar entry on September 15, 1655, in his relation written from the Onondaga prairies. Dablon and Father Joseph Chaumont came across a rotting animal carcass and, in their famished state, ate it. Dablon's description of this beast that "smelled very badly," is curious: "We devoured a wild cow, or species of hind,—these animals having horns like the stag's, and not like those of our European bull." In these instances of "wild cattle" or "wild cow," both Jesuit writers call them *vaches sauvages*. But it is plain these animals are not buffalo, but deer, elk, or caribou.[24]

However many buffalo may have been in the Alleghenies, by the mid-1700s their days were numbered. Other Pennsylvania fauna had vanished; more species soon would. Moose, elk, otters, fishers, parquets, pileated woodpeckers, panthers, wild pigeons, wolves—all suffered the same fate. Any buffalo that did graze the fields on the western borders of the Keystone state would have been killed off early.

Captain Daniel Brodhead, the commander at Fort Pitt, wrote to George Washington on December 7, 1780, about the vexing task of keeping his men fed. "I am so well convinced," Brodhead observed, "that the inhabitants on this side of the mountains cannot furnish half enough meat to supply the troops, that I have risked the sending of a party of hunters to kill buffalo at Little Kanawha." As historian Gail M. Gibson asserts, it is likely that "by 1780 . . . whatever buffalo had been in Pennsylvania had disappeared."[25]

Scouring of the First Far West

THE FRONTIER WAS IN SWIFT TRANSITION. LANDS WEST OF THE APPALA-chians swelled with settlers.

By 1785 the white population was growing north and south of Detroit and down the Ohio River. A string of French hamlets, with pastures, orchards, and windmills, lined the banks of Lake St. Clair, extending southward to the western end of Lake Erie. Kentucky's Bluegrass was filling in with immigrants. In Tennessee in the early 1780s, forts like Nashborough, Asher's, Union, Bledsoe's, Stone's River, Mansker's, Buchanan's, Freeland's, Eaton's, and Kilgore's gave refuge from raids.[1] In 1784 some of George Rogers Clark's men founded Clarksville, Indiana.[2]

The end of the war unleashed an armada of rafts, dugouts, canoes, bateaux, keelboats, and flatboats down the Ohio, many supplied like floating stores, and the murky river often ran red with blood. A flotsam of ransacked, half-sunk wrecks dotted the channel, creating barriers and snags; a jetsam of goods from the Monongahela littered the banks. Lock-jawed skulls stuck on stakes screamed silent howls of death at passersby. Indians used captives to cry for help as they hid, hoping crews would take the bait and pole their boats to shore. James Girty was a master of such tactics.

But dangers notwithstanding, Limestone became a key port of entry into the new West. "More than 12,000," Yale historian and author John Mack Faragher writes, "landed in Limestone from 1786 to 1788 alone."[3] The Ohio was a quicker route to the West than the traces blazed by Boone. Lexington too was a brisk, bustling town with surveyors and chain crews ready for hire to lead homesteaders to the best land.

Yet despite the Peace of Paris treaty in 1783, the British at Detroit fueled native hatred toward Americans. "Ye Indians was continually amongst us," wrote Isaac Ruddell from Limestone in 1785. "There is scarcely a day but they are seen in one part of our neighborhood or another."[4] Horses were whisked away, livestock slaughtered, slaves kidnaped; whites mysteriously vanished, and often Kentuckians forted up to wait out gathering storms of intrigue.

The last hour of Middle Ground Indians was nigh. Guns, powder and ball, tomahawks, scalping knives, rum, black and red war paint flowed in abundance, sparking a vicious era of hit-and-run raids. But the War of 1812 ended the British threat, and the defeat of Tecumseh on October 5, 1813, at the Battle of the Thames broke the might of the Woodland Indians forever.[5]

The land was being radically altered. Every April or May, settlers fired the winter-killed grass. From south of the Cumberland to beyond the Bluegrass, acrid smoke clouds rose as canebrakes and barrens torched into bonfires burned long and lit up the night, turning forage into blackened landscapes of soot and cinders that could be broken with iron plowshares.

Lashing flames from Kentucky's burning barrens in 1802 caused André Michaux to write that unless one had seen the "dreadful conflagrations," it was impossible to imagine such an inferno. Walls of fire raged for miles, pushed by gusts that stoked the blaze into such a fury that some "inhabitants, even on horseback, have become a prey to them."[6] In 1803 a traveler near Laurel Hill in Bedford County, Pennsylvania, watched from a pinnacle as ridges glowed for fifty miles. One man walking the shores of the Ohio said smoke was so dense that for an entire day he did not see the far bank. Gazing upon the Little Prairie of Illinois in 1821, William Hall called the wildfire "a most sublime spectacle." At dusk smoke obscured the horizon; the searing yellow-orange glare moved in a jagged line two or three miles long, "ranging towards you with increased fury, roaring, crackling, and thundering up the slope."[7] John Ross of Montgomery County, Tennessee, saw thirty-foot trees burst into flames: "No one who ever witnessed one of these great fires would ever afterward be at a loss to account for the scarcity of timber in the barrens, as trees of all kinds, when small, were destroyed by them."[8] In November 1818 William Faux spent the night near Vincennes, where men set fires to drive game into a clearing for a mob kill. Said Faux, "The prairie and forests were both enveloped in a wide-spreading, sky-reddening blaze, which the hunters had kindled."[9]

Indiana, Illinois, Kentucky, Tennessee, West Virginia, Pennsylvania, central Ohio, Georgia, Alabama, Mississippi, and Louisiana felt the flame's effect, clearing the way for the new agrarianism. Such a civilization,

Daniel Boone once complained to Peter Houston, "soured" him.[10] Yet Boone and the Long Hunters had helped bring about such change by killing off game herds and opening the new West to settlers lured into the once-teeming land. "This, we may note," states Francis Jennings in reference to the Middle Ground, "was the heritage of Daniel Boone, brought across the Ohio River from Kentucky."[11]

Indians fired their hunting grounds annually as their forebears had done. By 1805 farmers demanded that Indians cease torching the grass and cane, as it was igniting their farmlands. Indians, in turn, protested this intrusion on their way of life. One Algonquin argued that if they could not fire the grass to make pastures for the deer, elk, and buffalo, they could not live.[12]

Changes in native hunting sparked a rapid demise in game. Spurred by liquor and the ending of British aid that had once provided them with supplies, Indians turned with reckless zeal to the fur trade. One factor underlying the killing may have been the corrosive effect of the Church upon nativist culture and cosmology, especially its denunciation of shamanism. "The Indian lost faith in the traditional avenues of spiritual redress," theorizes historian Calvin Martin. Indians had succumbed to white religion, disease, and vice. No longer could they talk with animal spirit helpers—the Keepers of the Game. Cut off from game spirits, Indians ignored their own taboo and slaughtered animals, big and small, with no remorse. The hunt, once sacred, became profane.[13]

The Delaware were said to be "the earliest and most ruthless market-hunters." Said Moravian missionary David Ziesberger, "Deer are killed mainly for their hides . . . the meat is left in the woods. . . . Game must decrease." In 1787 the Miami refused to let the Delaware hunt on their land. So did the Ojibwa. "Delaware methods," notes Richard White, "had become widespread after the turn of the century."[14] By then, other groups were guilty of the same wantonness.

Native visionaries like Neolin the Delaware, the Ottawa holy man Trout, and the Shawnee brothers Tecumseh and Tenskwatawa saw the coming crisis and condemned the slaughter, calling for a rejection of white culture and a return to traditional paths.[15] Older nativist cults gained adherents as they invoked the Manitous. The secrecy shrouding the Midewiwin ceremonies of the Great Lakes is legendary, yet in 1804, Indians granted British officer Edward Walsh the rare privilege of witnessing a Midewiwin ritual. Walsh's description of the robe worn by the Miami shaman presiding over the rite indicates buffalo played a central role in the ceremony.

A white line divided the features into two equal parts—the right side was painted red with vermillion—the left black. His conjuring cap—which he afterward presented to me—was made of the shaggy skin of a buffalo's forehead with the ears and horns on. A Buffalo Robe hung on his broad shoulders the inside of which was worked in figures of sun, moon, stars and other Hieroglyphics.[16]

The painted and quilled robe validated the Midewiwin shaman's powers and served as a powerful metaphor to invoke the image and spirit of the rapidly disappearing animal.

From the Great Lakes to the Southeast, nativist revivalism and pan-Indianism erupted into a spirited resistance against Americans. But the prophetic native voices went unheeded, or tribal dissent thwarted their words, or vice, avarice, and defeat dulled and deafened ears that had once sought counsel.[17]

What immediate effect increased native hide hunting had on buffalo is not known; traders kept tallies of deer skins and peltry, not of buffalo or robes. Indian and white hunters averaged 150 deer every fall; every spring settlers and Indians torched the range. Loss of habitat, radical changes in Indian hunting, and the intrusion of white hunters, settlers, and farmers caused a rapid decline in game throughout the Mississippi Valley.

John Heckewelder (1743–1823) was a Moravian missionary who evangelized western Pennsylvania. Though he observed buffalo in Pennsylvania and Ohio, he never saw anything like the "vast herds" written about by Thomas Ashe and Henry W. Shoemaker years later.[18] He floated down the Ohio and rode along traces in Ohio and Indiana, reckoning that between 1762 and 1813 he crossed the Alleghenies thirty times and logged over thirty thousand miles. In 1792 he went to Vincennes and saw buffalo in Ohio, Indiana, West Virginia, and Kentucky, but the herds never numbered more than twenty head.

Along the Big Sandy dividing West Virginia and Kentucky, Heckewelder marveled at the wide traces. As his flotilla passed the Falls of the Ohio on August 19, he counted six droves shading themselves under the poplars along the banks. One typical herd was made up of "sixteen buffaloes and three calves." He "saw almost continually herds of buffaloes grazing along the banks," he wrote August 30.[19] Hunters sold wild beef for two pence a pound.

September 2: We overtook some people from Louisville with 4 buffaloes in their boat.

October 18: At the 18 Mile Island we met Kentucky hunters who had 2 large canoes loaded with buffalo meat, bear meat, and venison.[20]

On October 9 Heckewelder arrived at "the so-called Buffalo Salt Lick"—French Lick, Indiana—where "people say that 500 buffalo may be sometimes seen at one time." He doubted it. He saw only "many buffalo sculls & the skeletons of these animals which had been shot."

After trying a viscous glop of raw buffalo intestines—"I saw at once it was not for my stomach"—he rode for Vincennes and headed up a trace. Five miles later, several buffalo charged the party. His guides shot one and wounded one or two others to turn the beasts.[21] On his return trip to Pittsburgh, Heckewelder's last buffalo sighting was near Gallipolis, Ohio, on December 10, 1792: "One of the scouts here shot 8 buffaloes in this vicinity. He made about 80 dollars out of it."[22]

Heckewelder's memoirs show that in 1792 herds were getting smaller. And that wild beef was in demand, though cattle, hogs, goats, and chickens were abundant in settlements, signaled the death knell of the buffalo east of the Mississippi.

Much had changed in Kentucky by 1792, the year the Commonwealth became the fifteenth state of the new republic, the United States of America. Leadership shifted from frontiersmen like John Bowman, Daniel Boone, Simon Kenton, and George Rogers Clark to the more sophisticated and urbane, like George Nicholas, John Brown, and others.[23]

Kentucky's population soared. Americans poured into the West via the Wilderness Road, which Boone had blazed in 1775 and Kentuckians recleared and widened twenty years later. The official opening of the road—originally part trace, part Indian path, and now a wagon route—was announced October 15, 1796, in John Bradford's *Kentucky Gazette:* "The Wilderness Road from Cumberland Gap to the settlements in Kentucky is now completed. Wagons loaded with a ton weight may now pass with ease, with four good horses."[24] In 1790 Kentucky's population was 73,677, of which 61,133 were white, 12,430 were slaves, and 114 were free blacks. Ten years later, the number had risen to 220,955, of which 40,343 were slaves.[25]

Christopher Mann's father visited Boone in 1785 at Brushy Fork and watched him sit in his cabin and shoot a buffalo from out of his front

door. Mann said the herds had eaten a ditch four feet deep in the salty
earth around Boone's home.[26] William Sudduth shot a few buffalo near
Mount Sterling in March 1788 but said the beasts now had a hard time of
it and Indians were reduced to "chewing the green cornstalks which had
come up volunteer" around forts. In April 1786 near Strode's Station,
Sudduth spotted warriors making moccasins from a fresh buffalo hide.
One was shot; the others got away.[27]

In December 1790 Ben Allen went on his first buffalo hunt in Clark
County. Allen, his brother, and his father rendezvoused with other
hunters, and as the darkness came on and the fire burned low, Frank
Wyatt talked of the old days, of "big tales about killing buffalo." Allen
barely slept because of such talk.[28]

The next day Allen and his brother were captured by Shawnee. The
warriors were in good humor, so what could have been a brush with
death for the boys became high adventure. During his captivity, Ben saw
two herds of buffalo, one of which he counted at forty head. He was fed
on fat wild beef cut up and boiled with jerk and thickened cornmeal and
"thought it was elegant."

One Shawnee took Ben, dressed him in a red calico hunting shirt,
tied a blanket around him with a tug, and nicknamed him "Indian." This
same fellow, Um, shot a buffalo and pranced about the campfire,
chortling "Um kill buffalo," making everyone laugh. Ben watched his
captors slice silver-dollar-size hanks of hair and flesh off buffalo humps to
stretch and dry on six-inch willow frames. "It was my idea," Allen said,
"they meant to sell those scalps of the buffalo to the British for human
scalps." Weeks later rescuers shot Um and his band dead.

Daniel Boone sold pickled wild beef for three dollars a pound in 1794,
but at the headwaters of the Monongahela the price tripled because of
the dwindling supply.[29] Jesse Graddy, who settled on Glenn's Creek in
Woodford County and who used to go to Mann's Lick and Big Bone
Lick for salt, said that by 1787 "the buffalo were gone. Never saw a wild
one."[30] A man named Stites, who hunted the Licking, told John Shane
that in 1789 he saw only one poor bull.[31] At William Scholl's Station,
which later became Schollsville and was located near the headwaters of
Stoner Creek, reports were as dismal. John Hedges recalled that when he
came to Kentucky in 1791, the ground about Scholl's settlement was
covered with buffalo bones. "It was said that men used to come down
from Strode's Station . . . when the buffalo were poor, and kill them for
sport and leave them be."[32]

John Johnston (1775–1861) provided General Anthony Wayne's

army with supplies in the campaigns of 1793. From 1798 to 1812 he was a factor at Fort Wayne, and from 1812 to 1829 he was an Indian agent at Upper Piqua, Ohio. Johnston was a friend of Tecumseh's and a prolific recorder of native customs.[33] He wrote oral traditions passed down by the Shawnee, who knew early on that land and game were drawing whites westward. Johnston "was in Kentucky in the beginning of 1793. . . . The buffalo were nearly all destroyed." That year the last buffalo in Spencer County was killed.[34]

Francis Baily (1775–1844) voyaged to the United States in February 1796 and spent eighteen months on a grand tour. He flatboated down the Ohio to the Mississippi to New Orleans, then traveled the Natchez Trace. Baily saw traces and licks and met Daniel Boone. What is striking in his diary is that although he toured Kentucky, the Cumberland, and the old Southwest, he did not mention seeing even one buffalo.[35]

In 1773, two miles south of Midway, Hancock Taylor built a cabin and chinked it with mud mixed with buffalo hair. The site was at the crossroads of two lead traces—trails that became U.S. 62 and the Old Frankfort Pike. Indians killed Hancock in July 1774; Willis Lee, his cousin and a surveyor, inherited the place, but Indians killed him too, and it was to his memory that the settlement that grew up around the log house became known as Leestown. In 1802 Horatio Offutt refurbished the cabin and called it the Offutt Inn. John Kennedy and William Dailey rented it in 1804, and the Offutt Inn became the first stagecoach stop west of the Alleghenies. In 1812 the inn changed hands and was renamed Cole's Black Horse Tavern. The new owner was Richard Cole, Jr., whose granddaughter, Zerelda Cole James, was born there and became the mother of Frank and Jesse James. For travelers between Lexington and Frankfort, the inn's menu boasted of strong drink, berry pies, johnnycakes, venison, turkey, and buffalo steaks. The *Kentucky Gazette,* which carried advertisements for Cole's Tavern, does not list the cost of a buffalo steak, but by 1812 the price must have been high, as the buffalo were nearly killed out.[36]

André Michaux, who toured Kentucky and Tennessee in 1802, observed that the buffalo were nearly gone: "They did not fear the approach of the huntsmen, who sometimes shot them solely for the sake of having their tongue . . . there are scarcely any from Ohio to the river Illinois."[37] His observations were borne out by Fortescue Cumings, who traveled in the West from 1807 to 1809. On July 21, 1809, Cumings breakfasted at the tavern of Captain John Waller in Millersburg, in Nicholas County, Kentucky. Waller came to Limestone (present day Maysville) in 1775 with

Simon Kenton. As Cumings ate and asked about farmland, Waller explained that most of the farming had been begun within the past fifteen
years. Even after settlement, he said, people lived on game "until the poor
innocent buffaloes were completely extirpated."

> Those harmless and unsuspecting animals, used to stand gazing
> with apparent curiosity at their destroyer, until he was some-
> times within twenty yards of them, when he made it a rule to
> select the leader, which was always an old and fat female. If one
> of the common herd was the first victim of the rifle, the rest
> would immediately fly.[38]

The land was once covered in cane, he said, but now that was gone
too, devoured by plows, cattle, and fire.

At Wheeling in 1820 William Faux bought a buffalo robe for five
dollars. Faux knew he was buying a relic of the past. "When Kentucky
was first settled," he wrote, "buffaloes were shot by the settlers merely for
their tongues; the carcass and skin being thought worth nothing, were
left to rot where the animal fell."[39] When Faux bought his robe, buffalo
hides were being imported from west of the Mississippi. That same year
the last sighting of free-roaming buffalo in Kentucky was reported—
a small herd in Hart County seen near the Green River.[40]

In Tennessee, the tale of slaughter and despoliation is the same,
although the towns and counties that sprang up along its rivers, like
Cumberland, Duck, Tennessee, Watauga, Holston, Buffalo, and Harpeth,
as well as some of the hunters, are different.

One of the best-known travels through Tennessee was that by
Colonel John Donelson. Donelson's boat, the *Adventure,* headed a flotilla
of more than thirty vessels that "by God's permission" embarked from
Fort Patrick Henry on the Holston on December 22, 1779, to begin
their voyage down the Tennessee and up the Cumberland.[41] Donelson,
along with James Robertson, was in league with Richard Henderson,
whose Transylvania claim in Kentucky had been declared void by the
Virginia House of Delegates on November 4, 1778. Henderson, his
stockholders, Donelson, and Robertson hoped to establish a colony on
the Cumberland on the southernmost borders of Henderson's land. But
North Carolina voided Henderson's Tennessee claims in 1782, ending
forever his feudal schemes.[42]

Buffalo were not seen much on the first part of Donelson's trip. But wild beef kept the folks alive when supplies ran low. Donelson's journal from March 1780 mentions buffalo:

Sunday, 26th. Got under way early; procured some buffalo meat: though poor, it was palatable.
Tuesday, 28th. Set out very early this morning; killed some buffalo.
Thursday, 30th. Proceeded on our voyage. This day we killed some more buffalo.
Friday, 31st. We are now without bread and are compelled to hunt the buffalo to preserve life.[43]

The land around Nashville, he observed, was rutted with licks and buffalo paths. Cane towered in thickets jabbed in between traces.[44]

Donelson's voyage was a disaster: A slave froze to death, a baby died of exposure, smallpox ravaged some, Indians attacked, boats capsized, people went hungry. The trip ended on April 24, 1780, at Eaton's Station, in Sullivan County. On land owned by Michael Stoner, a signer of Henderson's Cumberland Compact, Donelson's party erected shelters, kindled fires, hung and salted meat, and dug furrows to plant corn. Donelson did not see the large herds observed by Mansker and the Long Hunters a decade earlier.

Thomas Spencer wintered in a sycamore at Bledsoe's Lick during the Hard Winter of 1780 and shot buffalo when he felt hungry.[45] That January, between the confluence of Obey's River and Big South Fork, Daniel Smith shot six buffalo. As Smith sat among the six carcasses, he noted the night was "clear and very cold." Smith felt the bite of the worst winter settlers in Tennessee and Kentucky ever endured. The Cumberland froze over, allowing James Robertson's party to cross on foot to establish Fort Nashborough.

The winter of 1782 twenty hunters from Eaton's Station paddled up the Cumberland to Caney Fork and Flynn's Lick Creek (roughly the area spanning Smith, Putnam, and Jackson Counties). They killed 175 bear, 100 deer, and 75 buffalo.[46]

In 1784 Major William Croghan kept a journal of a trip he made from Louisville to Nashville.

Monday, November 15th: Bogart went out hunting. . . . They killed a buffalo, part of which they carry with them.

Tuesday, 16th: Cut up and smoke the buffalo meat and render the tallow; about 16 pounds.

Wednesday, December 14th: About 12 miles from the mouth of Little River in the open Barrens killed 2 buffalo bulls. Made fire and stayed by them and eat hearty of them and the marrow bones all night.

Thursday, December 15th: Killed a buffalo and stayed all night.[47]

In 1784 John Lipscomb and his merry gang (who, according to Lipscomb's journal, did little else than ride through the countryside blasting away at wildlife, getting drunk, and frolicking with tavern girls) rode from Nashville up to the Little Barren River. At a salt lick on the Little Barren two of the men slipped off their horses and crept along to gun down whatever might be there, but they found the lick desolate and saw only bleached buffalo bones piled high—"there had been a great slaughter made amongst the Bufflelow." The men spied two bulls tailed by a wolf and, after holding "a Council of war," the men shot one bull and took the hump, a thigh, and the tongue. Near the Red River, in Sumner County, Tennessee, they chased a small drove and, being out of bullets, "shot wood slivers at them" but did not bring one down.[48]

Donelson's trip down the Cumberland, the establishment of Fort Nashborough, and Henderson's Cumberland Compact mark the beginning of American settlement in middle Tennessee. Indians shot Donelson in 1786. Robertson, a veteran of Lord Dunmore's War, fended off raids and pushed for settlement. He said that 1781 and 1782 were Tennessee's worst years for attacks; this was about the same time that William Calk rode along the Holston and saw that game was getting scarce.

Desperate, Indians took up the hatchet. In a burst of pan-Indian action, warriors stormed Buchanan's Station in September 1792. Tennesseans barely beat back four hundred to five hundred Chickamaugas and Cherokee, two hundred Creeks, and a score of Shawnee. Fort defenders shot fifteen Indians dead and wounded John Ross, leading man among the Cherokee. After the Coldwater campaign of 1787 and the Nickojack wars of 1794, the Indians' cause was irrevocably damaged; fighting stopped and dispossession followed. Woodsmen built new stations—Rain's, Pittman's, Ziegler's, and others—along traces to link Tennessee to the east.[49]

Statehood came in 1796. Names of the landed aristocracy, Overton, Polk, White, Sevier, and of course, Jackson, emerged. By 1797 horses pulled fancy carriages made in Philadelphia along streets in middle

Tennessee towns. In Sumner County in 1798, west of Gallatin, General James Winchester built the grandest home in the south, Cragfont. Cragfont was more than just a mansion—it was a symbol of the rising new South.[50]

In 1787 Sumner County merchants sold wild beef for three pence per pound; soon the price rose to six pence. In Montgomery County, John Dier contracted on October 4, 1793, to deliver "35 hundredweight of buffalo beef to John Edmundson at $2 a hundred." No one recorded how many hundred pounds Dier and his teamsters hauled in, but it is doubtful that they reached the quota; by 1793 herds in Tennessee had dramatically thinned.[51]

Joseph Bishop, who once hired himself out "slaying bears and buffaloes" and who was one of Tennessee's last meat hunters, does not mention killing buffalo in the Cumberland in 1791. In 1793 he and a hunter rode to Vincennes to hunt. After weeks of scouring the licks blanketing southern Indiana, the men shot fewer than ten buffalo.[52] Poor hunting forced them to try near Clarksville, Tennessee. There Bishop saw French and Spanish traders swapping beads, blankets, trinkets, and rum with the Indians for peltry, deer skins, and bear oil, but he saw no robes, tongues, or marrow bones traded. Disgusted, he rode back to middle Tennessee to plant corn. Bishop, like the beasts he hunted, was one of the last remnants of a vanishing breed east of the Mississippi.

Hugh Bell and John Montgomery hunted near Clarksville in 1793 but found no buffalo and got home "not a little emaciated." Montgomery tried again. Indians killed him on November 27, 1794, near Eddyville, Kentucky.[53] "Herds of buffalo," wrote Lewis Brantz near Nashville, "have been considerably hunted by the woodsmen and are diminished in number."[54] In the same region, André Michaux saw a few buffalo in June 1795. In December 1799 Abraham Steiner and Christian Frederic de Schweintz saw buffalo in Putnam County, though by then they "were rarely killed by hunters, as they are shy and fleet."[55]

Tradition says that John Young killed the last buffalo in Fentress County, but no one is sure when. "At this time," wrote historian John Haywood in 1823, "there is not one in the whole state of Tennessee."[56]

Lush prairies and dark, loamy soil caused settlers of the Illinois country to look upon its land as a paradise. Recorded buffalo sightings are few, but those that have been preserved show that Illinois was home to thousands of wild cattle.

Eighteenth-century Catholic fathers cite firsthand contacts with buffalo before settlement. In Illinois, as on the prairies of Wisconsin and Iowa, the French market hunters who shipped meat to New Orleans led in the early depletion of the herds. In 1763 an explorer of the upper Illinois and Mississippi named Hamburgh (his first name is lost to antiquity) saw buffalo from the Chicago River southward, the year Lieutenant Philip Pittman observed them in Kaskaskia. George Croghan saw "plenty" in 1765. "The herds were extraordinarily large and frequent to be seen," wrote Harry Gordon at the mouth of the Wabash, July 31, 1766. George Morgan slaughtered the herds from 1767 to 1769 for the tongue and tallow trade. George Rogers Clark and his army raged through southern Illinois to Vincennes in 1779 and lived on buffalo killed along the Wabash.[57]

In 1795 André Michaux saw buffalo near Fort Massac but did not say how many.[58] The last buffalo in Illinois reportedly was killed in 1808. In 1814 historian Henry M. Brackenridge wrote that the buffalo in Illinois were gone.[59]

There are few references to buffalo in Indiana. Certainly there were once thousands there. Their paths to and from the licks could be seen for years after their demise, and parts of Highway 150 from Louisville to Vincennes follow such a trace. Marquis Jean-François Rigaud de Vaudreuil (1718), Father de Charlevoix (1721), and George Croghan (1765) all saw buffalo in Indiana. While marching from Vincennes to the Ohio, Joseph Buell, who served under George Rogers Clark, wrote: "Came across five buffaloes. They tried to force a passage through our column. The general ordered the men to fire on them. Three were killed and the others wounded."[60] At French Lick in 1792 Heckewelder saw more buffalo bones than live buffalo. There is a vague account of a buffalo being spotted near Vincennes in 1808.

The lack of sightings makes it clear why in 1802 a delegation of Shawnee and Delaware told Indian agents their people were going hungry. William Henry "Old Tippecanoe" Harrison—Governor of the Indiana Territory, treaty breaker, despoiler of Indian land, and in 1841, short-lived Whig president—understood why. White settlers were crossing the Ohio to kill buffalo, he said, which once "being in great abundance a few years ago is now scarcely to be met with. One white hunter will destroy more game than five of the common Indians." Harrison heard more complaints from the Miami and Kickapoo living along the Wabash.[61]

In 1810 a hunter reportedly shot a buffalo at an unknown site in Indiana. Another killed a lone buffalo at French Lick in 1830—one of the last buffalo sightings east of the Mississippi, and the last one reported in Indiana.[62]

Of Ohio in the early 1700s, Philippe de Rigaud de Vaudreuil, the governor of New France, noted, "Thirty leagues up the Miami River at a place called La Glaise [Fort Defiance, west of Bellefontaine, near the headwaters of the Miami] buffaloes are always found." In 1765 George Croghan was near Antiquity, where he saw a "vast, migrating herd" of buffalo swim the Ohio. Harry Gordon traveled with Croghan in 1766; buffalo, he wrote, "were not so common, until we pass the Scioto," near Portsmouth. In April 1773 Heckewelder saw buffalo in eastern Ohio close to the Moravian mission, Gekelmuchpekink, noting "there are many hereabouts"; near Brokaw his Indian guides hunted buffalo. By the late 1700s buffalo in Ohio were something of a rarity. Across from Wheeling, West Virginia, in Mingo Bottom, John McQueen recalled in 1842 that years earlier "some few buffalo strayed up that way . . . but they were very seldom over there."[63]

At Fort Harmar, at the mouth of the Muskingum, near Marietta, "a buffalo was brought in" on March 27, 1787. Five more were shot on October 4; an old army journal describes the killing as "something of an event."[64] Hunters scored again near Fort Harmar on April 30, 1789. General Josiah Harmar sent wool samples to Michael Hillegas, continental treasurer, in New York.

> Dear Sir:
> I . . . now send you some more of the buffalo wool of a superior quality to the former. In the months of February and March is the time the wool is in proper season: I am apprehensive what was first sent will not answer your purpose. But few buffalo are killed in the vicinity of the Muskingum; I am sorry that it is not in my power to send you more than one pound of it at present, but I shall make it a point to send you the wool of one or two skins as soon as they can be procured.[65]

Just as buffalo east of the Mississippi were passing into extinction, the U.S. government was looking into the commercial prospects for buffalo wool. Whether Harmar sent more samples is not known; in October 1790 he and his army of 320 Regulars and 1,100 Kentuckians torched five Shawnee, Delaware, and Miami towns at the headwaters of the Maumee and were beaten in a bloodbath that disgraced Harmar forever.[66]

In November 1792 Heckewelder saw hunters cross the Ohio into Gallipolis to pursue some buffalo. That year a French New Yorker petitioned Congress and won a contract to write a pamphlet to induce folks to move west, buy land, and become Ohioans. How many did so is not known, but on one summer day in Gallipolis in 1795, townspeople heard a great noise wending its way down a main street. Charles Francis Duteil, a new arrival, had shot a buffalo.[67]

The event was so newsworthy that a parade was put together. A marching band, "playing violins, flutes, and oboes," led the way. Behind the band strode Duteil, gun shouldered, head high. Next came the dead buffalo hung upside down on a pole carried by strong men, its hooves lashed tight.

Spectators let loose a chorus of huzzahs. Duteil waved. Undoubtedly it was very fine.

"And for several days," wrote one who was at the gala affair, "there was feasting, as the first and the last buffalo of Gallipolis was served up in such a variety of ways and means as none but the French could devise." Charles Duteil went to his grave honored as the "renowned marksman" of the town, although, his title notwithstanding, his buffalo was not the first killed near Gallipolis. But it may have been the last.

Hunters shot two buffalo in 1800 in Jackson County. In 1806 a settler at the mouth of the Muskingum killed a buffalo. In 1808 the last known buffalo in Ohio was killed at Buffalo Fork, near Zanesville.[68]

"The history of the settlement of the western country is the history of his life," Judge John Coburn of Missouri wrote of Daniel Boone in 1812.[69] Crippled by rheumatism and scrofula, and his pale blue eyes turning weak, Boone laid down his rifle in 1817 and reminisced more than he hunted. Speaking wistfully of the old days, he once reportedly told John James Audubon, "There were then thousands of buffaloes on the hills in Kentucky; the land looked as if it would never be poor; and to hunt in those days was a pleasure indeed." Yet, as his work demanded, he had hunted buffalo and helped shoot them into oblivion.[70]

In 1790 one of Boone's sons took a wagonload of deer skins, peltry, and sundry goods to a Maryland fur buyer, Matthew Vanlear. Among the two hogsheads of ginseng and casks of tallow were 1,790 deer skins, 129 bear skins, and many fox, otter, and beaver pelts. This bounty came not from Kentucky, as the old hunter had left the Bluegrass in 1789, but from a land on the upper Ohio the Shawnee and Delaware called Tuenda-wie, "the meeting of waters." Whites knew it as the Kanawha

Valley of western Virginia. Fur was abundant there and dwindling game herds could still be hunted.[71]

One fall day in 1791 Boone killed nine buffalo near the mouth of Eighteen Mile Creek—"more than he had killed at any other time in the Kanawha country, only having killed one or two at other periods." Boone quartered them and hung the beef on tree scaffolds. Nathan said his father "killed buffalo for the meat—deer, beaver, and bear for skins and fur for sale." Yet when Boone moved to western Virginia, the buffalo were in their last hour. In 1797 Boone hunted the Big Sandy and canoed back to Limestone complaining "of having made a poor hunt."[72]

The herds between the Great and Little Kanawha were said to be abundant in 1784 by Albert Gallatin, who for eight months stayed there, living mostly off wild beef.[73] But one writer observed in 1795, "Buffalo have nearly disappeared from this region, where, less than thirty years before Croghan had found them in such vast numbers." In 1815 Archibald Price shot a buffalo on the banks of Little Sandy Creek of the Elk River, twelve miles below Charleston. In 1825 near the headwaters of the Kanawha, a buffalo cow and her calf were shot down, the last of their kind.[74]

In western Virginia, Boone sold hundreds of pounds of wild beef before moving back to Kentucky in 1795. In 1799 he moved again, leaving the Bluegrass for Spanish Missouri to hunt, trap, and live out his days. The land was wild, the Indians—Osage, Iowa, Sauk, and Fox—dangerous, the country teeming with game; Missouri was like Kentucky of old. It was a heady time for the old Long Hunter. Ironically, by the time of Boone's death in September 1820, the buffalo east of the Mississippi were just about gone too.

By 1730 the buffalo had been killed out in Virginia and the Tidewater; by the early 1770s few, if any, roamed the Carolinas, Florida, or Alabama. While touring the Little and Broad Rivers of the Georgia Piedmont in 1773, William Bartram wrote, "The buffalo (urus), once so very numerous, is not at this day to be seen in this part of the country."[75] Bartram was premature; a Georgia account in the early 1800s notes that "Mr. James Hamilton Couper shot a wild buffalo . . . near the headwaters of the Turtle River, not far from Brunswick, Georgia . . . the last known buffalo on the Atlantic coast." Colonel John Kelly reputedly shot the sole surviving Pennsylvania buffalo in 1801. The last buffalo in Louisiana was killed in 1803 near Monroe (Ouachita Parish). The last reported buffalo killing in Illinois was in 1808, the same year the last Ohio buffalo was killed. In Kentucky the last buffalo sighting was in 1820. Buffalo vanished from

Tennessee by 1823 and from western Virginia by 1825. In 1830 a hunter shot the last buffalo in Indiana. No one is sure when the beasts were killed out in the more northern states; one vague account asserts that in 1832 a band of Sioux in Wisconsin killed what are believed to have been the last two wild buffalo east of the Mississippi.[76]

Aside from a handful that settlers penned up and put on display as curios from the past, the eastern buffalo were gone. Yet the mindless slaughter was just a prelude to the savage butchery that occurred within the next seventy years to the buffalo west of the Mississippi.

Requiem

AND SO THE BUFFALO EAST OF THE MISSISSIPPI WERE GONE. IT TOOK LESS than three hundred years of slaughter and burning off the barrens and canelands. It might have taken less time had the European and Anglo-American settlements that began at the Tidewater spilled over the Appalachians more quickly to join the French and Spanish towns dotting the banks of the Mississippi from New Orleans to the Great Lakes. But Indian wars and the quest for independence changed all that.

Few missed the beasts. But for years people spoke in wonder about the meandering traces—the last sign that buffalo had once roamed there—and reminisced about the Indians and the game herds.

Several easterners attempted to breed buffalo commercially. Robert Wickliffe (1775–1859), of Lexington, Kentucky, an attorney, legislator, and staunch proslavery Democrat, was one of the first to try. By 1815 he had successfully crossbred buffalo imported from the Upper Missouri with cattle. And like the French a century before, he managed to break a few to a yoke for pulling wagons and carts, finding them "capable of making excellent oxen." He let them roam with his domestic cattle, but he was never able to tame the beasts fully, and his buffalo often tried to gore their keepers. Wickliffe experimented with his unique brand of bovine husbandry until 1845.

In Mercer County, Kentucky, near Shawnee Springs, George C. Thompson kept a small herd of buffalo on his farm from 1825 to 1875. In 1827 Thomas D. Carneal, a member of the Kentucky Legislature, owned a pair of buffalo, "which he kept for some time, for the purpose of improving his breed of draft."[1] In 1859, on his estate of several hundred acres near Belle Meade, Tennessee, General William G. Harding kept two hundred deer, twenty buffalo, and half a dozen elk. What Harding was doing with such a menagerie and the fate of his stock are not known, but the novelty of trying to tame buffalo and breed buffalo-cattle hybrids soon wore off; such oddities were not economically feasible, and so the experiments were abandoned.[2]

Buffalo abounded west of the Mississippi. Indeed, the truly huge buffalo herds first seen by Meriwether Lewis and William Clark in 1803, by the Mountain Men who followed in their wake and by those who fought in the Indian wars in the 1870s, numbered, by some inflated estimates, over sixty million. Such immense herds, by comparison, made the herds east of the Mississippi appear almost to be stragglers.[3]

Yet the vast throngs of buffalo that darkened the Great Plains, whose pounding hooves could be heard for miles, were doomed as surely as those in the East. Here the carnage was much worse, as there were so many more of them and guns had radically improved. Hard-hitting breechloaders replaced muzzleloaders—the Sharps and the Remington rolling block were two of the best, both of which reputedly could drop a buffalo half a mile off—spawning a new breed of professional "buffalo runners."[4] Markets for buffalo tongues, buffalo coats, and leather belts to turn the cogs of factory machinery opened in the East and in Europe.

Almost unbelievably, the extermination of the great herds in the West did not take as long as it had in the East. In less than a hundred years, as Americans moving west pushed the frontier past the Mississippi and Missouri Rivers and beyond the Rocky Mountains to the Pacific coast, the buffalo were destroyed. And with the buffalo vanished the glorious horse culture of the Plains Indians, who themselves were herded up and pushed onto reservations. By 1900 the ruminants overgrazing the plains, which were rapidly becoming fenced off into pastures, were mostly the cattle owned by homesteaders and ranchers.

Long before the days of ecological awareness, environmentalists, and corporate conservation, a few farsighted men like William T. Hornaday, Charles Jesse "Buffalo" Jones, Martin S. Garretson, Charles Goodnight, Michael Pablo, and others saw the desperate need to preserve the buffalo, corralled a few for breeding, and brought the animals back from certain extinction. Those seen today are descendants from that remnant stock.

Certainly the buffalo that stormed through the eastern canelands left their mark. In Kentucky, many of the Commonwealth's historic highway markers reflect the impact of the buffalo on the roads and highways winding throughout the Bluegrass State.[5]

In Scott County, Kentucky, on state route 227, near Stamping Ground, marker 217 reads:

This area first explored April 1775 by William McConnell, Charles Lecompte and party from Penn. Buffalo herds had stamped down undergrowth and ground around the spring—origin of town's name. McConnell and Lecompte in Blue Licks, 1782.

At least three sites in Kentucky were known as Stamping Ground, but the name survives only in Scott County. As buffalo licks were ideal pastureland, Stamping Ground became a fiercely contested piece of real estate, resulting in a long, complex series of lawsuits. One of the earliest, *John H. Craig vs. the McCracken Heirs*, was on the Franklin District Court docket from 1799 to 1802.[6]

One mile west of Stamping Ground at Lindsay's Station, at the junction of state route 227 and 368 in Cedar Park, a marker notes, "The station was on an old buffalo trace, leading north to the Ohio River, and was a regular stop for travelers and traders."

Marker 219, erected on a section of the famous Wilderness Road lying just on the outskirts of Louisville on state route 61, reads:

Trail of thousands of pioneers through here, 1775 to 1811. Made into wagon road by Act of the Legislature 1796. Lifeline for Gen. George Rogers Clark's army at Falls of Ohio, Louisville, 1778–83. Road abandoned 1840. It followed [an] ancient buffalo path.

In Louisville on June 10, 1938, a marker by the National Society of the Colonial Dames of America in the Commonwealth of Kentucky was unveiled.[7] Located on Thirty-first Street, about one hundred yards north of the Northwestern Parkway, it says:

THE BUFFALO FORD BELOW THE FALLS. Herds of buffalo from the Illinois Prairie forded the Ohio, seeking the Salt Licks and Bluegrass Lands of Kentucky. This Buffalo Trace along the Ridge of 26th St. became an Indian Trail, a Post Road to the Vincennes Garrison, via the Cane Run Road, and now is a Part of Highway 31 W. [Erected] 1938.

In Owensboro, in Daviess County, at the crossing of First and Frederica Streets, Kentucky historic marker 1307 reads:

Buffalo herds opened first road in wilderness to present site of Owensboro. Bill Smothers, the pioneer settler of Yellow Banks, followed trail from Rough Creek, near present-day Hartford, to Ohio River. Built his cabin at end of road, near here, 1797–98. An old court record says the buffalo road was a "place of great resort for that kind of game."

Just below the Ohio River, on U.S. 68 in Washington, four miles south of Maysville in Mason County, marker 1519 states:

This route follows the Buffalo Trace from the Ohio to Licking rivers and was first known as "Smith's Wagon Road." In 1829, President Andrew Jackson's Postmaster General, Wm. T. Barry, planned mail stage route, extension of branch of "National Pike," from Zanesville through Lexington to New Orleans. Maysville to Washington was the first macadamized road west of the Alleghenies.

A marker at the Johnson Creek Bridge in Alhambra, in Robertson County, about two miles northeast of state route 165, says of a portion of the old covered bridge: "It crosses Johnson Creek over an old Buffalo Trace, near Blue Licks Battlefield."

Kentucky is not alone in her debt to the buffalo for traces and paths that were made into roads. Tennessee, Ohio, Indiana, and other eastern states have highways, state roads, and railroad lines that meander along what were once buffalo paths. If one is diligent and looks hard enough, in overgrown lots, in pastures, and in the backyards of suburban homes, old buffalo traces—long silent from the pounding black hooves that dug the great furrows—can still be found.

And yet, though the days of the free-roaming wild cattle are gone forever, here and there, on public and private land from Florida to the Great Lakes, from the Mississippi to the Atlantic, one can see small herds of buffalo—transplants usually brought from the Dakotas—grazing behind barbed-wire fences. Most are butchered as yearlings and the beef sold to restaurants. But of the throngs of people who stop their cars and get out to snap pictures and gawk and hurl dirt clods at the brutes, few realize that in the same haunts many years ago the buffalo ran free.

Appendix

Chase the Buffalo

Oh, the hawk shot the buzzard and the buzzard shot the crow,
And we'll rally round the canebrake and chase the buffalo,
Oh, we'll chase the buffalo, we'll chase the buffalo,
And we'll rally round the canebrake and chase the buffalo.

Oh, the girls will sit and spin,
and the boys will stand and grin,
And we'll rally round the canebrake and chase the buffalo,
Oh, we'll chase the buffalo, we'll chase the buffalo,
And we'll rally round the canebrake and chase the buffalo.

Well, I will buy my wife a saddle
and a horse that she can ride,
And I'll buy me another and I'll ride by her side,
And we'll rally round the canebrake and chase the buffalo.
Oh, we'll chase the buffalo, we'll chase the buffalo,
And we'll rally round the canebrake and chase the buffalo.

Rise up, my dear, and present to me your hand.
We are traveling in succession to some far and distant land,
And we'll rally round the canebrake and chase the buffalo.
Oh, we'll chase the buffalo, we'll chase the buffalo,
And we'll rally round the canebrake and chase the buffalo.

From *Ballads of the Kentucky Highlands,*
by Harvey H. Fusion.
The Mitre Press, London: 1931.

Abbreviations

CAH: Charles A. Hanna, *The Wilderness Trail* (New York: Knicker-bocker Press, 1911)

CH: Charles Hudson

CJB: Charles J. Balesi, *The Time of the French in the Heart of North America 1673–1818* (Chicago: Alliance Française, 1992)

CWA: *Trade and Politics 1776–1769,* Collections of the Illinois State Historical Society, British Series, eds. Clarence Walworth Alvord and Clarence Edwin Carter (Springfield: Illinois State Historical Library, 1921)

DAD: David A. Dary, *The Buffalo Book: The Full Saga of the American Animal,* 2nd ed. (Athens, OH: Swallow Press, 1989)

DAWN: Samuel Cole Williams, *Dawn of Tennessee Valley and Tennessee History* (Johnson City, TN: Watauga Press, 1937)

DLR: Douglas L. Rights, "The Buffalo in North Carolina" *The North Carolina Historical Review* 9 (1932), 242–49.

DM: Draper Manuscripts, State Historical Society of Wisconsin, Madison

ER: Erhard Rostlund, "The Geographic Range of the Historic Bison in the Southeast," *Annals of the Association of American Geographers* 4 (1960)

EWC: Edward W. Chester, "The Kentucky Prairie Barrens of North-western and Middle Tennessee: An Historical and Floristic Perspective" (n.p.: 1988)

EWT: *Early Western Travels 1748–1846,* ed. Reuben Gold Thwaites (New York: American Manuscript Press, 1966)

FCHQ: *Filson Club History Quarterly*

FGR: Frank Gilbert Roe, *The North American Buffalo: A Critical Study of the Species in Its Wild State,* 2nd ed. (Toronto: University of Toronto Press, 1970)

FJ: Francis Jennings

GMB: George Michael Bedinger, interview with LCD, c. 1847
HFB: Hugh F. Bell, interview with LCD, c. 1843
HSA: Harriette Simpson Arnow, *Seedtime on the Cumberland,* 2nd ed. (Lexington: University Press of Kentucky, 1983)
HWS: Henry W. Shoemaker, *A Pennsylvania Bison Hunt* (Middleburg, PA: Middleburg Post Press, 1915)
JDS: John Dabney Shane
JH: John Heckewelder, *The Travels of John Heckewelder in Frontier America,* 2nd ed., ed. Paul A. W. Wallace (Pittsburgh, PA: University of Pittsburgh Press, 1985)
JRAD: *The Jesuit Relations and Allied Documents,* ed. Reuben Gold Thwaites, (New York: Pageant, 1959)
JRS-11: John R. Swanton, *Indian Tribes of the Lower Mississippi Valley and Adjacent Coast of the Gulf of Mexico,* Smithsonian Institution, Bureau of American Ethnology, Bulletin 43 (Washington, DC: Government Printing Office, 1911)
JRS-46: John R. Swanton, *The Indians of the Southeastern United States,* Smithsonian Institution, Bureau of American Ethnology, Bulletin 137, 2nd ed. (Washington, DC: Smithsonian Institution Press, 1979; originally published 1946)
JSB: John Spencer Bassett, *The Writings of Colonel William Byrd of Westover in Virginia, Esquire,* 2nd ed., ed. John Spencer Bassett (New York: Burt Franklin, 1970)
JSJ: J. Stoddard Johnson, *First Explorations of Kentucky* (Louisville, KY: John P. Morgan and Company, 1898)
KY: *The Kentucky Encyclopedia,* ed. John E. Kleber (Lexington: University Press of Kentucky, 1992)
LCD: Lyman Copeland Draper
LH: Father Louis Hennepin, *A Description of Louisiana, "Translated from the Edition of 1683, and Compared with the Nouvelle Decouverte, the La Salle Documents and Other Contemporaneous Papers,"* 2nd ed., ed. John Gilmary Shea (Ann Arbor, MI: University Microfilms, 1966)
LIFE: "The Life of Boone," incomplete manuscript by LCD
MSG: Martin S. Garretson, *The American Bison: The Study of Its Extermination as a Wild Species and Its Restoration under Federal Protection* (New York: New York Zoological Society, 1938)
NB: Nathan and Olive Boone, interview with LCD, c. 1851
NOH: Neal Owen Hammon
RKHS: *Register of the Kentucky Historical Society*

RW: Richard White

SCW: Samuel Cole Williams, *Early Travels in the Tennessee Country 1540–1800* (Johnson City, TN: Watauga Press, 1928)

SZ: Stephanie Zebrowski, "Debunking a Myth: Were There Really Buffalo in Pennsylvania?" *The Journal* 39 (1989), 11–23.

WC: "Reverend John D. Shane's Interview with Pioneer William Clinkenbeard," c. 1843, ed. Lucien Beckner, *FCHQ* 2 (1928): 95–128.

WEM: William E. Myer, *Indian Trails of the Southeast,* 2nd ed. (Nashville, TN: Blue and Gray Press, 1971)

WTH: William T. Hornaday, *The Extermination of the American Bison* (Washington, DC: Government Printing Office, 1889)

Notes

CHAPTER 1. THE WILD CATTLE OF NORTH AMERICA

1. For Beringia, see John A. Garraty and Peter Gay, eds., *The Columbia History of the World*, 2nd ed. (New York: Harper and Row, 1981), 18–22; FJ, *The Founders of America: From the Earliest Migrations to the Present* (New York: W. W. Norton and Company, 1993) 25–35; for weaponry, see George C. Frison, *Prehistoric Hunters of the High Plains* (New York: Academic Press, 1978), 147–248; for evolution, see Tom McHugh, *The Time of the Buffalo* (Lincoln, NE: Bison Books, 1979), 27–38; for analysis of the data concerning extinct and extant bison, see Larry Barsness, *Heads, Hides, and Horns: The Compleat Buffalo Book* (Fort Worth: Texas Christian University Press, 1985), 27–30, 37–40; for crossbreeding, management, and diseases of *B. athabascae*, see E. Broughton, "Wood Bison—*Bison bison athabascae*," *Source Conservation Comment* No. 125, quoted in *Buffalo!* 18 (April–June 1990): 22–25; the most complete work to date on bison evolution and morphology is Jerry N. McDonald, *North American Bison: Their Classification and Evolution* (Berkeley: University of California Press, 1981).
2. Charles Jesse "Buffalo" Jones, quoted in Barsness, *Compleat Buffalo*, 35.
3. FJ, *The Invasion of America: Indians, Colonialism, and the Cant of Conquest* (New York: Norton, 1976), 20–21.
4. McHugh, *Buffalo*, 83–109; DAD, 52–68. This glimpse of buffalo and Plains Indians is by necessity brief. Regarding the buffalo's impact on less nomadic tribes, see RW, *The Roots of Dependency: Subsistence, Environment, and Social Change among the Choctaws, Pawnees, and Navajos* (Lincoln: University of Nebraska Press, 1983), 147–211; for Comanches and a scholarly, revisionist look at bison ecology and herd counts in the Southern Plains, see Dan Flores, "Bison Ecology and Bison Diplomacy: The Southern Plains from 1800 to 1850," *The Journal of American History* 4(1991): 465–85.

5. LH, 147.

6. For buffalo hide boats west of the Mississippi, see Hiram Martin Chittenden, *History of Early Steamboat Navigation on the Missouri River: Life and Adventures of Joseph La Barge* (Minneapolis, MN: Ross and Haines, 1962) 1:96–102; Hiram Martin Chittenden, *The American Fur Trade of the Far West* (Stanford, CA: Academic Reprints, 1954) 1:35.

7. Meriwether Lewis, May 29, 1805, quoted in John Bakeless, ed., *The Journals of Lewis and Clark* (New York: New American Library, 1964), 155–56.

8. John James Audubon, quoted in McHugh, *Buffalo,* 85.

9. Flores, *Ecology,* 471; see also McHugh, *Buffalo,* 16–17.

10. For theories concerning the development of the ecosystem that permitted Great Plains bison to enter the American Southeast, see ER, 395–407; RW, *Dependency,* 10–15; and Daniel H. Usner, Jr., *Indians, Settlers, and Slaves in a Frontier Exchange Economy: The Lower Mississippi Valley Before 1783* (Chapel Hill: University of North Carolina Press, 1994), 152.

11. Unless otherwise stated, all quotes are from ER, 399, 405.

12. Quoted in Archer Butler Hulbert, *Historic Highways of America* (Cleveland, OH: Frontier Press, 1967), 1:140; ER, 223–25.

13. FGR, 247, 707.

14. Quoted in FGR, 230.

15. FGR, 231.

16. Quoted in WTH, 386.

17. John Spencer Bassett, ed., *The Writings of Colonel William Byrd of Westover in Virginia, Esquire,* 2nd ed. (New York: Burt Franklin, 1970), 127.

18. ER, 397; quoted in ER, 405.

19. References to these alleged remains are from ER, 402.

20. FGR, 27; also see Lucien Beckner, "The Moundbuilders," *FCHQ* 29(1955): 203–55.

21. Quoted in MSG, 18.

CHAPTER 2. INDIANS, BARRENS, TRACES, AND WILD COWS

1. Timothy Silver, *A New Face on the Countryside: Indians, Colonists, and Slaves in the South Atlantic Forests, 1500–1800* (New York: Cambridge University Press, 1993), 104.

2. CH, ed., *Four Centuries of Southern Indians* (Athens, University of Georgia Press, 1975, 1; FJ, *Invasion,* 16, 30.

3. For Indian usage and description of flint corn varieties up to the historic era, see Edgar Anderson and William L. Brown, "The Northern Flint Corns," *Annals of the Missouri Botanical Garden* 34(1947): 1–20;

JRS-46: 268, 269, 274, 281, 288, 289, 296, 351–59, 373. For southeastern varieties, see Joan Green and H. F. Robinson, "Maize Was Our Life: A History of Cherokee Corn," *Journal of Cherokee Studies* 9(1986): 40–49.

4. Captain Thomas Nairne, *Nairne's Muskhogean Journals: The 1708 Expedition to the Mississippi River,* ed. Alexander Moore (Jackson: University Press of Mississippi, 1988), 52; for Catawba fire hunting, see James H. Merrell, *The Indians' New World: Catawbas and Their Neighbors from European Contact through the Era of Removal* (Chapel Hill: University of North Carolina Press, 1989), 35.

5. Quoted in RW, *Dependency,* 11.

6. For Indian uses of fire, see RW, *Dependency,* 10, 11, 21; CH, *The Southeastern Indians* (Knoxville: University of Tennessee Press, 1992), 19, 177, 276–77, 525; Silver, *Countryside,* 59–64; William Cronon, *Changes in the Land: Indians, Colonists, and the Ecology of New England* (New York: Hill and Wang, 1992), 13, 28, 47–51, 57–58, 90–91, 118–19.

7. Quoted in Paul M. Angle, ed., *Prairie State: Impressions of Illinois, 1673–1967, by Travelers and Other Observers* (Chicago: University of Chicago Press, 1968), 12.

8. George Croghan, June 23, 1765, *EWT,* 1:145.

9. Quoted in Hugh Cleland, *George Washington in the Ohio Valley* (Pittsburgh, PA: University of Pittsburgh Press, 1955), 266.

10. James Monroe to Thomas Jefferson, January 19, 1786, *The Papers of Thomas Jefferson,* ed. Julien P. Boyd (Princeton, NJ: Princeton University Press, 1954), 9:189.

11. John Ross, 1812, quoted in EWC, 152.

12. EWC, 147–51. Further citations regarding the barrens and Michaux, unless otherwise stated, are from EWC, 145–65; see also HSA, 20–21.

13. John A. Jakle, *Images of the Ohio Valley: A Historical Geography of Travel, 1740 to 1860* (New York: Oxford University Press, 1977), 56.

14. LIFE, DM 3B:57; another version in LIFE, DM 3B:126–27; James Dysart to LCD, March 27, 1849, DM 5C:60(2).

15. NOH, "Historic Lawsuits of the Eighteenth Century Locating 'The Stamping Ground,'" *RKHS* 69(1971): 197.

16. Marquis Calme, spring 1775, quoted in NOH, *RKHS* 69(1971): 204.

17. Flores, *Ecology,* 467.

18. CH, *Indians,* 65–66, 77, 88–90, 313; JRS-46: 736–42; FJ, *Founders,* 52, 65–66, 79; Kathryn E. Holland Braund, *Deerskins and Duffels: Creek Indian Trade with Anglo-America, 1685–1815,* (Lincoln: University of Nebraska Press, 1993), 26–27. For more on the ceremonial

importance of the yaupon holly, see CH, ed., *Black Drink: A Native American Tea,* (Athens: University of Georgia Press, 1979).

19. J. G. M. Ramsey, *The Annals of Tennessee to the End of the Eighteenth Century,* 2nd ed. (Kingsport, TN: Kingsport Press, 1967), 88.
20. NOH, *RKHS* 68(1970): 92.
21. WEM, 77–80; *DAWN,* 59–60.
22. Simon Kenton, deposition given June 5, 1824, DM 15C:25(1); see also John D. Barnhart, ed., *Henry Hamilton and George Rogers Clark in the American Revolution with the Unpublished Journal of Lieut. Gov. Henry Hamilton* (Crawfordsville, IN: R. E. Banta, 1951), 198.
23. "For Untold Centuries the Buffalo Roamed Kentucky," *The Kentucky Explorer* 7(1992): 64–65.
24. Quoted in JSJ, 185; see Hulbert, *Highways,* 1:120.
25. CH, *Centuries,* 2–3.
26. For an exhaustive study of these and other tribes, see JRS-11; JRS-46: 292; for estimates of Creek, Choctaw, and Cherokee populations, see Braund, *Deerskins,* 8–9; CH, *Centuries,* 3.
27. JRS-11: 146–49.
28. Du Pratz quoted in JRS-46: 261.
29. JRS-46: 249.
30. Quoted in JRS-46: 471; Adair, *Adair's History of the American Indians,* 2nd ed., ed. Samuel Cole Williams (New York: Argonaut Press, 1966).
31. CH, *Indians,* 268–69, 322.
32. JRS-11: 51, 60–61, 64–65, 112, 118, 277; JRS-46: 249, 292, 326, 439, 443, 449–50, 458, 523, 546, 588, 601.
33. William M. Darlington, *An Account of the Remarkable Occurrences in the Life and Travel of Col. James Smith* (Cincinnati: Robert Clark, 1870), 21–23; Wellborn Coffey to LCD, September 28, 1884, DM 19C:240.
34. John Lawson, *A New Voyage to Carolina,* 12th ed., reprint of 1709 edition, ed. Hugh Talmage Lefler (Chapel Hill: University of North Carolina Press, 1967), 54. Unless otherwise noted, all references to Lawson come from this work. See also W. P. Cumming, S. E. Hillier, D. B. Quinn, and G. Williams, eds., *The Exploration of North America* (New York: G. P. Putnam's Sons, 1974), 200.
35. HFB, DM 30S:261; see also Daniel Trabue, *Westward into Kentucky: The Memoirs of Daniel Trabue,* ed. Chester Raymond Young (Lexington: University Press of Kentucky, 1981), 74.
36. LIFE, 4B:142–43; John Bakeless, *Daniel Boone: Master of the Wilderness,* 3rd ed. (Lincoln, NE: Bison Books, 1989), 37; GMB, July 3, 1847, DM 1A:18; JH, 52–53.

37. Chittenden, *Missouri,* 1:96–102; Chittenden, *Fur Trade,* 1:35. For buf-
    falo hide boats in the East, see Thomas Rodgers, September 1797,
    DM 19S:168. NB quoted in E. Douglas Branch, *The Hunting of the
    Buffalo,* 2nd ed. (Lincoln, NE: Bison Books, 1962), 111–12; LIFE, DM
    4B:165.
38. RW, *The Middle Ground: Indians, Empires, and Republics in the Great Lakes
    Region, 1650–1815,* 2nd ed. (Cambridge, England: Cambridge Uni-
    versity Press, 1993), 137, 482.
39. RW, *Ground,* 42.
40. Father le Petit to Baron d'Avaugour, July 12, 1730, *JRAD,* 68:133.
41. CH, *Indians,* 403.
42. JRS-46: 249.
43. Quoted in RW, *Middle Ground,* 341.
44. FJ, *Founders,* 16.

CHAPTER 3. BUFFALO AND SPANISH INVADERS
 1. Regarding Columbus and subsequent events, my debt to FJ, *Founders,*
    101–51, is obvious.
 2. Quoted in DAD, 7; De Solis's account of Cortés (written in 1684, 1691,
    or 1724) may be apocryphal, see FGR, 206–7; WTH, 373.
 3. Quoted in DAD, 8; also in MSG, 11–12.
 4. For more on Núñez, see Buckingham Smith, trans., *Relation of Alvar
    Núñez Cabeza De Vaca* (Washington, DC: Library of Congress, 1871),
    available from Ann Arbor, MI: University Microfilms.
 5. For more on Coronado's men and their arms and accoutrements, see
    Antonio de Mendoza, *The Muster Roll and Equipment of the Expedition
    of Francisco Vasquez de Coronado,* Bulletin No. 30 (Ann Arbor, MI:
    William Clements Library, 1939).
 6. For fray Marcos de Niza, Coronado, and the Seven Cities of Cíbola,
    see Herbert E. Bolton, *Coronado: Knight of Pueblos and Plains,* 2nd ed.
    (Albuquerque: University of New Mexico Press, 1964); FJ, *Founders,*
    140, 165.
 7. Quoted in CH, *Indians,* 20.
 8. Quoted in *DAWN,* 5–7; also in HSA, 58–59.
 9. CH, *Indians,* 115–16.
10. Material on Hernando de Soto was taken from CH, *Indians,* 107–15;
    FJ, *Founders,* 140–41; JRS-46: 39–56; RW, *Dependency,* 2–3, 8–9, 11.
11. ER, 401.
12. FJ, *Founders,* 165–66; CH, *Indians,* 429, 432; Menéndez's letter quoted
    in FGR, 213–15.

13. Carl Ortwin Saur, *Sixteenth Century North America: The Land and People as Seen by the Europeans* (Berkeley: University of California Press, 1971), 214–18.
14. Quoted in ER, 400. Unless otherwise noted, all Spanish observations of buffalo are excerpted from ER, 395–407.
15. Quoted in Mark F. Boyd, "The Occurrence of the American Bison in Alabama and Florida," *Science* 84(1936): 203; see also ER, 395; JRS-46: 63, 121.
16. ER, 397; JRS-46: 326.
17. Quotes excerpted from Mark F. Boyd, "Diego Peña's Expedition," *The Florida Historical Quarterly* 28(1949):1–27.
18. Saur, *Sixteenth Century,* 219–20; JRS-46: 101, 133–34, 141.
19. For a general summation of much of the evidence of buffalo in the Southeast, see ER, 400–5; McHugh, *Buffalo,* 24–26; CH, *Indians,* 20; RW, *Dependency,* 1–2, 8, 10, 17.

CHAPTER 4. FLEUR-DE-LIS AND LES BOEUFS SAUVAGES
1. Quoted in C. Keith Wilbur, *Early Explorations of North America* (Chester, CT: The Globe Pequot Press, 1989), 110.
2. Quoted in Samuel Eliot Morison, *The European Discovery of America: The Northern Voyages* (New York: Oxford University Press, 1971), 354.
3. Nicholas Le Challeux, quoted in ER, 400–401.
4. Concerning these descriptions in the writings of Le Challeux (1575) and in the memoirs of d' Escalante Fontaneda (1566), Erhard Rostlund theorizes that both men may have seen early-arriving buffalo that had roamed east either contemporaneously with or just after de Soto's expedition. "It seems reasonable to think that among these early arrivals [buffalo] were the *vacas lanudas* of Fontaneda and the *grande beste* of Le Challeux." Rostlund contends that such hints, taken in the overall historical context of early buffalo sightings, add greater credibility to the claims by Pedro Menéndez de Avilés in 1565 of shipments from New France of "6,000 bison skins." For Menéndez see chapter 3, note 12; also see ER, 400–401.
5. For voyageurs, see Grace Nute, *The Voyageur* (St. Paul: Minnesota Historical Society, 1955); Dr. James A. Hanson, *The Voyageur's Sketchbook* (Chadron, NE: The Fur Press, 1981); Louis Antoine de Bougainville, *Adventures in the Wilderness: The American Journals of Louis Antoine de Bougainville, 1756–1760* (Norman: University of Oklahoma Press, 1964): 288.
6. DAD, 10–11; FTR, 681–84; see also *JRAD,* 9:310, 15:249.
7. Reverend David Jones, June 18, 1772, quoted in MSG, 20–21.

8. Quoted in Nute, *Voyageur,* 212–13.

9. Quoted in FGR, 254–55.

10. Quoted in *JRAD,* 47:316.

11. François Xavier, "Relation of 1670–71," *JRAD,* 55:195–97.

12. Jacques Marquette, June 1673, *JRAD,* 59:111–13; for dissenting opinions regarding Marquette's location, see FGR, 223–25.

13. Louis Jolliet to Claude Dablon, August 1, 1674, *JRAD,* 58:105–9; also quoted in Paul M. Angle, ed., *Prairie State: Impressions of Illinois, 1673–1967, by Travelers and Other Observers* (Chicago: University of Chicago Press, 1968), 11–12.

14. Jacques Marquette, June 1673, *JRAD,* 59:111–13.

15. For one of the best renderings of La Salle's exploits from a decidedly French perspective, see CJB, 28–65.

16. LH, 60–61.

17. CJB, 112.

18. Usner, *Settlers,* 14.

19. LH, 144–46.

20. LH, 142–43.

21. LH, 143, 152–53.

22. French historian Pierre Margry cites this figure as "two hundred." See LH, 143, note 3.

23. LH, 146, 147, 265.

24. Sebastian Rale to "Monsieur his Brother, at Narantsouak," Abenaki mission in Maine, October 12, 1723, *JRAD,* 67:169.

25. De Gannes, *Memoir of De Gannes, Concerning the Illinois Country,* published as "The Illinois Country in the Late 1600s," in *The Black Powder Report* 12(1983): 1:4–5.

26. Quoted in ER, 399.

27. Quoted in JRS-46: 327.

28. CJB, 112; for buffalo sightings from d'Iberville's journal see ER, 396–97.

29. Andre Penicaut, *Fleur de Lys and Calumet: Being the Penicaut Narrative of French Adventure in Louisiana,* trans. Richebourg Gaillard McWilliams (Tuscaloosa: University of Alabama Press, 1981), 12, 19, 48, 81–82, 89, 138–39, 146; ER, 397; WTH, 381.

30. McWilliams, *Calumet,* 112.

31. LH, 148.

32. Gabriel Marest to Bartholomew Germon, November 9, 1712, *JRAD,* 66:225.

33. Monsieur de Remonville to the Count de Pontchartrain, December 10, 1697, quoted in WTH, 380.

34. FGR, 707; WTH, 379.

35. Le Moyne d'Iberville, quoted in CJB, 127. During the colonial era, a livre was a close equivalent of an English pound. A French livre equals 489.506 grams, as compared to 453.6 grams, the weight of an avoirdupois pound. The livre was reduced in value and replaced by the franc. A sol is a small coin made of silver, later of copper. Gun expert T. M. Hamilton notes: "Actually, the pound was only 92.6% as heavy as the livre. The monetary unit, the livre, equaled 20 sous, which, in turn, equaled 12 deniers." The sol was superseded by the sou. Voyageurs made capote buttons from sou coins. For monetary exchanges and early fur trade era guns, see T. M. Hamilton, *Colonial Frontier Guns*, 2nd. ed. (Union City, TN: Pioneer Press, 1987), 7, 12. The breadth and scope of Hamilton's *Colonial Frontier Guns* makes it authoritative in its field.

36. LH, 151; A literal rendering of *boucanneer* is "to smoke on a frame." According to linguist and translator Richebourg McWilliams, "Boucan is a South American Tupi word meaning a 'wooden lattice frame for the smoking of meat.'" See McWilliams, *Calumet*, 19.

37. Julien Binneteau "to a Father of the same Society," January 1699, *JRAD*, 65:73–75; for more on Binneteau's observations, see FGR, 29.

38. Quoted in CJB, 160; quoted in Dale Van Every, *Forth to the Wilderness* (New York: Quill, 1961), 28; for Pierre de Charlevoix, see RW, *Middle Ground*, 131, 147, 161, 183.

39. Jacques Gravier to Jean de Lamberville, February 11, 1701, *JRAD*, 65:105; *JRAD*, 66:247.

40. For observations of Antoine Simon Le Page du Pratz, see *The History of Louisiana: Translated from the French of M. Le Page du Pratz*, ed. Joseph G. Tregle, Jr. (Baton Rouge: Louisiana State University Press, 1775), 136–38, 139–41, 174, 255, 300.

41. Quotes regarding D'Artaguiette are from *Travels in the American Colonies*, ed. Newton D. Mereness (New York: Macmillan, 1916), 15–16, 22, 32, 40–87; see also SCW, 73–82 and CJB, 147–49; FGR, 239.

42. This and subsequent inventory vouchers are quoted in Natalia Maree Belting, *Kaskaskia Under the French Regime* (New Orleans, LA: Polyanthos, 1975), 46, 66–67.

43. Usner, *Settlers*, 255.

44. CJB, 129–30, 133; see also John M. Lansden, *A History of the City of Cairo, Illinois*, 2nd ed. (Carbondale: Southern Illinois University Press, 1976), 21; for the Fox wars, see R. David Edmunds, *The Fox Wars: The Mesquakie Challenge to New France* (Norman: University of Oklahoma

Press, 1993). According to local lore, the sunken remnants of Juchereau's tanning vats are still visible.

45. CJB, 147; Jeanne Poisson Pompadour "to Father," c. 1716–27, *JRAD*, 67:285; see also FGR, 239.

46. Estimates of Native American population in the Lower Mississippi Valley are from Usner, *Settlers,* 17, 25, 31–32; D'Artaguiette's 1723 census appears in Belting, *Kaskaskia,* 13.

47. Quoted in Usner, *Settlers,* 33.

48. CJB, 146, 151; HSA, 127, note 58.

49. Quoted from Richard Taylor, *Girty* (Frankfort, KY: Gnomon Press, 1990), 51.

50. Taylor, *Girty,* 51.

51. For Bonnecamp's journal of this entire episode, see "Account of the Voyage of the Beautiful River Made in 1749, under the Direction of Monsieur de Celeron, by Father Bonnecamps," *JRAD,* 69:151–99, 179. It is odd that Bonnecamps did not see a greater number of buffalo herds along the Ohio; buffalo were plentiful in that region, as later accounts testify.

52. RW, *Middle Ground,* 48.

53. Jean-Bernard Bossu, *Travels in the Interior of North America: 1751–1762,* trans. and ed. Seymour Feiler (Norman: University of Oklahoma Press, 1962), 64, 68, 77, 198.

54. Bossu, *Interior,* 117.

55. Jean-Bernard Bossu, *New Travels in North America: 1770–1771,* ed. Samuel Dorris Dickinson (Natchitoches, LA: Northwestern State University Press, 1982). For biographical information on Bossu and his literary works, see v–xi; for Bossu's observations of buffalo and re-lated anecdotes, see 36–37, 40–41; for Bossu's equipment, dress, arms and accoutrements, see 90, 112, 127. Dialogue in the narrative is quoted directly from Bossu's letters.

56. "Jolicoeur" Charles Bonin, *Memoir of a French and Indian War Soldier,* ed. Andrew Gallup (Bowie, MD: Heritage Books, 1993).

57. "Synethnic," meaning "of mixed genetic and ethnic stocks," is adapted from FJ, *Founders,* 196; regarding the tenuous French-Algonquin alliance and the diverse factors sustaining it, see RW, *Middle Ground,* 32.

CHAPTER 5. ENGLISHMEN AND WILD CATTLE

1. FJ, *Founders,* 180.

2. Cronon, *Changes,* 50–81, 146; see FJ, *Founders,* 153; for a global perspective of this phenomenon, see Alfred W. Crosby, *Ecological Imperialism: The Biological Expansion of Europe, 900–1900* (New York: Cambridge University Press, 1986); see chapter 2, note 1.

3. Arthur Barlowe, July 1584, "Barlowe's Description of the North Carolina Coast," quoted in *The Ocean Highway: New Brunswick, New Jersey to Jacksonville, Florida,* 2nd ed., ed. Charles C. Terry, Jr. (New York: Modern Age Books, 1972), 218.

4. Quoted in DAD, 9; FTR, 213–14; MSG, 16–17; WTH, 375.

5. Quoted in WTH, 378; quoted in Branch, *Buffalo,* 55.

6. Abraham Wood to John Richards, August 22, 1674, quoted in Clarence Walworth Alvord and Lee Bidgood, *The First Explorations of the Trans-Allegheny Region by the Virginians 1650–1674* (Cleveland, OH: Arthur H. Clark, 1912), 213; see also C. S. Shoup, "Notes from the Background of Our Knowledge of the Zoology of Tennessee," *Journal of the Tennessee Academy of Science* 19(1944): 126.

7. F. Ralph Randolph, *British Travelers among the Southern Indians, 1660–1763* (Norman: University of Oklahoma Press, 1973), 26–27.

8. Lawson, *Voyage,* 107–8.

9. Lawson, *Voyage,* 120–21.

10. How John Lawson died remains a mystery. On November 3, 1711, Christopher Gale reported that an Indian who witnessed Lawson's death told him the Tuscarora warriors "stuck him [Lawson] full of fine small splinters of torch wood like hog's bristles and so gradually set them afire." In 1727 Colonel William Byrd asserted that of "Mr. Lawson," the Indians "waylaid him and cut his throat from ear to ear." Another thirdhand account, allegedly from one of the slaves who was captured and released, reported that Lawson was hanged by his captors—a very non-Indian mode of execution. Baron Christopher Von Graffenried, who was captured with Lawson but released, wrote that "The Indians kept that execution very secret." See Lawson, *Voyage,* xxxi–xxxix; William K. Boyd, *William Byrd's Histories of the Dividing Line betwixt Virginia and North Carolina* (Raleigh: North Carolina Historical Commission, 1929), 290.

11. Nairne, *Journals,* 73.

12. Nairne, *Journals,* 46, 57.

13. Nairne, *Journals,* 52.

14. Nairne, *Journals,* 52–53.

15. Biographical information for Thomas Nairne taken from Nairne's *Journals;* see also CH, *Indians,* 439; Merrell, *Catawbas,* 66; Tom Hatley,

The Dividing Paths: Cherokees and South Carolinians through the Revolutionary War Era (New York: Oxford University Press, 1995), 18, 21, 25, 68; for Yamasee War, see CH, *Indians,* 438–39, 452; Merrell, *Catawba,* 66–75.

16. Quotes from the South Carolina Commissioners of the Indian Trade and inventory list taken from W. L. McDowell, ed., *Colonial Records of South Carolina: Journals of the Commissioners of the Indian Trade, September 20, 1710–August 29, 1718* (Columbia: South Carolina Archives Department, 1955), 77, 88, 316.

17. Mark Catesby, *The Natural History of Carolina, Florida, and the Bahama Islands* (London, 1731–1743), 2:27; LCD, n.d., DM 8C:199–199(1); see also ER, 399.

18. JSB, November 11, 1728, 224–26. See also Boyd, *Histories,* x–xxvii, 157, 166, 168–69, 176, 286–89, 315.

19. JSB, 226, 312.

20. Quoted in WTH, 376; JSB, 311–12.

21. JSB, 225; see also DLR, 246–48.

22. Lawson, *Voyage,* lii–liii.

23. Quoted in DLR, 247–48; LCD, n.d., DM 8C:199–199(1).

24. Quoted in DAD, 11–12.

25. Unless otherwise stated, subsequent English observations of buffalo taken from ER, 395–407; see also FTR, 242–45.

26. Quoted in DM 1B:121; see also LIFE, DM 5B:2; for a similar incident in 1738 involving a certain Hugh Paul Taylor, see LCD, n.d., DM 21U:1–3.

27. Quoted in MSG, 21; see also J. A. Allen, "The American Bison," in *The Kentucky Geological Survey, 1876,* transcribed by LCD, DM 8C:199–199(1); quoted in DLR, 248–49.

28. Quoted in WTH, 381; see FTR, 241–42.

29. CH, *Indians,* 11; biographical information on James Adair taken from James Adair, *Adair's History of the American Indians,* 2nd ed., ed. Samuel Cole Williams (New York: Argonaut Press, 1966).

30. CH, *Indians,* 436; Braund, *Deerskins,* 53.

31. Adair, *History,* 8, 11, 19, 33, 119.

32. Adair, *History,* 27, 32–33, 200.

33. Adair, *History,* 457.

34. Adair, *History,* 446–47.

35. Silver, *Countryside,* 100; L.C.D., N.D. DM 8C:199–199(1); LIFE, DM 2B:39.

36. Quoted in ER, 400.

37. For estimates and actual counts of the quantities of deer skins that were shipped annually from North America, see Braund, *Deerskins,* 69–73, 88–89, 104–5; see Usner, *Settlers,* 244–75.
38. Inventory appears in Usner, *Settlers,* 260. Original source cited as "Archives des Colonies, Paris, Series C13A, XXXIII, 230v."
39. Inventory appears Braund, *Deerskins,* 128. Original source cited as "Journal of the Superintendent's Proceedings, April 24, 1767–June 6, 1767, Gage Papers, William L. Clements Library, Ann Arbor, Michigan."
40. Quoted in Allan W. Eckert, *Wilderness Empire,* 4th ed. (New York: Bantam Books, 1979), 135.

CHAPTER 6. SPECULATORS, TRADERS, LONG KNIVES, AND WAR IN THE WEST

1. Charles G. Talbert, "Ohio Company," *KY,* 689; quoted in JSJ, 88.
2. Quoted in JSJ, 6; quoted in JSJ, 90. *First Explorations* contains both the journals of Dr. Thomas Walker and Christopher Gist.
3. John Mack Faragher, *Daniel Boone: The Life and Legend of an American Pioneer* (New York: Henry B. Holt and Company, 1992), 39.
4. Christopher Gist, November 25, 1750, JSJ, 110.
5. Christopher Gist, February 17, 1751, JSJ, 132–33.
6. Christopher Gist, March 4, 1751, JSJ, 147.
7. Christopher Gist, February 17, 1751, JSJ, 133.
8. Christopher Gist, March 25, 1751, JSJ, 154.
9. Thomas Walker, March 6, 1750, JSJ, 33–34.
10. Thomas Walker, March 15, 1750, JSJ, 37.
11. Thomas Walker, April 13, 1750, JSJ, 47–48.
12. Thomas Walker, April 17, 1750, JSJ, 50.
13. Many credit Dr. Thomas Walker as its discoverer. But white men as far back as Father Marquette in 1673 had heard reports of it. It was the French who first saw the "Rivière des Anciens Chouanons" (River of the old Shawnee), which is how it appeared on cartographer Jacques Bellin's 1755 map of Louisiana. See HSA, 74–75; CAH, 2:126–27; *DAWN,* 58; regarding Bellin's map, see NOH, "Early Roads into Kentucky," *RKHS* 68(1970): 100, note 18.
14. Thomas Walker, April 19, 1750, JSJ, 51.
15. J. Stoddard Johnston observes: "The Indian Road which he [Dr. Thomas Walker] struck here was that which crossed the Cumberland River below Clover Creek, the trail by which immigration came in later, and the Old Wilderness State Road. It is the main road of that county now [1898], along which the Louisville and Nashville Railroad runs." Quoted in JSJ, 57, note 1.

16. Thomas Walker, May 18, 1750, JSJ, 61.

17. Thomas Walker, June 4, 1750, JSJ, 66.

18. Thomas Walker, June 19, 1750, JSJ, 70.

19. Thomas Walker, July 13, 1750, JSJ, 75.

20. R. S. Cotterill, 1921, quoted in "Ben Franklin Published First Map of Kentucky in 1755," *The Kentucky Explorer* 7(1992): 20–24.

21. Quoted in Faragher, *Boone*, 71.

22. Clarence Walworth Alvord, "Virginia and the West: An Interpretation," *The Mississippi Valley Historical Review* 3(1916): 21–22, quoted in William Stewart Lester, *The Transylvania Colony* (Spencer, IN: Samuel R. Guard, 1935), 15.

23. Robert E. Rennick, "Eskippakithiki," *KY*, 297; see also Lucien Beckner, "Eskippakithiki: The Last Indian Town in Kentucky," *FCHQ* 6(1932): 355–82.

24. NB to LCD, LIFE, DM 2B:171.

25. JSJ, 70; LCD, c. 1851, DM 1U:1(1), 1(11).

26. For a succinct account of Fort Loudoun, see *DAWN*, 193–271; for more on Henry Timberlake's mission, see *DAWN*, 272–83.

27. Henry Timberlake, December 7–8, 1761, *Lieut. Henry Timberlake's Memoirs, 1756–1765,* 2nd ed., ed. Samuel Cole Williams (Marietta, GA: Continental Book Company, 1948), 47; Henry Timberlake, January 2, 1762, *Memoirs*, 71.

28. Henry Timberlake, March 12, 1762, *Memoirs*, 120–21.

29. SCW, 211, 214–15; Robert Farmer to John Stuart, December 16, 1765, quoted in SCW, 216.

30. CAH, 1:131; Ramsey, *Annals*, 45.

31. Remington Kellogg, "Annotated List of Tennessee Mammals," Smithsonian Institution, *Proceedings of the National Museum* 86(1939): 297; ER, 403.

32. CAH, 2:1–86.

33. George Croghan, May 19, 1765, *EWT*, 1:130–32.

34. George Croghan, May 31, 1765, *EWT*, 1:135; June 13, 1765, *EWT*, 1:140.

35. Harry Gordon, June 23, 1766, CAH, 2:41. Gordon's journal also appears in Mereness, *Travels*, 457–89.

36. Harry Gordon, July 16, 1766, CAH, 2:42.

37. Harry Gordon, July 31, 1766, CAH, 2:44.

38. LCD, n.d., DM 6XX:37(1–2), 38, 50(1–6); Ramsey, *Annals*, 192–94; J. C. Guild, *Old Times in Tennessee,* 2nd ed. (Knoxville: Tenase Company, 1971), 310–13; *DAWN*, 324–26.

39. LCD, n.d., DM 6XX:50(6), 37(1), 38.

40. Quoted in *DAWN*, 293.

41. Captain Philip Pittman, c. 1763, *The Present State of the European Settlements on the Mississippi,* 3rd ed. (Gainesville: University of Florida Press, 1973), 40, 51.
42. Ben Franklin to W. Franklin, November 25, 1767, CWA, 3:xvi, 77–81, 180.
43. Nicholas B. Wainwright, *George Croghan: Wilderness Diplomat* (Chapel Hill: University of North Carolina Press), 233; for listings of goods from Baynton, Wharton, and Morgan, see CWA, 230–31, 391–405; for fur prices see CWA, 234–35; for the inventories of Baynton, Wharton, and Morgan listed in subsequent paragraphs, see CWA 163, 230–31, 391–405.
44. CAH, 2:38; see also HSA, 117–18.
45. George Morgan to John Baynton and Samuel Wharton, December 16, 1767, CWA, 141.
46. George Morgan to John Baynton and Samuel Wharton, December 16, 1767, CWA, 143.
47. Marion W. Mitchell, 1985, *Fort de Chartres 1718–1772: Its Place in the Big Picture* (privately published, n.d.); Wainwright, *Wilderness Diplomat,* 201–38; see also Belting, *Kaskaskia,* 18–19. A partially finished, historically accurate stone re-creation of the 1756 edition of Fort de Chartres (complete with the fort's original powder magazine), built on its original site, was flooded out the summer of 1993. The old fortress has been refurbished but seasonal threats from high water are a perpetual problem.
48. Thomas Gage to Sir William Johnson, October 10, 1768, CWA, 417.
49. George Morgan to John Baynton and Samuel Wharton, December 10, 1767, CWA, 132.
50. Quoted in HSA, 126.
51. George Morgan to John Baynton and Samuel Wharton, July 20, 1768, CWA, 354, 362; Consul Wilshire Butterfield, *History of the Girtys,* 2nd ed. (Columbus, OH: Long's College Book Co., 1950), 37, 57, 346.
52. John Wilkins to Thomas Gage, August 15, 1768, CWA, 376.
53. George Butricke to Thomas Barnsley, September 15, 1768, CWA, 409.
54. Quoted in HSA, 127, note 58; for more on trade with the West Indies, see CWA, 116, 200.
55. George Morgan to John Baynton and Samuel Wharton, December 16, 1767, CWA, 143.
56. George Morgan to John Baynton and Samuel Wharton, April 5, 1768, CWA, 222–24; George Morgan to Molly Morgan, n.d., but after September 5, 1768, CWA, 481–82.

57. George Morgan to John Baynton and Samuel Wharton, October 30, 1768, CWA, 443; George Morgan to John Baynton, October 30, 1768, CWA, 435.

58. SCW, 216–18; Kellogg, "Annotated List," 301; John Jennings, June 28, 1768, quoted in SCW, 220–21.

59. George Butricke to Thomas Barnsley, February 12, 1769, CWA, 498–99; George Morgan to John Baynton and Samuel Wharton, October 30, 1768, CWA, 440–41; HSA, 127, 130–31.

60. *DAWN,* 305–6; for more on Hutchins's surveys of the Cumberland and the Tennessee in 1768–69, see *DAWN,* 304–10.

61. John Wilkins to William Wildman Barrington, December 5, 1769, CWA, 634.

62. Bernard and Michael Gratz to William Murray, August 31, 1768, CWA, 387–88.

CHAPTER 7. LONG HUNTERS, MEAT GETTERS, AND MARKET HUNTERS

1. Bord, *Dividing Line,* 92.

2. David Barrow, c. 1795, DM 12CC:193.

3. James Wade to JDS, c. 1843–49, DM 12CC:39.

4. Material on Long Hunters from LIFE, DM 3B:47ff; DM 6XX; Joseph Doddridge, *Notes on the Settlement and Indian Wars of the Western Parts of Virginia and Pennsylvania* (1824), in Samuel Kercheval, *A History of the Valley of Virginia,* 4th ed. (Strasburg, VA: Shenandoah Publishing, 1925), 250–52, 257–63; Brent Altsheler, "The Long Hunters and James Knox Their Leader," *FCHQ* 5(1931): 167–85; HSA, 134–71; for more on lifestyle, food, skills, and related topics, see Ted Franklin Belue, "Indian-Influenced Woodsmen of the Cane," *The Book of Buckskinning VII,* ed. William H. Scurlock (Texarkana, TX: Scurlock Publishing, 1995): 42–77.

5. Faragher, *Boone,* 31.

6. LIFE, DM 2B:181; Daniel Boone ledger entry, July 19, 1790, DM 27C:23(22); Daniel Bryan to LCD, n.d., DM 31C:50; regarding winter-tanned hides, see Harold Peterson, *The Last of the Mountain Men: The True Story of a Living American Legend* (New York: Charles Scribner's Sons, 1969), 23–24.

7. Jordan, "Kenny," 26–27. Author's note: I tried this several times on trees, including black locust, oak, hickory, elm, and maple. It did not work for me.

8. LIFE, DM 2B:181; Daniel Bryan to LCD, n.d., DM 31C:50.

9. James Wade to JDS, c. 1842, DM 12CC:18.

10. ER, 403, note 44; see LIFE, DM 2B:182; also chapter 5, note 16; for buffalo beef, see Jordan, "Kenny," 39–40.
11. LCD interview with George Edwards, c. 1863, DM 19S:83.
12. Thomas Rodgers to LCD, n.d., DM 19S:168.
13. Quoted in Branch, *Buffalo,* 111–12.
14. J. D. Spears to LCD, March 24, 1887, DM 20C:75; HSA, 111–12.
15. LCD, n.d. DM 6XX:72; see also HSA, 166.
16. Lucien Beckner, "A Sketch of the Early Adventures of William Sudduth in Kentucky," *FCHQ* 2(1928): 53–54.
17. LCD interview with William Champ, September 1863, DM 15C:31; JDS interview with James Lane, c. 1840s, DM12CC:56–57. Open-faced log huts may have had their origin in Scandinavia. As late as 1910 such shelters were used in the Savo-Karelian region of Kainuu Province, Finland. See Terry G. Jordan and Matti Kaups, *The American Backwoods Frontier: An Ethnic and Ecological Interpretation* (Baltimore, MD: Johns Hopkins University Press, 1989), 41–42.
18. "John D. Shane's Interview with Benjamin Allen, Clark County," ed. Lucien Beckner, *FCHQ* 5(1941): 68–69.
19. Jordan and Kaups, *Backwoods,* 219–20.
20. GMB to LCD, DM 1A:38; Trabue, *Westward,* 74; HSA, 166; *DAWN,* 331; LIFE, DM 3B:52ff; David Thompson to JDS, c. 1843–49, DM 12CC:200.
21. Elizabeth Hain to LCD, May 3, 1884, 14C:30(2); HFB to LCD, DM 30S:261.
22. GMB to LCD, DM 1A:14.
23. Evisa Lydia Coshow to LCD, May 28, 1884, DM 21C:43, 48.
24. GMB to LCD, DM 1A:35.
25. *The Journal of Nicholas Cresswell,* 1774–1777, 2nd ed. (New York: Dial Press, 1928), 75–76.
26. HFB to LCD, DM 30S:262–63.
27. JDS interview with John McQueen, c. 1842, DM 13CC:127; LCD interview with NB, DM 6S:237; LIFE, DM 5B:16; GMB to LCD, DM 1A:36; John Fitch to JDS, c. 1842, 8CC:107.
28. Henry A. Logan to LCD, January 5, 1884, DM 16C:13(2).
29. Mrs. [first name illegible] Black to JDS, c. 1842, DM 12CC:151.
30. Quoted in LCD, *King's Mountain and its Heroes,* 2nd ed. (Baltimore: Genealogical Publishing Company, 1967), 404.
31. John Ray to LCD, February 20, 1843, DM 12C:16(3); for snakes, see LCD interview with John Cuppy, August 1860, DM 9S:21, 36–37; see Laurence M. Klauber, *Rattlesnakes: Their Habits, Life Histories, and Influence on Mankind,* 2nd ed. (Berkeley: University of California Press,

1972), 2:984–85; see also Ted Franklin Belue, "The Memoirs of John Cuppy: Frontier Spy," *Muzzleloader,* July–August, 1991:35–39; HFB to LCD, DM 30S:264.

32. Thomas Walker, May 10 and 11, 1750, JSJ, 59–60.

33. Quoted in FJ, *Cant,* 92.

34. Harry G. Enoch, "The Travels of John Hanks: Recollections of a Kentucky Pioneer," *RKHS* 92(1994): 139; for more on cappo-coats, c. 1778, see John Cuppy to LCD, c. 1860, DM 9S:36–37; see also Alexander McConnell to JDS, c. 1842, DM 13CC:142; for a definitive treatise on capotes, see Francis Black, "The Canadian Capot (Capote)," *The Museum of the Fur Trade Quarterly* 27(1991): 4–15.

35. GMB to LCD, DM 1A:44–45.

36. Doddridge, in Kercheval, *Virginia,* 251.

37. Trabue, *Westward,* 74.

38. HFB to LCD, DM 30S:260–61.

39. Philip Bruner to LCD, December 15–16, 1864, DM 20S:217.

40. Cresswell, 82–84; quoted in *The Voice of the Frontier: John Bradford's Notes of Kentucky,* ed. Thomas D. Clark (Lexington: University Press of Kentucky, 1993), 92; Doddridge, in Kercheval, *Virginia,* 251.

41. Thomas Rodgers to LCD, n.d., DM 19S:168; Eyewitness accounts of Daniel Boone's appearance and dress vary. As Boone is the best-known Long Hunter and has become the archetypal American frontiersman, a summary of these firsthand observations of Boone is useful. In 1774 he was seen near the Holston wearing a buckskin hunting shirt "dyed black," most likely sewn from leather dyed in a broth of black-walnut hulls. In 1780 John Redd saw Boone at Richmond while serving in the Virginia legislature as a representative of Kentucky: "He was dressed in real backwoods style, he had on a common jeans suit, with buckskin leggings beaded very neatly ... manufactured by the Indians." In 1782 he was reportedly "dressed in a deerskin shirt and breeches." Christopher Mann told Lyman Draper that he saw once saw Boone "dressed in leather." On occasion Boone wore a scarlet weskit with sterling buttons engraved with his name; the buttons were a gift from his nephew Daniel Bryan, who had made them in the fall of 1783. In 1791 Thomas Rodgers saw Boone at Maysville wearing a "linen hunting shirt and moccasins the color of leaves." Fielding Belt saw him at the Upper Blue Licks in 1799 dressed as "the poorest hunter" with his powderhorn, shot bag, rifle, and hunting shirt. Reverend James E. Welch described Boone in 1818 as "rather low of stature, broad shouldered, high cheek bones, very mild countenance [and] fair complexion." Reverend Timothy Flint, author of *Life and Exploits of*

Col. Dan'l Boone, interviewed Boone in 1818 and observed that he had "what phrenologists would have considered a model head—with a forehead peculiarly high, noble and bold—thin compressed lips—a mild clear blue eye—a large prominent chin, and a general expression of countenance in which fearlessness and courage sat enthroned. . . . Never was old age more green or gray hairs more graceful. His high, calm bold forehead seemed converted by his years into iron."

In an interview in 1851, Nathan Boone told Draper that his father stood five feet, eight inches and weighed 175 pounds but that near his death his weight dropped to 155 pounds. In 1868 Elijah Bryan told Draper that Boone "was one of the most powerful made men he ever knew—very straight, 5'8"—heavy-made, thick thighs and very small ankles." William S. Bryan (1846–1940), coauthor of *Pioneer Families of Missouri,* related that Elijah Bryan said Boone was "scarcely five feet eight inches . . . stout and heavy, and, until the last year or two of his life, inclined to corpulancy. His eyes were deep blue, and very brilliant, and were always on the alert. . . . His hair was gray, but had been originally light brown to flaxen, and was fine and soft."

For "dyed black," see Thwaites, *Boone,* 110; John Redd to LCD, c. 1848–49, DM 10NN:101; John Jones to LCD, 1868, DM 23S:207; Christopher Mann to LCD, October 15, 1883; Daniel Bryan to LCD, April 1844, DM 22C:14(14); Thomas Rodgers to LCD, 1863, DM 19S:168; Fielding Belt to LCD, 1866, DM 21S:204; James E. Welch, *Christian Repository,* Louisville, KY, March 1860, DM 16C:47–48; Timothy Flint, *Life and Exploits of Col. Dan'l Boone* (Philadelphia: H. M. Rulison, 1856), 249–50; NB to LCD, 1851, 6S:281; Elijah Bryan to LCD, c. 1868, DM 23S:243; William S. Bryan quoted in Lilian Hays Oliver, *Some Boone Descendants and Kindred of the St. Charles District* (Cordova, CA: Dean Publication, 1984), 11–12.

42. Henry J. Kauffman, *The Pennsylvania-Kentucky Rifle* (New York: Bonanza, 1960), v–vi; see also Charles Hanson, Jr., "The Guns," *The Book of Buckskinning,* ed. William H. Scurlock (Texarkana, TX: Rebel Publishing, 1980), 82–84.

43. JDS, c. 1843–49, DM 11CC:35–36; for more on Linn, see *Kaskaskia Records, Virginia Series,* Volume II, ed. Clarence Walworth Alvord (Springfield: Illinois State Historical Library, 1909), xvii–xx.

44. Z. Taylor to LCD, October 30, 1848, DM 5B:37(1–3); see also LIFE, DM 3B:45.

45. LIFE, DM 3B:47–62. For an alternate interpretation and ancillary biographical date, see HSA, 158–69.

46. LIFE, DM 3B:50.
47. LIFE, DM 3B:52.
48. DAD, 12; DLR, 248–49.
49. Joseph Martin to Patrick Henry, July 2, 1789, Joseph Martin to Patrick Henry, January 18, 1791, DM 1XX:30–31, 37; Nathaniel Green to William Preston, n.d., DM 2XX:37(1–3); a handwritten transcription of Donelson's journal by LCD, n.d., DM 11ZZ:14.
50. This entire episode is found in LIFE, DM 3B:55–65; for another version see John B. Dysart to LCD, March 27, 1849, DM 5C:60(2)–61(2); also General William Hall, *Early History of the South-West,* 2nd ed. (Nashville, TN: Parthenon Press, 1968), 33–36.
51. LIFE, DM 3B:57; see also "Letters of Thomas Perkins to Gen. Joseph Palmer, Lincoln County, Kentucky, 1785," ed. James R. Bently, *FCHQ* 49(1975): 145.
52. LIFE, DM 3B:58–59.
53. HFB to LCD, DM 30S:263.
54. Robert Wickcliffe to LCD, January 28, 1884, DM 5C:54(3); John Hanks to JDS, c. 1842, DM 12CC:144; JDS interview with John McQueen, c. 1842, DM 13CC:122–23.
55. LIFE, DM 3B:60; regarding Captain Will Emery, see Robert M. Addington, *History of Scott County, Virginia* (Baltimore, MD: Regional Publishing, 1977), 35; see also Robert Hancock to LCD, c. 1853, DM 24C:17(2).
56. LIFE, DM 3B:63.
57. LIFE, DM 3B:65.
58. Ramsey, *Annals,* 144, 193.
59. Stephen Aron, "The Significance of the Kentucky Frontier," *RKHS* 91(1993): 308.
60. John Lipscomb, August 30, 1784, quoted in SCW, 279.

CHAPTER 8. KENTUCKY I

1. Frederick Jackson Turner, *The Significance of the Frontier in American History,* 2nd. ed. (New York: Unger, 1963), 35.
2. Aron, "Kentucky Frontier," 323.
3. For a synthesis of the Shawnee fight for Kentucky, see Aron, "Kentucky Frontier," 298–323.
4. William C. Sturtevant, ed. *Handbook of North American Indians* (20 vols.; Washington, DC: Smithsonian Institution, 1978), Bruce G. Trigger, ed., *Northeast* (1978), 622–35.
5. Lester, *Transylvania,* 35; Faragher, *Boone,* 111–12; regarding the Dark and Bloody Ground motif, see A. Gwynn Henderson, "Dispelling the

Myth: Seventeenth- and Eighteenth-Century Indian Life in Kentucky," *RKHS* 90(1992): 1–25.

6. James McCague, *The Cumberland* (New York: Holt, Rinehart and Winston, 1973) 32–34; Ramsey, *Annals,* 68; HSA, 145–47; Carolyn D. Wallin, *Elisha Wallen: The Long Hunter* (Johnson City, TN: Overmountain Press, 1990), 84–85.

7. LIFE, DM 3B:54–55.

8. George Washington, November 2, 1770, quoted in Hugh Cleland, *George Washington in the Ohio Valley* (Pittsburgh, PA: University of Pittsburgh Press, 1955), 261.

9. George Washington, October 29, 1770, Cleland, *Washington,* 259.

10. George Washington, November 19, 1770, Cleland, *Washington,* 266–67; George Washington to James Cleveland, January 10, 1775, in John C. Fitzpatrick, ed., *The Writings of George Washington* (Washington, DC: U.S. Printing Office, 1931), 3:260–61; regarding buffalo hair, see George Washington to David Bowers, May 28, 1779, 15:175–76; see also George Washington to Andrew Lewis, February 1, 1788, 29:397. Washington was not the only Virginian curious about buffalo. On October 12, 1783, Thomas Jefferson received a letter from Archibald Cary that said he "weighed a bull buffalo far from being fat, at 1150 [pounds], [but he] had killed much larger." Archibald Cary to Thomas Jefferson, October 12, 1783, in Julian P. Boyd, ed., *The Papers of Thomas Jefferson,* (New Jersey: Princeton University Press, 1952), 6:343; see also William Short to Thomas Jefferson, February 11, 1789, 14:543.

11. NOH, "Thomas Bullitt," *KY,* 139–40; concerning the relationship of Bullitt and Lord Dunmore, see Otis Rice, *Frontier Kentucky,* 2nd ed. (Lexington: University Press of Kentucky, 1992), 47–50; James C. Klotter, "James Harrod," *KY,* 413–14; "Robert McAfee," *KY,* 589; Thomas D. Clark, *A History of Kentucky* (Lexington, KY: John Bradford Press, 1960), 35–37.

12. Quoted in NOH, *RKHS* 69(1971): 202–3.

13. John Poage, February 3, 1853, "Ironton Register," DM 16E:1.

14. Thomas Hanson, c. 1774, DM 24CC:18; see also Lester, *Transylvania,* 52–55.

15. Deposition of Daniel Boone, Fayette County, Kentucky, Complete Book B, 211, quoted in NOH, "Pioneer Kentucky History: Separating the Facts from the Myths," n.p.; see also NOH, "The Fincastle Surveyors at the Falls of the Ohio, 1774," *FCHQ* 47(1973): 14–28.

16. LIFE, DM 3B:126–27.

17. Elizabeth A. Moize, "Daniel Boone: First Hero of the Frontier," *National*

Geographic 168 (December 1985): 812. Unless otherwise stated, material on Boone was drawn from LIFE; other works consulted were Bakeless, *Daniel Boone,* and Faragher, *Boone.*

18. Quoted in Lawrence Elliott, *The Long Hunter: A New Life of Daniel Boone* (New York: Reader's Digest, 1976), 43.
19. LIFE, DM 2B:138–39.
20. LIFE, DM 2B:152–53; LCD to Benson J. Lossing, January 22, 1853, DM 4C:29(2), 30–31.
21. Daniel Boone to John Filson, *The Discovery, Settlement and Present State of Kentucke,* originally published in 1784, many editions available (New York: Corinth Books, 1962), 50–51.
22. David Thompson to JDS, c. 1843, DM 12CC:199.
23. FJ, *Founders,* 314–15.
24. Filson, *Kentucke,* 54.
25. Elijah Bryan to LCD, December 16, 1884, DM 4C:36(3); see also Jacob Boone to LCD, January 4–5, 1890, DM 14C:84; Daniel Bryan to LCD, October 24, 1843, DM 22C:9(1).
26. Quoted in George W. Ranck, *Boonesborough,* 2nd ed. (Salem, NH: Ayer, 1986), 151.
27. For new interpretations of the complexities of the Sycamore Shoals treaty, see Tom Hatley, *The Dividing Paths: Cherokees and South Carolinians through the Revolutionary Era* (New York: Oxford University Press, 1995), 217–221; Colin G. Calloway, *The American Revolution in Indian Country: Crisis and Diversity in Native American Communities* (New York: Cambridge University Press, 1995), 189–90; for an expanded rendering of the history of the Transylvania Company, the March 1775 conference, the terms of the treaty, and the personnel involved, see Lester, *Transylvania,* 1–47.
28. Quoted in Faragher, *Boone,* 111; quoted in Duane H. King, "The Origin of the Eastern Cherokees as a Social and Political Entity." Duane H. King, ed., *The Cherokee Nation: A Troubled History,* (Knoxville: University of Tennessee Press, 1979), 164.
29. For Dragging Canoe, see Charles Robertson to Arthur Campbell, October 3, 1777, DM 1CC:184; quoted in Faragher, *Boone,* 124.
30. Other woodcutters included Captain William Twitty, Colonel Richard Callaway, Squire Boone, John Kennedy, William Bush, Michael Stoner, Samuel Coburn, James Bridges, Thomas Johnson, John Hart, William Hicks, James Peeke, and Felix Walker. See Lester, *Transylvania,* 59.
31. Unless otherwise cited, material for the Wilderness Road, Skaggs' Trace, and Boone's Trace was taken from Myer, *Indian Trails,* 59–66;

NOH, *RKHS* 68(1970): 91–131; Hanna, *Wilderness Trail*, 2:244–45; NOH, "Boone's Trace," *KY,* 101–2; NOH, "Skaggs Trace," *KY,* 825; see also biographies cited for Daniel Boone.

32. Henry Hamilton, April 24, 1779, quoted in *Hamilton,* ed. Barnhart, 198.
33. Richard Henderson, June 1775, LIFE, DM 4:25.
34. William Bush, quoted in NOH, "The First Trip to Boonesborough," *FCHQ* 45(1971): 256; David Lynch, quoted in NOH, *FCHQ* 45(1971): 259.
35. Samuel Estill, quoted in NOH, *FCHQ,* 45(1971): 257.
36. Quoted in Robert M. Coates, *The Outlaw Years: The History of the Land Pirates of the Natchez Trace* (New York: Macaulay Company, 1930), 5.
37. Ranck, *Boonesborough,* 11–13: Lester, *Transylvania,* 62–64.
38. S. Callaway to LCD, August 21, 1884, DM 7C:65(2–3); for another version see Septimus Schull, c. 1833, DM 11CC:51.
39 Felix Walker, LIFE, DM 3B:182–83; Lester, *Transylvania,* 65.
40. For the best accounts of the early beginnings of Boonesborough, see Lester, *Transylvania,* 78–98; also see Ranck, *Boonesborough,* 27–41.
41. James Nourse, June 5, 1775, "Journey to Kentucky in 1775: Diary of James Nourse," *The Journal of American History* 29 (1925):256; Nourse's description of Harrod's Town may be open to dispute. When Nourse returned to Harrod's Landing and described the Harrod's Town settlement to Nicholas Cresswell, who at that time had not seen it, Cresswell recorded a conflicting description of Harrod's Town in his journal on June 6, 1775: "Mr. Nourse informs me there is about thirty cabins in it [Harrod's Town], all built of logs and covered with clapboards, but not a nail in the whole town." Nicholas Cresswell, *Journal,* 82.
42. Simon Kenton, land depositions, August 23, 1821, and June 5, 1824, in DM 15C:25(1–2); see also the depositions of Daniel Boone, given June 20, 1817, DM 15C:25(5); see also Joshua McQueen to JDS, c. 1842, DM 13CC:121.
43. Quoted in NOH, *FCHQ* 45(1971): 261.
44. Nathan Reid to LCD, March 7, 1849, DM 10NN:149–50.
45. Richard Henderson, May 9, 1775, LIFE, DM 3B:205–6.
46. Richard Henderson, May 17, 1775, LIFE, DM 3B:210; Richard Henderson, May 20, 1775, LIFE, DM 4B:6–8; see also Lester, *Transylvania,* 94–95.
47. Richard Henderson, July 7, 1775, LIFE, DM 4B:25.
48. Quoted in FGR, 235; for more purported accounts about Kenton and buffalo, see Edna Kenton, *Simon Kenton: His Life and Period, 1755–1836,*

Reprint Edition (Salem, NH: Ayer Company, 1993), 5, 63, 70, 72, 84, 92.

49. James Wade to JDS, c. 1843, DM 12CC:16.
50. Quoted in Lester, *Transylvania*, 243.
51. LIFE, DM 4B:142–43; William Fleming, c. 1779–80, DM 2ZZ:74(1–2).
52. WC, 114–15, 119; for "bodkoos," see William T. Lamme to LCD, n.d., DM 5S:43(47); JDS, c. 1843, DM 11CC:282; William Fleming, c. 1779–80, DM 2ZZ:75(9).
53. Unless otherwise stated, excerpts by Nourse are taken from "Diary," 29: 121–38; 251–60; 351–64; see also NOH, *RKHS* 69(1971): 198–203.
54. James Nourse, May 28, 1775, "Diary," 29: 251–52.
55. James Nourse, June 3, 1775, "Diary," 29: 256.
56. James Nourse, June 18, 1775, "Diary," 29: 258–60.
57. James Nourse, June 25, 1775, "Diary," 29: 352–53.
58. James Nourse, June 25, 1775, "Diary," 29: 352.
59. James Nourse, June 23, 1775, "Diary," 29: 260.
60. James Nourse, June 28, 1775 "Diary," 29: 361.
61. James Nourse, June 28-29, 1775, "Diary," 29: 361–62.
62. James Nourse, June 28, 1775, "Diary," 29: 361.
63. James Nourse, June 28, 1775, "Diary," 29: 362.
64. Unless otherwise stated, excerpts by Cresswell are taken from *Journal*, 62–95.
65. Nicholas Cresswell, May 17, 1775, *Journal*, 75–77.
66. Nicholas Cresswell, May 23-24, 1775, *Journal*, 77–79.
67. Nicholas Cresswell, June 11, 1775, *Journal*, 84–85.
68. Nicholas Cresswell, June 19, 1775, *Journal*, 82–83.
69. Nicholas Cresswell, May 25 and 28, 1775, *Journal*, 79–80.
70. Nicholas Cresswell, June 1, 2, 11, and 16, 1775, *Journal*, 81, 84, 88.
71. Nicholas Cresswell, June 14, 1775, *Journal*, 86.
72. Stories of white buffalo west of the Mississippi are well known; in the East such tales are rare.
73. Nicholas Cresswell, July 2, 1775, *Journal*, 94.

CHAPTER 9. KENTUCKY II

1. JDS interview with Sarah Graham, c. 1840s, DM 12CC:45; see also Faragher, *Boone*, 146–47.
2. Trabue, *Westward*, 48.
3. LIFE, DM 4B:62.
4. Richard Holder to LCD, October 8, 1850, DM 24C:29; Samuel Dixon to LCD, February 3, 1852.

5. Bakeless, *Daniel Boone,* 142, 144–45.
6. Deposition of George Phelps, October 1796, in Jefferson County Kentucky Minutes, book 4, 331.
7. Nicholas Proctor, deposition given on June 8, 1816, DM 1A:194.
8. Spencer Records, c. 1842, DM 23CC:39–40.
9. GMB to LCD, DM 1A:17–18, 95; for "buffler knives" see *The Papers of Henry Laurens,* ed. Philip M. Hamer (Columbia: University of South Carolina Press, 1968), 1:378.
10. Daniel Bryan to LCD, n.d., DM 22C:14(9).
11. Spencer Records, c. 1842, DM 23CC:36–38.
12. LIFE, DM 4B:149–50; for the fullest account to date on the fate of Boone's salt boilers, see Ted Franklin Belue, "Terror in the Canelands: The Fate of Daniel Boone's Salt Boilers," *FCHQ* 68(1994), 3–34.
13. Josiah Collins, March 26, 1778, quoted in Lester, *Transylvania,* 195; Trabue, *Westward,* 47.
14. Quoted in Jack M. Sosin, *The Revolutionary Frontier: 1763–1783* (New York: Holt, Rinehart and Winston, 1967), 106.
15. Trabue, *Westward,* 54.
16. Josiah Collins to JDS, c. 1843–49, DM 12CC:63.
17. Sarah Graham to JDS, c. 1843–49, DM 12CC:45; George Graves to JDS, c. 1843–49, DM 11CC:122–23; Levi Todd, August 18, 1787, DM 18CC:6; Ephraim Sadowsky to JDS, c. 1843–49, DM 11CC:142, 145.
18. Trabue, *Westward,* 166, f. 46.
19. Quoted in FGR, 229.
20. James Alton James, ed., *George Rogers Clark Papers 1781–1784,* (Springfield, IL: American Manuscript Society Press, 1972), 2:ix, 260–61, 334, 352–53, 361.
21. John Donne, November 23, 1780, Fort Jefferson, from George Rogers Clark Papers, Archives Branch, Archives and Records Division: Virginia State Library, Richmond, n.p. Copies from box 14A, Department of Archaeology, Murray State University, Murray, Kentucky, repository for the copies and indexed by Dr. Kenneth C. Carstens. Unless otherwise stated, subsequent quotes on Fort Jefferson are from this collection.
22. John Donne, March 17, 1781, Fort Jefferson.
23. Captain Robert George, March 27, 1781, Fort Jefferson.
24. Leonard Helm to George Slaughter, October 29, 1780, Fort Jefferson.
25. Trabue, *Westward,* 75.
26. A. Campbell, c. 1780, DM 13CC:82–87.
27. Filson, *Kentucke,* 73.
28. December 27, 1780, delivery by Joshua Archer to Fort Jefferson.

29. Daniel Bryan to LCD, n.d., DM 22C:14(9).

30. LCD interview with Moses Boone, c. 1846, DM 19C:28.

31. Spencer Records, c. 1842, DM 23CC:33–35; WC to JDS, 104–6, 112.

32. William Fleming, March 20, 1780, Mereness, *Travels,* 636.

33. James and Samuel McAfee, c. 1842, DM 14CC:115.

34. Rachel Denton to LCD, January 5, 1856, DM 23C:104(2).

35. Quoted in FGR, 235.

36. Trabue, *Westward,* 75.

37. This and subsequent quotes by John Floyd are taken from Hambleton Tapp, "Colonel John Floyd, Kentucky Pioneer," *FCHQ* 15(1941): 1–24.

38. Simon Girty, c. 1781, quoted in Consul Willshire Butterfield, *History of the Girtys,* 2nd ed. (Columbus, OH: Long's College Book Company, 1950), 190–91.

39. John Crawford to JDS, c. 1843–48, DM 12CC:161. Maligned, misunderstood, and hated, Girty emerged by the early 1800s as the prototypical "white savage renegade." Through eighteenth-century American eyes it is not hard to see why Girty—Patriot turned Tory, defender of Indian rights, willing tool of the British Indian Department—was hated. Yet Girty helped those he could. He befriended Daniel Boone during his Shawnee days, was a sworn brother to Simon Kenton, and saved Kenton's life. John Burkhart, Thomas Ridout, Samuel Murphy, William May, Margaret Handley Erksine, Henry Baker, and at least a dozen more captives were saved by his efforts. For a balanced overview of Girty's life, see Phillip Hoffman, "Simon Girty," *The American Revolution: 1775–1783, An Encyclopedia,* ed. Richard L. Blanco (New York: Garland Publishing, 1993), I:660–64 Belue, *Buckskinning VII,* 58–59.

40. JDS interview with Ben Guthrie, in Mrs. William H. Coffman, ed., "Big Crossing Station, Built by Robert Johnson," *FCHQ* 5(1931): 9.

41. Reverend John Brown to William Preston, May 5, 1775, in Reuben Gold Thwaites and Louise Phelps Kellogg, eds., *Revolution in the Upper Ohio, 1775–1777,* (Madison: State Historical Society of Wisconsin, 1908), 10.

42. Lester, *Transylvania,* 86–87.

43. This and subsequent quotes by Houston regarding tanning are from Peter Houston to F. W. Houston, c. 1842, DM 20C:84(24–26). In another contemporary account of the era, it is observed that frontier attire for most women in Kentucky was "nothing but a petticoat over their shift and a handkerchief round their necks"; such feminine dress might be adorned with trade silver confiscated from Indians or pewter

brooches cut from old plates. In 1768 in backcountry South Carolina, Reverend Charles Woodmason observed that "females . . . come to Service in their Shifts and short petticoat only, barefooted and Barelegged—Without caps or Handkerchiefs—dress'd only in their hair." See Roseann R. Hogan, "Buffaloes in the Corn: James Wade's Account of Pioneer Kentucky, *RKHS* 89(1991): 23; for brooches, see George Yocum to JDS, c. 1843–49, DM 12CC:150, Woodmason quoted in Kay Moss and Kathryn Hoffman, *The Backcountry Housewife* (Charlotte, NC: Schiele Museum, 1994), 4.

44. Scooped out hollows of what may be bark tanyards can still be seen among the overgrown remnants of Boone's Station, near Athens.
45. John Evans Finlay, 1790, DM 12ZZ:77.
46. John Bradford, November 17, 1826, quoted in *Bradford's Notes,* 52–53; David Thompson to JDS, c. 1843, DM 12CC:199.
47. Thomas D. Clark, "Salt: A Factor in the Settlement of Kentucky," *FCHQ* 12(1938): 42–52; see also Frederick Jackson Turner, *The Frontier in American History,* 3rd ed. (Malabar, FL: Robert E. Krieger, 1985), 17–18.
48. Robert E. McDowell, "The Wilderness Road in Jefferson County," *Louisville* (June 20, 1967), 7–15.
49. Robert E. McDowell, "Bullitt's Lick: The Related Saltworks and Settlements," *FCHQ* 30(1956): 241–59.
50. Parts of the old trace weave in and out of Old Shepherdsville Road and Preston Highway and on to downtown Louisville.
51. For William Fleming's travels in 1779–80, see Fleming's journal in DM 2ZZ:74ff; see also Mereness, *Travels,* 617–58.
52. Roy E. Appleman, "Joseph and Reuben Field: Kentucky Frontiersmen of the Lewis and Clark Expedition and their father, Abraham," *FCHQ* 49(1975): 16–18; see also NOH, *FCHQ* 52(1978): 147–165.
53. Thomas Perkins to Joseph Palmer, July 24, 1785, quoted in "Letters of Thomas Perkins to Gen. Joseph Palmer, Lincoln County, Kentucky, 1785," ed. James E. Bentley, *FCHQ* 49(1975): 147.
54. FGR, 235; for William Sudduth, see Lucien Beckner, "A Sketch of the Early Adventures of William Sudduth in Kentucky," *FCHQ* 2(1928): 47; for Ben Guthrie, see LCD, n.d., DM 14C:6; for letter, author unknown, February 21, 1786, DM 3U:207.
55. LIFE, DM 4B:90.
56. John Haywood, *The Civil and Political History of the State of Tennessee,* 2nd ed. (Knoxville, TN: Tenase, 1969), 94; see also HSA, 209.
57. Edward Bryan to LCD, October 2, 1863, DM 30S:257.
58. M. M. Henkle, April 20, 1843, Obituary of Ann Harrod, Harrodsburg,

Kentucky, *Western Christian Advocate,* May 12,1843, DM 12C:25; see also Trabue, *Westward,* 56, 169.

59. Mrs. Kitty Phillips interview by JDS, c. 1843, DM 16CC:291.

60. Trabue, *Westward,* 48; for Joel Sappington, see Joshua McQueen, c. 1842, DM 13CC:122; for Nathan Boone, see DM 6S:208; for Simon Kenton, see Fielding Belt to LCD, n.d., DM21S:208–09.

61. GMB to LCD, DM 1A:19.

62. NB to LCD, DM 6S:240–41.

63. NB to LCD, DM 6S:159–60.

64. HFB to LCD, DM 30S:257–260.

65. HFB to LCD, DM 30S:260.

66. WC to JDS, 104.

67. WC to JDS, 104.

68. WC to JDS, 108.

69. WC to JDS, 104.

70. GMB to LCD, DM 1A:35–36.

71. Isaac Cunningham to JDS, c. 1843–49, DM 11CC:26; Walker Kelso to JDS, c. 1843–49, DM 12CC:42; James Wade to JDS, c. 1843–49, DM 12CC:29.

72. Enoch, "John Hanks," 140.

73. Trabue, *Westward,* 72, 74.

74. Trabue, *Westward,* 74; James Wade to JDS, c. 1843–49, DM 12CC:29.

75. Joshua McQueen to JDS, c. 1842, DM 13CC:119, 121.

76. WC to JDS, 114–15, 123.

77. For an analysis of Filson's *Kentucke* compared to John Trumball's plagiarized version, see Michael A. Lofaro, "The Eighteenth Century 'Autobiographies' of Daniel Boone," *FCHQ* 76(1978): 85–97.

78. Filson, *Kentucke,* 27.

79. Quoted in Jakle, *Images,* 49–50.

80. Faragher, *Boone,* 77; WC to JDS, 98.

CHAPTER 10. PENNSYLVANIA'S "VAST HERDS"

1. That Reverend Ettwein observed land beneath the woodland canopy that appeared as "cleared fields" actually suggests that portions of the landscape had been subjected to repeated controlled burnings.

2. HWS, 23–24.

3. HWS, 17.

4. HWS, 11–12, 16–18; For a critical analysis of Shoemaker's book, see FGR, 28ff, 248–56.

5. Quoted in John E. Guilday, "Evidence for Buffalo in Prehistoric Pennsylvania," *Pennsylvania Archaeologist* 33(1963): 135; SZ, 11.

6. Guilday, "Evidence," 136; SZ, 131.

7. HWS, 11–12, 16–18.

8. HWS, 24–25.

9. Jakle, *Images*, 54.

10. HWS, 28–36; also quoted in DAD, 14–18.

11. HWS, 43.

12. SZ, 15.

13. HWS, 38–43.

14. Gabriel Thomas, *An Historical and Geographical Account of the Province and Country of Pennsylvania; and of West-New-Jersey in America,* 2nd ed. (New York: New York Historical Society, 1848), A2, 15, 43, 45.

15. For Thomas Penn, see Pennsylvania State Archives Group 17: Land Office Surveyor General Journals: Penn Journal C, 20; for Hugh Gibson's memoirs, see "An Account of the Captivity of Hugh Gibson among the Delaware Indians," *Collections of the Massachusetts Historical Society* 6(1837): 148; see also John W. Jordan, ed., "Journal of James Kenny, 1761–1763," *The Pennsylvania Magazine of History and Biography* 37(1913): 13. All three references are quoted by Gail M. Gibson, in "Historical Evidence of the Buffalo in Pennsylvania," *The Pennsylvania Magazine of History and Biography* 63(1969): 157–58.

16. Charles Hamilton, ed., *Braddock's Defeat: The Journal of Captain Robert Cholmley's Batman; The Journal of a British Officer; Halkett's Orderly Book,* (Norman: University of Oklahoma Press, 1959), 19, 21, 24–25, 47.

17. Gibson, "Historical Evidence," 159.

18. Gordon and Collins quoted in Gibson, "Historical Evidence," 159–60. Stephanie Zebrowski argues that these sightings may have been in Maryland or West Virginia. See SZ, 19–21.

19. "Account of the Voyage of the Beautiful River Made in 1749, under the Direction of Monsieur de Celeron, by Father Bonnecamps," *JRAD,* 69:151–99.

20. See Samuel N. Rhoads, *The Mammals of Pennsylvania and New Jersey* (Philadelphia: privately published, 1903), 5, 47–51, 239; for early discoveries of buffalo fossils in Pennsylvania, see Samuel N. Rhoads, "Distribution of the American Bison in Pennsylvania with Remarks on a New Fossil Species," *Proceedings, Academy of Natural Sciences* (Philadelphia, 1895), 244–48.

21. See John E. Guilday, "Evidence for Buffalo," *Pennsylvania Archaeologist,* 135–39; for a similar conclusion, see A. W. Schroger, "The Validity of *Bison bison pennsylvanicus,*" *Journal of Mammalogy* 25(1944): 313–15; for a scientific listing and discussion of what animal remains and arti-

facts were found at a representative dig site, see James B. Bressler, "Excavation of the Bull Run Site 36LY119, *Pennsylvania Archaeologist* 50, no. 4: 31–63.

22. For Father Jean de Breboeuf, see *JRAD* 1:21–26, 4:181, 5:57, 73, 257–65; for his torturous end, see *JRAD* 34: 25–27; see also Francis Parkman, *France and England in North America,* 3rd. ed. (New York: The Library of America, 1983), 1:670–74; Dr. William Egle quoted in SZ, 12; for the relevance of place names as proof of the existence of buffalo in Pennsylvania, see Gibson, "Historical Evidence," 151–60; SZ, personal correspondence, April 4, 1995.

23. Quoted in SZ, 16.

24. Father Simon Le Moine, September 2, 1654, *JRAD,* 41: 126–29; Father Claude Dablon, September 15, 1655, *JRAD,* 42: 62–65; see also Gibson, "Historical Evidence," 157–58.

25. Quoted in Gibson, "Historical Evidence," 160.

CHAPTER 11. SCOURING OF THE FIRST FAR WEST

1. Lester, *Transylvania,* 265.

2. *Atlas of Great Lakes Indian History,* ed. Helen Hornbeck Tanner (Norman: University of Oklahoma Press, 1987), 84–86.

3. Faragher, *Boone,* 249.

4. Isaac Ruddell to "Col. Mutir," September 12, 1785, quoted in Bakeless, *Daniel Boone,* 315.

5. *Atlas,* ed. Hornbeck, 87–121.

6. André Michaux, 1802, *EWT,* 3:221.

7. Quoted in Jakle, *Images,* 54–57.

8. John Ross, 1812, quoted in EWC, 152.

9. William Faux, *EWT,* 2:210.

10. Peter Houston, c. 1842, DM 20C:84(54).

11. FJ, *Founders,* 323.

12. Quoted in White, *Middle Ground,* 490

13. For a cogent analysis of this theory, see Calvin Martin, *Keepers of the Game: Indian-Animal Relationships and the Fur Trade* (Berkeley: University of California Press, 1982), ix, 146–49.

14. White, *Middle Ground,* 488–90.

15. For Tenskwatawa, see R. David Edmunds, *The Shawnee Prophet* (Lincoln: University of Nebraska Press, 1983); for Tecumseh, see R. David Edmunds, *Tecumseh and the Quest for Indian Leadership* (Boston: Little, Brown and Company, 1984).

16. Quoted by Edward Walsh, 1804, in Dr. Ruth B. Phillips, *Patterns of Power* (Kleinburg, ON: McMichael Canadian Collection, 1984), 28.
17. See Gregory Evans Dowd, *A Spirited Resistance: The North American Indian Struggle For Unity, 1745–1815* (Baltimore, MD: Johns Hopkins University Press, 1992).
18. JH, c. 1773, 108–9.
19. JH, August 28–29, 1792, 278.
20. JH, September 2 and October 18, 1792, 279, 286.
21. JH, October 7–9, 1792, 284–85.
22. JH, December 10, 1792, 291.
23. Thomas D. Clark, *KY,* xix.
24. Quoted in NOH, *RKHS* 68(1970): 124.
25. Thomas D. Clark, *KY,* xx.
26. Christopher Mann to LCD, October 15, 1883, DM 15C:26(1).
27. Lucien Beckner, *FCHQ* 2(1928): 48, 52.
28. Lucien Beckner, ed., "John D. Shane's Interview with Benjamin Allen, Clark County," *FCHQ* 5(1931): 69–77.
29. Daniel Boone's ledger book, November 1, 1794, DM 27C:47.
30. "John D. Shane's Interview with Jesse Graddy of Woodford County," ed. Lucien Beckner, *FCHQ* 20(1946): 13.
31. JDS interview with M. Stites, c. 1842, DM 13CC:107.
32. John Hedges to JDS, c. 1843–49, DM 11CC:20.
33. John Johnston to LCD, December 29, 1847, DM 11YY:32–32(1).
34. Brent Altsheler, *FCHQ* 5(1931): 174.
35. Francis Baily, *Journal of a Tour in the Unsettled Parts of North America in 1796 and 1797,* ed. Jack D. L. Holmes (Carbondale: Southern Illinois University Press, 1969).
36. Byron Crawford, "Inn the Old Days: Tavern on Buffalo Trails May Reopen," *The Courier-Journal,* March 14, 1983: B1, B2.
37. André Michaux, c. 1802, *EWT,* 3:233–34; see also FGR, 233.
38. Fortescue Cumings, July 21, 1809, *EWT,* 4:177–78.
39. William Faux, January 22, 1820, *EWT,* 12:19–20.
40. Robert W. Kingsolver, "Buffalo," *KY,* 138; see also FGR, 237.
41. Donelson's narrative is found in SCW, 231–42; for an alternate rendering with commentary, see HSA, 235–40.
42. Lester, *Transylvania,* 268-269; see also HSA, 228–29.
43. John Donelson, March 26, 1780, quoted in SCW, 240–41.
44. Quoted in MSG, 22–23; see also FTR, 237.
45. Sampson Williams to T. H. Williams, May 7, 1840, DM 5XX:19.

46. Quoted in HSA, 233; Ramsey, *Annals,* 450.
47. William Croghan's diary, November–December, 1784, DM 1N:6–11.
48. John Lipscomb, June 24, 1784, quoted in SCW, 276. Lipscomb's journal appears in SCW, 269–79; John Lipscomb, August 7, 1784, quoted in SCW, 278.
49. HSA, 296–99.
50. HSA, 262–63; 336.
51. Quoted in Remington Kellogg, "Annotated List," 300.
52. John W. Gray, *The Life of Joseph Bishop,* 2nd ed. (Spartanburg, SC: Reprint Company, 1974), 48, 86, 94–97, 106, 116–17, 122–23.
53. HFB to LCD, DM 30S:268–70; General William Hall to LCD, c. 1841–44, DM 3B:81.
54. Lewis Brantz, December 1785, quoted in SCW, 285.
55. Quoted in Kellogg, "Annotated List," 300.
56. Haywood, *Tennessee,* 234.
57. All quotes cited in previous chapters.
58. Quoted in FGR, 232.
59. FGR, 229–230.
60. Joseph Buell, October 14, year unknown, quoted in Hulbert, *Highways,* 1:114.
61. Quoted in R. David Edmunds, *Tecumseh and the Quest for Indian Leadership,* ed. Oscar Handlin (Boston, MA: Little, Brown, and Company, 1984), 63–64.
62. FGR, 230.
63. FGR, 230–31, note 28; for George Croghan, see Brent Altsheler, *FCHQ* 5(1931): 173; JH, April 24, 1773, 108; JDS interview with Joshua McQueen, c. 1842, DM 13CC:121.
64. Quoted in FGR, 232.
65. Josiah Harmar to Michael Hillegas, April 30, 1789, DM 2W:37–38.
66. *Atlas,* ed. Hornbeck, 72–73, 89.
67. DAD, 13–14; McHugh, *Buffalo,* 271–72.
68. James Mooney, *Myths of the Cherokee and Sacred Formulas of the Cherokees,* 2nd ed. (Nashville, TN: Charles Elder, 1972), 447; FGR, 232; see also McHugh, *Buffalo,* 272.
69. Quoted in H. Addington Bruce, *Daniel Boone and the Wilderness Road* (New York: Macmillan, 1910), 330; see also Faragher, *Boone,* 227–33.
70. Quoted in Faragher, *Boone,* 272. Originally appeared in John James Audubon, *Delineations of American Scenery and Character* (New York: G. A. Baker, 1926), 115.

71. M. W. Vanlear to Daniel Boone, April 27, 1790, DM 27C:6; M. W. Vanlear to Daniel Boone, March 6, 1792, DM 27C:10; Faragher, *Boone,* 264–65; see also FGR, 232, 247.
72. NB to LCD, DM 6S:197; Thomas Rodgers to LCD, n.d., DM 19S:168.
73. In 1786 Gallatin recorded one of the earliest attempts at propagating hybrids between buffalo and domestic cattle. Such mixed-breed bovine, he said, were common.
74. FRG, 231–32, 247, 707; see also John P. Hale, *Trans-Allegheny Pioneers: Historical Sketches of the First White Settlements West of the Alleghenies 1748 and After,* 2nd. ed. (Bowie, MD: Heritage Books, 1988), 2.
75. Mark Van Doren, ed., *The Travels of William Bartram* (New York: Barnes and Noble, 1940), 62; ER, 399.
76. ER, 406, note 58; DAD, 19; for a discussion regarding the last buffalo killed east of the Mississippi, see FGR, 226, 230.

CHAPTER 12: REQUIEM
1. Quoted in DAD, 243–44, 272–74; Kingsolver, *KY,* 138; FGR, 707, 709, 711.
2. Kellogg, "Annotated List," 300.
3. DAD, 20–29, 117, 286–89; McHugh, *Buffalo,* 13–17, 26.
4. For a firsthand, unabashedly gut-wrenching look at the grim business and lifestyle of Great Plains buffalo runners during the late 1800s, see Frank H. Mayer and Charles B. Roth, *The Buffalo Harvest,* 2nd. ed. (Union City, TN: Pioneer Press, 1995), 33, 37–42.
5. All historic highway markers are from Mary Lou S. Madigan and Diane Wells, *Update: Guide to Kentucky Historical Markers* (Frankfort: Kentucky Historical Society, 1983), sign numbers 217–19, 1307, 1519, 1567.
6. NOH, *RKHS* 69(1971): 201–202.
7. Otto A. Rothert, "News and Comments," *FCHQ* 12 (1938): 170–71.

A Selected Annotated
Bibliography

MOST OF THE EYEWITNESS ACCOUNTS OF BUFFALO IN KENTUCKY, TEN-
nessee, Illinois, and western Virginia came from memoirs, narratives,
muster rolls, and other records found in the Draper Manuscript Collection.
Those especially rich in buffalo lore are the George M. Bedinger Papers,
Draper's unfinished "Life of Boone," the Daniel Boone Papers, William
Croghan Papers, Draper's Notes, Frontier Wars Papers, Kentucky Papers,
Robert Patterson Papers, Tennessee Papers, and Virginia Papers. Another
major source for firsthand accounts is *The Jesuit Relations and Allied
Documents.*

Primary sources that were especially helpful are the writings and
narratives from Diron D'Artaguiette, Nathan Boone, Colonel William
Byrd, George Rogers Clark, William Clinkenbeard, Nicholas Cresswell,
George Croghan, Pierre Le Moyne Sieur d'Iberville, John Donelson,
John Filson, Christopher Gist, John Heckewelder, Richard Henderson,
Louis Hennepin, Louis Jolliet, John Lawson, Jacques Marquette, George
Morgan, James Nourse, Diego Peña, Jean Penicant, Antoine Simone Le
Page du Pratz, Henry Timberlake, Daniel Trabue, Felix Walker, and
Thomas Walker.

Other useful primary and secondary accounts are included in works
by Clarence Walworth Alvord, Harriette Simpson Arnow, John Bakeless,
Charles J. Balesi, Edward Chester, W. P. Cumming, David A. Dary, John
Mack Faragher, Martin S. Garretson, Charles A. Hanna, William T. Hor-
naday, John Alton James, T. Stoddard Johnson, Remington Kellogg,
William Stewart Lester, Samuel N. Rhoads, Douglas L. Rights, Frank
Gilbert Roe, Reuben Gold Thwaites, and Samuel Cole Williams.

For southeastern Native Americans, major works consulted were
John R. Swanton's ethnographies, especially *The Indians of the Southeastern
United States,* and Charles Hudson's *The Southeastern Indians.* Regarding
Indians and the environment, see works by Kathryn E. Holland Braund,

William Cronon, Tom Hatley, Francis Jennings, Calvin Martin, James Merrell, Timothy Silver, Daniel Usner, and Richard White.

For traces and trails, see works by Harriette Simpson Arnow, Neal O. Hammon, Charles Hanna, Archer Butler Hulbert, J. Stoddard Johnson, Mary Lou Madigan, Robert E. McDowell, Otto A. Rothert, and Dianne Wells. Neal O. Hammon's essays are the best source on traces and roads in Kentucky. An extensive work on paths in the eastern United States is William E. Myers's *Indian Trails of the Southeast.*

The work of Erhard Rostland contains a comprehensive collection of firsthand accounts of the Spanish in the Southeast. References regarding the range of eastern buffalo are found in the writings of John W. Allen, Roy E. Appleton, Mark F. Boyd, Colonel William Byrd, Martin S. Garretson, William T. Hornaday, Samuel N. Rhoads, Douglas L. Rights, Frank Gilbert Roe, and Reuben Gold Thwaites.

Few books on buffalo in the West are listed. Frank Gilbert Roe's *The North American Buffalo: A Critical Study of the Species in Its Wild State* is still the authoritative standard. Others include *The Buffalo Book: The Full Saga of the American Animal,* by David A. Dary, and *Head, Hides and Horns: The Complete Buffalo Book,* by Larry Barsness.

The following selected lists are far from exhaustive. See notes for a comprehensive listing.

MANUSCRIPTS

George Rogers Clark Papers, Archives Branch, Archives and Records Division: Virginia State Library, Richmond. Copies from Box 14A, Department of Archaeology, Murray State University, Murray, Kentucky, repository for the copies and indexed by Dr. Kenneth C. Carstens.

Contains data on Clark's Fort Jefferson occupation c.1780–81.

Lyman C. Draper Manuscript Collection. 486 vols. Microfilm ed. Madison: The State Historical Society of Wisconsin, 1980.

The scope and content of this extensive collection is immense. Dr. Lyman Copeland Draper records the reflections, memoirs, diaries, narratives, and other such documents of pioneers.

John Floyd Papers. Transcribed from the Draper Manuscript Collection by Neal O. Hammon and housed in the Filson Club.

Contains John Floyd's (1750–83) Kentucky correspondence.

PAPERS

Carstens, Kenneth C. "Fact vs. Fiction: Military Engagements At George Rogers Clark's Fort Jefferson, 1780–1781." 1991.

This essay, presented at the George Rogers Clark Trans-Appalachian Frontier History Conference in 1989 at Vincennes University, Indiana, is a succinct summary of the history of Fort Jefferson, located at the confluence of the Ohio and Mississippi in 1780–81.

Chester, Edward W. "The Kentucky Prairie Barrens of Northwestern Middle Tennessee: An Historical and Floristic Perspective." Paper presented at the Proceeding of the First Annual Symposium, sponsored by TVA's Land Between the Lakes, 1988.

This monograph on the prairie barrens of Tennessee discusses the parameters of the grasslands, their floristic composition, and the barrens.

De Jong, C. G. van Zyell. "Historical Geographic Variation in North American Bison and the Taxonomic Status of Remnant Populations of Wood Bison." Paper presented at the North American Bison Workshop, September 9–10, 1987.

A brief discussion on the morphological differences between *Bison bison bison* and *Bison bison athabascae.*

ARTICLES

Altsheler, Brent. "The Long Hunters and James Knox Their Leader." *FCHQ* 5(1931): 167–85.

A generally accurate account of the Long Hunters of Kentucky and Tennessee and buffalo hunting.

Appleman, Roy E. "Joseph and Reuben Field: Kentucky Frontiersmen of the Lewis and Clark Expedition and Their Father, Abraham." *FCHQ* 49(1975): 5–36.

Tells of the demise of the buffalo in Jefferson and Bullitt Counties of Kentucky and provides data on buffalo behavior and traces.

Beckner, Lucien. "John D. Shane's Interview with Benjamin Allen, Clark County." *FCHQ* 5(1931): 63–98. Originally found in DM 11CC: 67–69.

Allen lived near present-day Richmond, Kentucky, in 1790, and his recollections are full of stories of Indian and hunting, including a description of how Indians made fake scalps from buffalo wool to sell to the British.

_____. "John D. Shane's Interview with Jesse Graddy of Woodford County." *FCHQ* 20(1946): 10–17. Originally found in DM 13CC: 130–34.

This memoir contains Jesse Graddy's statement that by 1787 "the buffalo were gone. Never saw a wild one."

_____. "John D. Shane's Interview with Pioneer William Clinkenbeard." *FCHQ* 2(1928): 95–128. Originally found in DM 11CC:54–66.

Features tales of Indian warfare, insights on frontier life, and much buffalo lore.

_____. "The Moundbuilders." *FCHQ* 29(1955): 203–25.
Information on the prehistory of Kentucky, traces, and evidence suggesting the late arrival of the buffalo east of the Mississippi.

_____. "A Sketch of the Early Adventures of William Suddeth in Kentucky." *FCHQ* 2(1928): 95–128.
Includes a few incidents of buffalo hunting in Clark County, Kentucky, after 1783.

Bentley, James R. "Letters of Thomas Perkins to General Joseph Palmer, Lincoln County, Kentucky, 1785." *FCHQ* 49(1975): 141–51.
Contains a few excerpts about buffalo and salt licks.

Boyd, Mark F. "The Occurrence of the American Bison in Alabama and Florida." *Science* 84(1936): 203.
An essay on the expedition of Marcos Delgado in Florida and Alabama from "Apalachee to the Creek country in 1686." Boyd mentions William Hornaday's thesis that there are no records of buffalo in the Deep South of North America.

Clark, Thomas D. "Salt, a Factor in the Settlement of Kentucky." *FCHQ* 12(1938): 42–52.
Describes the importance of salt to the early (1770s) settlers of Kentucky.

Coffman, Mrs. William H. "Big River Crossing: Built by Robert Johnson." *FCHQ* 5(1931): 1–15. Originally found in DM 11CC:76–79.
Consists of an interview with Kentucky pioneer Ben Guthrie. Graphic accounts of buffalo hunting in Kentucky (c. 1780s) and Indian activity.

Crawford, Byron. "Inn the Old Days: Tavern on Buffalo Trails May Reopen." *Louisville Courier-Journal* (March 14 1983):B1.
The Offutt-Cole tavern, according to Crawford, was "The first stagecoach stop west of the Alleghenies." It was erected on an original survey by Hancock Taylor between Lexington and Frankfort. It is thought that in 1773 Taylor and his band of Fincastle, Virginia, surveyors used the cabin for shelter. The National Heritage Commission has declared that the tavern is "the oldest existing log building in Kentucky." The chinking between the logs in the walls is made from mud and buffalo wool.

Hammon, Neal O. "Early Louisville and the Beargrass Stations." *FCHQ* 52(1978): 147–65.
Includes references to traces in Bullitt and Jefferson County that were developed into roads.

_____. "Early Roads into Kentucky." *RKHS* 68(1970): 91–131.

A summary of Indian paths and traces that led into eastern and central Kentucky, such as Boone's Trace, Skaggs' Trace, the road from Cumberland Gap to Flat Lick, and many more. Includes a number of excerpts from eighteenth-century narratives that feature eyewitness accounts of buffalo.

_____. "The Fincastle Surveyors at the Falls of the Ohio, 1774." *FCHQ* 47(1973): 14–28.

Discusses the party of thirty-six surveyors that came down the Ohio to Kentucky by way of Point Pleasant, western Virginia, and the plats of their surveys. Some of those mentioned are John Floyd, James Harrod, Isaac Hite, Hancock Taylor, James Douglas, and James Knox. Includes data on buffalo traces and Hammon's diagrams of the original survey lines in relation to modern-day Louisville.

_____. "The First Trip to Boonesborough." *FCHQ* 45(1971): 249–63.

An annotated account of the narrative of Felix Walker, a roadcutter for Daniel Boone in 1775. Includes maps and textual material from Hammon on traces, comments on the settlers' use of buffalo roads, and information on herds.

_____. "Historic Lawsuits of the Eighteenth Century Locating the 'Stamping Ground.'" *RKHS* 69(1971): 197–215.

A listing of eighteenth-century lawsuits for the contested Stamping Ground in Scott County, Kentucky. Although the legal aspect of this material may be of passing interest to researchers, this essay includes many firsthand observations of buffalo and traces.

Kellogg, Remington. "Annotated List of Tennessee Mammals." Smithsonian Institution, *Proceedings of the National Museum* 86 (1939): 245–303.

Includes accounts of buffalo in the Cumberland from prehistory to the animal's extermination in Tennessee in 1819.

McDowell, Robert E. "Bullitt's Lick: The Related Saltworks and Settlements." *FCHQ* 30(1956): 241–69.

An interesting account on the importance of salt on the frontier. Includes information on buffalo herds and traces in Bullitt County, Kentucky, c. 1778–79.

_____. "The Wilderness Road in Jefferson County." *Louisville* Vol. 20 (June 1967): 7–15.

This essay by the late editor of the *Filson Club History Quarterly* retraces the western prong of the Wilderness Trail in Jefferson and Bullitt Counties, Kentucky. Mentioned are Squire Boone, George Rogers

Clark, William Preston, William Fleming, Joseph Brooks, James Francis Moore, Alexander Breckinridge, John Floyd, and others. Complete with aerial photographs, photos of old traces and buffalo fords, maps, and a generous helping of frontier Kentuckiana c. 1780, this article is helpful in understanding the location of the Beargrass settlements, the Fish Pools, and other outposts in the region.

Nourse, James. "Journey to Kentucky in 1775." *The Journal of American History* 29 (1925): 121–38; 251–60; 351–64.

Nourse left London for Virginia on March 16, 1769, and in 1775 floated down the Ohio by dugout with a company of men with the intent to get land. Nourse and his party, which included Nicholas Cresswell, went to Harrod's Town and Boonesborough, traveling the Kentucky River, and returned to the eastern settlements the same year. Nourse's laconic writings, as compared with the much more eloquent narrative of the same trip by Cresswell, include many entries about buffalo in Kentucky.

Rhoads, Samuel N. "Distribution of the American Bison in Pennsylvania with Remarks on a New Fossil Species." *Proceedings of the Academy of Natural Sciences,* Philadelphia, Pennsylvania (1895): 244–48.

In this examination of bison molars and bones found in Pennsylvania, Rhoads asserts that most of the fragments inspected are *Bison bison* and extends its easternmost wanderings to the Delaware Valley.

Rights, Douglas L. "The Buffalo in North Carolina." *North Carolina Historical Review* 9(1932): 242–49.

An overview of primary source observations of buffalo in North Carolina from 1521 to 1730.

Rostlund, Erhard. "The Geographic Range of the Historic Bison in the Southeast." *Annals of the Association of American Geographers* 4(1960): 395–407.

Lists numerous eyewitness sightings of buffalo herds and Indian-made buffalo wares in Georgia, Louisiana, Florida, Alabama, and North and South Carolina. The accounts range from the 1575 memoirs of Do. d'Escalante Fontaneda to the 18th-century writings of Alexander Hewat. This is the most detailed study of the southeastern range of the eastern buffalo yet published. Earlier boundaries established by William Hornaday (1889) and Dr. Joel A. Allen (1876) excluded southern Louisiana, Alabama, half of Georgia, and Florida; Frank Gilbert Roe in *The North American Buffalo* (1951) did likewise. Rostlund cites dozens of buffalo sightings well beyond the limits of the Allen-Hornaday boundary.

Rothert, Otto A. "News and Comments." *FCHQ* 12(1938): 170–71.
Mentions how a buffalo trace in Jefferson County, Kentucky, was developed by early road builders and later became U.S. Highway 31W.
_____. "Solon Robinson: Pioneer and Agriculturist." *FCHQ* 10(1936): 185–202.
Selected writings from Solon Robinson—an 19th-century Kentuckian—regarding travel along buffalo traces.

Rucker, Tom. "News from Forest Resources Development." *Tennessee Valley Authority* 1(1992): 1–2.
Discusses the environmental impact fire had on native trees.

Shoup, C. S. "Notes from the Background of Our Knowledge of the Zoology of Tennessee." *Tennessee Academy of Science* 19(1944): 126–36.
A summary of observations of Tennessee wildlife. Includes a few mentions of buffalo, mostly from James Needham (1673) and John Donelson (1780).

Zebrowski, Stephanie. "Debunking a Myth—Were There Really Buffalo in Pennsylvania?" *The Journal,* Lycoming County Historical Society, Williamsport, Pennsylvania 39(1989): 11–23.
Essential to any study of eastern buffalo, Zebrowski's essay deals a death blow to the claims of writers who have reported that Pennsylvania during the historic period was teeming with buffalo.

BOOKS

Alvord, Clarence Walworth. *The Illinois Country 1673–1818.* Chicago: A. G. McClurg and Company, 1922.
Presents a good overview of life in Illinois prior to statehood, including the impact of George Croghan and the firm Baynton, Wharton, and Morgan on the old Northwest.

Alvord, Clarence Walworth, and Clarence Edwin Carter, eds. *Trade and Politics 1767–1769.* Collections of the Illinois State Historical Society, Springfield, IL: Illinois State Historical Library, 1921. British Series, vol. 3.
Includes the correspondence between George Morgan in Illinois and the Philadelphia firm of Baynton, Wharton, and Morgan. Many references to buffalo.

Arnow, Harriette Simpson. *Seedtime on the Cumberland.* 2nd ed. Lexington: University Press of Kentucky, 1983.
Includes many graphic pioneer accounts of life in Kentucky and Tennessee. Numerous references to buffalo hunting, many of which were drawn from the Draper Manuscript Collection.

Baily, Francis. *Journal of a Tour in Unsettled Parts of North America in 1796 and 1797*. Edited by Jack D. L. Holmes. Carbondale: Southern Illinois University Press, 1969.

Documents Baily's travels throughout the Ohio Valley, featuring an interview with Daniel Boone. Is striking for its lack of buffalo sightings.

Balesi, Charles J. *The Time of the French in the Heart of North America, 1673–1818*. Chicago: Alliance Française, 1992.

A dependable, well-written exegesis of the French intrusion in North America. Highlighted are the settlements of Illinois, a history of Fort de Chartres, and the cultural relations among the settlers, priests, voyageurs, coureurs de bois, and Métis. Includes excerpts from the journals of La Salle, D'Artaguiette, Jolliet, Tonty, and d'Iberville.

Barsness, Larry. *Heads, Hides and Horns: The Compleat Buffalo Book*. Fort Worth: Texas Christian University Press, 1985.

Deals mostly with trans-Mississippian buffalo. Included here because of its extensive bibliography.

Bassett, John Spencer, ed. *The Writings of Colonel William Byrd*. New York: Burt Franklin, 1970.

Byrd's 1728 writings on buffalo.

Braund, Kathryn E. Holland. *Deerskins and Duffels: Creek Indian Trade with Anglo-America, 1685–1815*. Lincoln: University of Nebraska Press, 1993.

Examines the mechanics and impact of the deer-skin trade between Creek Indians and Anglo-American traders in the Southeast.

Cleland, Hugh. *George Washington in the Ohio Valley*. Pittsburgh, PA: University of Pittsburgh Press, 1955.

Includes excerpts from the diary of George Washington written on a surveying expedition in the Ohio Valley in October–December 1770. Washington records the size of the buffalo herds he encountered.

Cresswell, Nicholas. *The Journal of Nicholas Cresswell 1774–1777*. 2nd ed. New York: Dial Press, 1928.

Cresswell came to America in 1774 to buy land. Taking up with James Nourse and others heading down the Ohio to Kentucky in April 1775, Cresswell kept a daily log of his adventures. His entries during this phase of his travels are rich in buffalo lore.

Cumming, W. P., S. E. Hillier, D. B. Quinn, and G. Williams, eds. *The Exploration of North America 1630–1776*. New York: G. P. Putnam's Sons, 1974.

A collection of memoirs, narratives, and journals, featuring, among others, accounts from Jolliet and Marquette, Mark Catesby, Gabriel Arthur, John Lawson, William Byrd, Thomas Walker, Christopher Gist, George Croghan, Daniel Boone, and William Bartram.

Dary, David A. *The Buffalo Book: The Full Saga of an American Animal.* 2nd ed. Athens, OH: Swallow Press, 1989.
The first chapter deals with the eastern buffalo.

Faragher, John Mack. *Daniel Boone: The Life and Legend of an American Pioneer.* New York: Henry B. Holt and Company, 1992.
A useful work on Boone.

Filson, John. *The Discovery, Settlement and Present State of Kentucke.* 2nd ed. Louisville, KY: John P. Morgan and Company, 1929.
This book, published in 1784, brought Daniel Boone international acclaim. Includes Boone's observations of Kentucky game herds.

Garretson, Martin S. *The American Bison: The Story of Its Extermination as a Wild Species and Its Restoration under Federal Protection.* New York: New York Zoological Society, 1938.
A summary of the history of the killing of the buffalo by the secretary of the American Bison Society. Chapter 6 is devoted to the eastern buffalo.

Gray, John W. *The Life of Joseph Bishop.* 2nd ed. Spartanburg, SC: The Reprint Company, 1974.
About a hunter in the Cumberland in the 1790s who witnessed the last days of the buffalo.

Hall, General William. *Early History of the Southwest.* 2nd ed. Nashville, TN: Parthenon Press, 1968.
General Hall's account of Tennessee's Indian wars in Sumner County in 1787–95. A map of the area pinpoints a trace.

Hanna, Charles A. *The Wilderness Trail.* 2 vols. New York: Knickerbocker Press, 1911.
An overview of the trans-Allegheny replete with portrayals of famous French, British, and American leaders and frontiersmen, and tales of Indian wars. Includes many references to buffalo and traces.

Hennepin, Louis. *A Description of Louisiana.* Translated by John Gilmary Shea. 2nd ed. Ann Arbor, MI: University Microfilms. 1966.
An early account (1678–80) of the Louisiana Territory. Includes graphic observations of buffalo, especially along the upper Mississippi drainage.

Hornaday, William T. *The Extermination of the American Bison.* Washington, DC: Government Printing Office, 1889.
One of the classics. Hornaday's efforts during the late nineteenth and

twentieth century were a major factor in saving the buffalo from extinction. Although much of the text in this dated work focuses on
the West, there are several pages on buffalo in the East.

Hulbert, Archer Butler. *Historic Highways of America.* 2nd ed. 16 vols. New
York: American Manuscript Press, 1971.
A dated series on the evolution of American roadways. Volume 1,
"Paths of the Mound-Building Indians and Great Game Animals,"
and volume 2, "Indian Thoroughfares," are useful, but many claims
are inflated.

James, Alton James, ed. *George Rogers Clark Papers 1781–1784.* 2 vols.
Springfield, IL: American Manuscript Society Press, 1972.
James lists many entries about buying wild meat to feed troops and
theorizes about the depletion of the herds.

Johnson, J. Stoddard. *First Explorations of Kentucky.* (Louisville, KY: John P.
Morgan, 1898).

Klos, Heinz-Georg, and Arnfried Wunshmann. "The Wild and Domes-
tic Oxen." In *Grzimek's Animal Life Encyclopedia,* edited by Dr.
H. C. Bernhard Grzimek, Vol. 13:331–98. New York: Van Nostrand
Reinhold, 1968.
A good overview of the buffalo and its Old World ancestor, the
wisent *(Bison bonasus).*

Lawson, John. *A New Voyage to Carolina.* Edited by Hugh Talmage Lefler.
Chapel Hill: University of North Carolina Press, 1967.
This immensely popular and often plagiarized work was first published in London in 1709. Since its first printing, it has gone through
at least a dozen editions, including two German translations. Lawson
toured the Piedmont of North and South Carolina between 1700
and 1701 and wrote about the "wild cattle" that he encountered. His
work is one of the few reliable primary source documents on buffalo
east of the Appalachians.

Lester, William Stewart. *The Transylvania Colony.* Spencer, IN: Samuel
Guard, 1935.
One of the foremost books on Richard Henderson's proposed
"fourteenth colony" in Kentucky. A major contribution to American
history.

Mereness, Newton D. *Travels in the American Colonies.* New York: Macmil-
lan Company, 1916.
A collection of original memoirs ranging from Cuthbert Potter's
"Journal of a Journey from Virginia to New England, 1690" to
"Colonel William Fleming's Journal of Travels in Kentucky, 1783."
Also included are the journals of Diron D'Artaguiette, Captain Harry

Gordon, General James Oglethorpe, and many others. Numerous first-hand sightings of buffalo are mentioned.

Myer, William E. *Indian Trails of the Southeast.* 2nd ed. Nashville: Blue and Gray Press, 1971.

A listing of trails and traces used by Indians and explorers. The map accompanying the text illustrates the extensive web of native "road-ways" in use prior to European intrusion.

Penicaut, André. *Fleur de Lys and Calumet: Being the Penicaut Narrative of French Adventure in Louisiana.* Translated by Richebourg Gaillard McWilliams. Tuscaloosa: Univeristy of Alabama Press, 1981.

Penicaut's observations and adventures during his travels in Alabama, Louisiana, and up the Mississippi to the Illinois country, written from 1698 to 1723. Many references to buffalo.

Pittman, Captain Philip. *The Present State of the European Settlements on the Mississippi.* 2nd ed. Gainesville: University of Florida Press, 1973.

In this facsimile version of the 1770 edition, Captain Pittman, of His Majesty's Fifteenth Regiment of Foot, describes his five-month journey in 1763 from St. Augustine, Florida, to Mobile, Alabama, and up the Mississippi to Fort de Chartres, Illinois.

Rhoads, Samuel N. *The Mammals of Pennsylvania and New Jersey.* Philadelphia: Wickersham Printing, 1903.

Rhoads contends that the historic buffalo in Pennsylvania were *Bison bison.* Although he lists no historic buffalo sightings in New Jersey, evidence of buffalo in at least twenty Pennsylvania counties is barely documented. Some lore later quoted by Shoemaker also appears here.

Roe, Frank Gilbert. *The North American Buffalo: A Critical Study of the Species in Its Wild State.* 2nd ed. Toronto: University of Toronto Press, 1970.

This book is well researched, annotated, and footnoted, and has an extensive bibliography. Of all the buffalo books encountered in the course of this study, *The North American Buffalo* includes the most critical analysis of the data concerning the buffalo east of the Mississippi. Important topics include speciation controversies of the eastern buffalo, *Bison bison,* versus other North American variants; a critique of Henry W. Shoemaker's work; herd size, migration theories, and buffalo demographics in the East; and buffalo habitat and historical chronology east of the Mississippi. Recent scholarship has proven Roe to be in error regarding the presence of buffalo in Florida and in other parts of the animal's extreme southeastern range.

Shoemaker, Henry W. *A Pennsylvania Bison Hunt.* Middleburg, PA: Middleburg Post Press, 1915.

Pure fiction. Shoemaker contends that the Pennsylvania buffalo was the wood bison, basing his case on the thirdhand remembrances of eighty-nine-year-old Jacob Quiggle (1821–1911).

Silver, Timothy. *A New Face on the Countryside: Indians, Colonists, and Slaves in the South Atlantic Forests, 1500–1800.* New York: Cambridge University Press, 1993.

An important piece of environmental history that shows how human habitation, regardless of ethnic group, altered the diverse, constantly changing ecosystems of the countryside.

Swanton, John R. *The Indians of the Southeastern United States.* 2nd ed. Washington DC: Smithsonian Institution Press, 1979.

Thwaites, Reuben Gold, ed. *Early Western Travels 1748–1846.* 32 vols. New York: American Manuscript Press, 1966. 32 vols.

Includes the journals of George Croghan and André Michaux, buffalo lore, numerous references to Long Hunters and early trans-Appalachian explorers, and discussions of Indian relations and the demise of the game herds.

_____. *The Jesuit Relations and Allied Documents.* 73 vols. New York: Pageant Books, 1959.

Storehouses of information on the cultural and social relationships between the Great Lake and Ohio Valley Indians and the Jesuit missionaries. Numerous references to buffalo.

Timberlake, Henry. *Lieut. Henry Timberlake's Memoirs, 1756–1765.* 2nd ed. Edited by Samuel Cole Williams. Marietta, GA: Continental Book Company, 1948.

The journal of Timberlake's forays into the Cumberland in 1762, in which he charted the rivers he navigated and recorded much of what he saw. This was the first Tennessee survey deemed as authoritative. His narrative has many references to buffalo.

Van Doran, Mark, ed. *The Travels of William Bartram.* New York: Barnes and Noble, 1940.

Bartram was a famous naturalist of the late 1700s whose narratives note the demise of the herds.

Wainwright, Nicholas B. *George Croghan: Wilderness Diplomat.* Chapel Hill: University of North Carolina Press, 1959.

Croghan was an English trader from Pennsylvania who traveled extensively in the Ohio Valley during the 1750s to 1760s. He made many observations about buffalo and traces.

Wallace, Paul A. W., ed. *Thirty Thousand Miles with John Heckewelder.* Pittsburgh, PA: University of Pittsburgh Press, 1958.

Heckewelder was a Moravian missionary to Indians throughout Pennsylvania, Ohio, and Virginia during the late 1700s. He frequently saw buffalo.

White, Richard. *The Middle Ground: Indians, Empires, and Republics in the Great Lakes Region, 1650–1815.* New York: Cambridge University Press, 1993.

A landmark work critical in attempting to understand the tenuous cultural accommodations, search for commonality, and conflicts arising between Indians and whites living in the upper Mississippi Valley.

_____. *The Roots of Dependency: Subsistence, Environment, and Social Change among the Choctaws, Pawnees, and Navajos.* Lincoln: University of Nebraska Press, 1988.

New historical, anthropological, and ecological thought concerning the collapse of these three representative native subsistence economies in the wake of the European invasion. White argues that buffalo came east after the time of de Soto and other Spanish invaders. This work is useful in helping determine the demographics of white-tailed deer herds at the time of contact.

Williams, Samuel Cole. *Dawn of Tennessee Valley and Tennessee History.* Johnson City, TN: Watauga Press, 1937.

An overview of Tennessee history from Hernando de Soto to statehood. Chapter 5 deals with traces in the Southeast. The book also discusses Long Hunters.

_____. *Early Travels in the Tennessee Country 1540–1800.* Johnson City, TN: Watauga Press, 1928.

This volume consists of journals of expeditions into Tennessee, including the explorations of Diron D'Artaguiette (1722–23), John Donelson (1779–80), John Lipscomb (1784), and Lewis Brantz (1785).

Young, Chester Raymond, ed. *Westward into Kentucky: The Narrative of Daniel Trabue.* Lexington: University Press of Kentucky, 1981. Originally found in DM 57J.

Trabue, a contemporary of Daniel Boone's, provides graphic testimony of buffalo hunting in eastern and central Kentucky during settlement.

Glossary

Algonquin: One of the largest Indian linguistic stocks of North America, spanning the area from Virginia to the St. Lawrence and west to the Mississippi River and beyond. Well-known eastern Algonquin tribes are the Shawnee, Delaware, Ottawa, Kickapoo, Potawatomi, Sauk, and Fox; western tribes include the Cheyenne, Arapaho, and Blackfeet. In the eighteenth century, the upper Ohio Valley was densely populated with Algonquin groups.

arquebus: An archaic muzzleloading blackpowder gun supported on a forked rest or shot off-hand. It was used by Europeans from the times of the conquistadors to the 1600s. Ignition at the breech is achieved by a slow fuse, or "match" (hence matchlock, another name for these guns). Contrary to claims that they are clumsy and inaccurate, the smooth-bored arquebus, equipped with front and rear sights, was the assault weapon of its day and was capable of inflicting considerable damage. Also known as *harquebus.*

barrens: Extensive grasslands once spanning broad patches of the Mississippi Valley. Indians, managing their environment by burning, helped create these vast savannas as grazing grounds for game herds. Settlers moving into such regions believed the land was infertile because of the lack of trees and few watercourses, so they settled the wooded areas first, but they later learned that the barrens were quite fertile.

bateaux: Flat-bottomed, square-nosed boats of plank construction, made in a variety of lengths and drafts, and used throughout the eastern fur trade. Although often cordelled, poled, or rowed, most were equipped with a crude, hand-hewn hardwood mast, up which could be run a sail in times of favorable winds, and canvas awnings aft for shade and privacy and to keep men, goods, and peltry dry. For firepower and defense, travelers mounted small cannon, called swivels or swivel guns, which were capable of shooting up to a four-pound projectile, on bows of some bateaux and high sides to ward off bullets from attackers along riverbanks. Bateaux of twelve tons' burden averaged forty feet in length, nine feet in beam, and four feet from gunwales to hull.

Demi-galeres, or decked bateaux, weighed twice as much and housed a crew of sixty-four. On August 4, 1761, James Kenny observed a mechanized bateaux near Fort Pitt built by one William Ramsey who joined two small boats at their square sterns and equipped them with

> an Engine that goes with Wheels inclose'd in a Box to be worked by one Man by sitting on ye end of ye Box & treding on Traddles at bottom with his feet setts ye wheels agoing which works scullers or short Paddles fixed over ye gunnels turning them Round ye under ones always laying hold in ye water will make ye Battoe goe as if two men Rowed & ye can steer at ye same time by lines like plow lines.

bear bacon: Salted bear meat, a primary staple east of the Mississippi and a big trade item for meat markets from the Tidewater to Illinois and south to New Orleans.

Black Robes: Indian term for Jesuits, identifiable by their long dark cassocks.

blaze marks: Marks chopped into trees along a forest path. Blazing a trail refers to chopping such marks.

bodkoos: A buffalo hide bag laced together with tugs—hide strips made into ropes—and used for carrying buffalo tallow or stores of wild meat. Two bodkoos could be made from one adult buffalo hide.

boskoyas: Meaning "bags of grease," boskoyas were skin bags or buffalo intestines packed with rendered buffalo tallow and carried by early French explorers and hunters.

boucanned: French for dried meat or jerk. *Buccaneers* was an early name for Frenchmen in the Caribbean who processed dried meat in *boucans* (smokehouses). The term later became identified with pirates who frequented the area.

Braddock's Defeat: The worst rout of the English army during the French and Indian War (1754–63). On July 9, 1755, near Fort Duquesne (Pittsburgh), 1,500 English troops led by Major General Edward Braddock collided with Captain Daniel de Beaujeu's force of 72 French marines, 146 Canadian militia, and 637 Indians. Crown troops killed Beaujeu in the first volley of the ambush, but his men rallied. Braddock was shot and died July 13. Only 538 British emerged unhurt; French and Indian casualties were light.

Brown Bess: This nickname for the English Long Land Pattern musket first appeared in print in 1785 in *A Classical Dictionary of the Vulgar Tongue,* by Frances Grose. "A soldier's firelock. To hug Brown Bess . . . to carry a firelock or serve as a private soldier." The term "brown musket" is noted in 1708, but "Brown Bess" does not appear in the official records of the British army until the 1850s. Some say the name referred to the gun's walnut stock, others to browning the barrel. By 1815 induced rusting, or browning, of the barrel was the norm; before then, except in a few cases, barrels were not blued or browned. Various Brown Bess models were used from 1730 to 1815.

budget: A burden, pack, or bundle toted high on one's back in a pack-frame or slung with a "hoppus" strap, usually made of animal hide such as deer, buffalo, bear, or elk, or of finger-woven wool blended with hemp or nettle.

buffalo hide boat: Indian buffalo hide boats used east of the Mississippi were small, often made of one or two bull hides stretched with the hair inside over a willow frame and lashed with sinew or tugs. Such a craft could float a load weighing up to eight hundred pounds. To make the craft water-resistant, builders caulked the seams with a mixture of ashes and tallow. Trappers made bigger hide boats by stitching more hides together and binding them to a stouter frame.

cane, canebrake: Cane *(Arundinaria gigantea)* is an indigenous bamboo of the eastern United States. During the 1700s cane grew in dense thickets, known as canebrakes, blanketing much of the Southeast up to the southern Middle Ground. Both Indians and whites sought canebrakes for cover, backing into them with ramrods in hand to flip up the cane to cover their trails as they plunged deep into the brake. In winter cane provided buffalo with forage. Early travelers often commented on "an abundance of cane" and of the "fine cane lands." To Anglo settlers, canebrakes were an indicator of soil fertility. Reports of cane growing forty feet tall and two inches in diameter and of canebrakes spanning many miles are common. Cane still grows on less arable lands and creek banks in small stands from six to ten feet tall, but in these times of rampant habitat destruction, vacillating state, local, and federal legislation concerning private land use and impact studies, and backlashes against environmentalists from certain well-financed interest groups, American cane, like many types of flora and fauna worldwide, is reaching an endangered status. Already in Florida, cane is protected and cutting it is prohibited. Unfortunately, such laws are rarely enforced and are easily circumvented.

chain carrier: Chaining was an integral part of eighteenth-century surveying, and each surveying team of four or five men employed at least one chain carrier. Surveying chains were links of forged, reed-thin steel rods sixteen inches long, joined at the ends in hook and eye fashion, and were four poles long. (A pole equals one rod, or five and a half yards.) Such chains were used to mark linear boundaries in surveys; measurements of land lines were recorded in increments of poles. Many surveys were inaccurate because the chain was kinked and worn from being dragged, and because deputy surveyors were poorly trained. In rugged terrain, chaining was done carelessly, if at all.

Conquistadors: Spanish and Portuguese fighting men who sailed to North and South America following the voyages of Columbus. Conquistadors—their very name defines their roles as an antagonistic, conquering breed—plundered and pillaged their way through the Aztec, Inca, and Maya empires, then did the same in the U.S. Southwest and Southeast. Cortés, Pizarro, Narváez, de Soto, Coronado, de León all were conquistadors.

Coureurs de bois: Unlicensed French-Canadian trappers who roamed much of eastern North America from New Orleans to Canada during the colonial period. Their independence, illegal hunting, ambivalent alliances, and maverick activities were problematic for the Canadian government. Coureur de bois sold pelts and skins to the highest bidder, whether French, Spanish, Dutch, or British. These intrepid men lived with Indians, and some played key roles between races as interpreters and diplomats.

dugout: A slender log canoe hewn from the trunk of poplar, cypress, or white pine. Eastern Woodland Indians and, after Anglo contact, white settlers made these craft, which often measured over thirty feet.

elm-bark canoe: Canoes built of elm, spruce, or birch bark were a native expedient for travel. Though some bark canoes were hastily made craft used for emergency travel (experienced builders with readily available raw materials could easily construct such a craft in half a day or less), other types of bark canoes, like the sturdily built Iroquois elm-bark canoe, called a ga-o-wo, were more lasting. Elm-bark canoes carried up to forty people, depending on the boat's size and draft. By the early 1800s, Anglo encroachment and deforestation made it increasingly difficult to find suitable bark, and the art of bark canoe building died out. Dugouts came to replace bark canoes.

Es-kip-pa-ki-thi-ki: Founded in 1718, Es-kip-pa-ki-thi-ki, Shawnee for "a place of blue licks," is thought to have been the last Shawnee settlement in Kentucky during the historic period and has reached almost mythical status in Kentucky lore. According to sketchy accounts, a palisade surrounded the one-acre village situated on a thirty-five-hundred-acre floodplain near Howard and Lulbegrud Creeks in Clark County. A 1736 French census lists its population at two hundred families. John Findley, whose colorful tales of Kentucky strongly influenced Daniel Boone to explore beyond the Blue Ridge, visited the Indian town in 1752. By 1754 the Shawnee living at Es-kip-pa-ki-thi-ki joined their kinsmen in towns on the north shore of the Ohio and its tributaries, thus ending the occupation of Es-kip-pa-ki-thi-ki.

Falls of the Ohio: "The falls," as the rapids were commonly known to Kentuckians, hunters, settlers, boatmen, and traders along the Ohio, were a series of cataracts at Louisville between present-day river markers 604 and 606. In this two-mile stretch of whitewater, the river cascading over the shoals dropped thirty feet. The falls were the only river obstruction on the waterway from Pittsburgh to New Orleans. In the 1830s engineers dug canals to bypass the falls. The construction of the McAlpine Dam in 1964 obliterated them.

flintlock: A firearm ignition system consisting of a cock, which holds a sharply knapped (chipped) flint in its jaws, and a steel striker, called a frizzen. When the trigger is squeezed, the cock strikes the frizzen, causing sparks to ignite the priming in the frizzen pan and flash through the touchhole in the breech, thus firing the gun. Gun historians theorize that the flintlock mechanism was a French innovation in existence by the early 1600s. By the mid-1800s the percussion cap system largely replaced the flintlock, and gunsmiths converted many rifles to the newer style. But even late in the fur trade, which ended in the 1840s, more seasoned Rocky Mountain beaver trappers like William "Old Bill" Williams—the archetypal "mountain man"—favored the older flintlock system because indigenous flint or chert was readily available, whereas in the remote Far West percussion caps might be hard to get.

French and Indian War: Also known as the Seven Years War, the French and Indian War (1755–63) was the final war between France and England over control of North America. The European wars of conquest in North America—King William's War (1689–97), Queen Anne's War (1702–13), and King George's War (1744–48)—were preludes to the French and Indian War.

have one's gun in order: A common frontier phrase for having one's flintlock rifle or musket loaded, primed, and ready to fire. Blackpowder is hydroscopic, or water absorbing. Any moisture—from dew, rain, snow, or humidity—leaking into the priming pan could dampen the priming powder, resulting in delayed ignition, called a "hangfire"; a "flash in the pan," meaning that the priming burned off but the charge did not fire; or no flash or spark at all.

hoppus: A burden strap used by woodsmen and Indians for carrying bags. A hoppus could be up to fifteen feet long and was made of hemp or buffalo wool interwoven with nettle. The hoppus's center three-foot section was two and a half inches wide; from there it tapered to one inch at the ends. While carrying (called "hoppusing") a burden, the wide part of the strap lay across the forehead or chest so that the burden, or "budget," rode high on the back. This also helped protect the carrier from being shot in the back. Also known as a sapper's string or tumpline.

hunting shirt: In his *Notes on the Settlement and Indian Wars of the Western Parts of Virginia and Pennsylvania, 1763–1783,* published in 1824, Reverend Joseph Doddridge wrote: "The hunting shirt was universally worn. This was a kind of loose frock, reaching half way down the thighs, with large sleeves, open before and so wide as to lap over a foot or more when belted." Doddridge notes that to close such a garment, hunters wore a "belt, which was always tied behind." This "belt" was a woolen sash. Hunters also tied sashes off to the side (as seen in Peter Rindis-bacher's nineteenth-century sketches of voyageurs) or in back to keep loose ends out of the way. In a letter from Isaac Leffler to Lyman Draper dated June 6, 1862, he notes that once Indians attacked him and Edmund Butts, and an Indian "caught the end of his belt, and it, being tied in a bow knot, it drew out" (DM 6E:85{19}). Paintings rendered from life show Daniel Boone and David Crockett wearing hunting shirts with leather belts buckled in front. Hunting shirts were commodious and were sometimes caped and "handsomely fringed." They became an identifying badge of an eastern woodsman, but contrary to Doddridge's observation, hunting shirts were not "universally worn."

Iroquois: Also known as the Five Nations, the Iroquois league was composed of the Mohawk, Seneca, Cayuga, Oneida, and Onondaga; the Tuscarora joined in 1722. The Iroquois lived from New York to the eastern reaches of the Great Lakes and were often bitter foes of Algonquin tribes. To this day, longhouse ceremonies, the religion of Handsome Lake, and elaborate false-face rituals are important parts of Iroquois culture.

Jäeger **rifle:** In central Europe from the late seventeenth to the early eighteenth centuries, the *Jäeger* rifle was the preferred hunting gun. It had a short (thirty- to thirty-six-inch) octagonal swamped barrel and was of heavy caliber, usually .62 to .75. Pennsylvania gunsmiths modified this design for frontier use, and it evolved into the distinctly American long rifle—the famed Kentucky rifle.

jerk: Dried and smoked wild meat, usually deer or buffalo. The drying and smoking process was known as jerking. Jerk kept for months and could still be palatable. Often it was broken up and boiled with fresh meat, parched corn, or other food for a quick meal on the trail.

Kentucky rifle: A uniquely American rifle was developed by Pennsylvania gunsmiths in the 1760s and often exhibited features of both German and English firearms. Most were over .50 caliber and usually stocked with curly maple (though cherry, walnut, and other woods also were used), with brass furniture and hand-forged barrels up to fifty inches or more. By the 1780s such guns featured intricate brass patch boxes inlaid on the lock side of the butt. During 1780 to 1820, the "golden age" of the

American long rifle, guns were elaborately decorated and engraved and featured silver and gold inlay and rococo relief carving. In 1822 Noah Ludlow popularized the theatrical frontier ballad "The Hunters of Kentucky," the song that made the phrase "Kentucky rifle" an enduring part of Americana.

Long Hunters: Professional hide hunters of the eastern American frontier whose long hunts would last for months, or even years, as in the case of Daniel Boone, who hunted in Kentucky from 1769 to 1771. Their primary quarry was the white-tailed deer. Dressed deer hides were common currency in the colonies, one large deer skin being deemed "one buck."

marrow bones: Buffalo femurs and shank bones, which Indians and Anglo hunters would roast, split and scrape out the marrow. These were prized as delicacies, and settlers often used buffalo marrow as a butter substitute.

meat getter: An old term for an eighteenth-century market hunter.

Middle Ground: Bordered on the south by the Ohio, on the west by the Mississippi, and in the north by the Great Lakes to the western tip of Lake Ontario, the Middle Ground was a true ethnic melting pot of Indians and Europeans. The culturally diverse soil of the Middle Ground, which the French called the *pays d'en haut,* spawned some of the most colorful characters on the frontier.

shoepacs: An Anglo adaptation of Indian moccasins, consisting of a tanned or half-dressed leather upper and sole, sewn and/or laced together, with leather thongs for ties. Shoepacs were functional, plain, utilitarian, comfortable, easily made, and sturdier than their native counterparts, but just as moccasins did, they still got soggy and did little to keep their wearer's feet dry in wet conditions.

Tuckehoe: Eighteenth-century frontier term for Virginian.

tugs: Hide ropes made by cutting fresh deer skins or buffalo hides round and round into long, hairy strips. Dry buffalo tugs were nearly indestructible and were in common use by both Indians and whites living east of the Mississippi.

wild beef: Frontier term for buffalo meat.

Year of Blood: In Kentucky 1782 was a bloodier year than most in the pivotal years leading to statehood. James Estill and his men were attacked by a band of Wyandots at the Battle of Little Mountain, also known as Estill's Defeat, as Estill was killed, casualties were high, and the whites fled the battlefield. Several other Kentucky forts were besieged as well. That August, following the siege of Bryan's Station, the Battle of Blue Licks made many frontier widows and ignited skirmishes along the trans-Appalachian ridge.

Year of the Hard Winter: West of the Appalachians, the winter of 1780 was the hardest settlers endured. The Ohio and Cumberland froze over and animals froze to death. Many settlers died from sickness, starvation, or exposure.

Year of the Three Sevens: For Kentuckians in the Bluegrass, 1777 was a memorably bloody year fraught with Indian attacks emanating from north of the Ohio. A chronological precursor to the Year of Blood.

Yellow Boys: A eighteenth-century term for Indians. Whites also called Indians terms like Injuns, reds, red devils, red rascals, and savages. Indians called their Kentucky foes Kentuckians, whites, white men, white-eyes, Long Knives, or any number of profane terms learned from whites.

Index

231

de Coronado, Franciso Vásquez, 25–26
de Delondarce de la Hontan, Armaud Lonis, 8
de Echagaray, Martin, 29
De Gannes, 40–41
de León, Juan Ponce, 28
de Luna, Tristán, 28
De Monbruen, Jacques Timothy Boucher, 79, 95
de Narváez, Pánfilo, 24
de Niza, Marcos, 25
de Pez, Andrés, 30
de Remonville, Monsieur, 43
de Rigaud de Vaudreuil, Philippe, 161
de Sigüenza y Góngora, Don Carlos, 29–30
de St. Denys, Charles Juchereau, 47
de Schweintz, Christian Frederic, 159
De Solis, 24
de Soto, Hernando, 26–28
de Toni, Henry, 41
Deer skins, 87
Delaware Indians, 19, 151
  Wolf clan, 124
Delgado, Marcus, 29
Description of South Carolina (Milligen), 65
d'Iberville, Sieur, 41–42, 43
Dier, John, 159
The Discovery, Settlement, and Present State of Kentucke (Filson), 132–34
Dobyns, Henry, 11
Doddridge, Joseph, 92
Dogs, hunting, 128
Donelson, John, 156–57, 158
Donne, John, 122
Dragging Canoe, 105
Drake, Joseph, 94
Draper, Lyman, 76, 100
Drayton, John, 65
du Pratz, Antoine Simon Le Page, 18, 44
Dutch Station, 122
Duteil, Charles Francis, 162
Dysart, James, 94

Edmundson, John, 159
Egle, William, 145–46
Emery, Will, 95, 102
Escopeta, 26
Es-kip-pa-ki-thi-ki settlement, 75
Estill's Defeat, 124
Ettwein, John, 135
European Wars, 74–75
European wisent, 3
Evans, Lewis, 74
Ewing, Charles, 95

Faragher, John Mack, 70, 149
Farmer, Robert, 76
Faux, William, 150, 156

Fields, Abraham, 127
Fields, Lewis, hunting experience, 130
Filson, John, 101, 102, 132–34
Finch, John, 122
Findley, John, 75, 102
Firearms, 25–26
  Long Hunters, 92
Fire-hunting, 12
Fitch, John, 90
Fleete, Henry, 56
Fleming, William, 127
Flores, Dan, 7, 15
Florida, demise of buffalo in, 163
Floyd, John, 100, 105, 123–24, 127
Fontaneda, Hernando d'Escalante, 31–32
Fort Cavendish, 82
Fort de Chartres, 82
Fort Jefferson, 122, 123
Fort Le Boeuf, 145–46
Fort Nashborough, 158
Fort St. Vincent, 47
Fort Stanwix Treaty of 1768, 78
Fowler, Henry, 63
Fox Indians, 20
Fraser, John, 69
French and Indian War, 75–78
Frontiersmen, 67
Fur trade, 51–53, 65–67
  standard prices in, 45

Gage, Thomas, 82
Galissoniere, Marquis de la, declaration of, 48
Gallatin, Albert, 163
Galphin, George, 64
Garretson, Martin S., 166
George, Robert, 122
Georgia, demise of buffalo in, 163
Gibson, Gail M., on buffalo in Pennsylvania, 147
Gibson, Hugh, 142
Girty, James, 126, 149
Girty, Simon, 82
  fueling war flames, 124
Gist, Christopher, 70–71, 74
  route of (map), 73
Glen, James, 65
Goodnight, Charles, 166
Gorbes, Gordon, 82
Gordon, Harry, 78–79, 143, 160, 161
Graddy, Jesse, 154
Graham, Sarah, 119
Gravier, Jacques, 41, 43–44
Great War Path, 16
Groghan, George, 69, 143
Guild, Joseph, 79
Guilday, John E., 144–45
Guthrie, Ben, 127